vatican II

vatican II

Volume I: The First Session

by Antoine Wenger, a.a.

TRANSLATED BY ROBERT J. OLSEN

THE NEWMAN PRESS
WESTMINSTER, MARYLAND
1966

282.0023
W485E
V. 1

171387

The present work is a translation of *VATICAN II: PREMIERE SESSION* by Antoine Wenger, a. a. © 1963 Editions Centurion, Bonne Presse, Paris.

Nihil Obstat: Very Rev. Carroll E. Satterfield, J.C.D.
    Censor Librorum

Imprimatur: His Eminence, Lawrence Cardinal Shehan
    Archbishop of Baltimore
    September 27, 1966

The *Nihil Obstat* and *Imprimatur* are official declarations that a book or pamphlet is free of doctrinal and moral error. No implication is contained therein that those who have granted the *Nihil Obstat* and *Imprimatur* agree with the opinions expressed.

Copyright © 1966 by THE MISSIONARY SOCIETY OF SAINT PAUL THE APOSTLE IN THE STATE OF NEW YORK. *Library of Congress Catalog Card Number:* 66–16573. Printed in the United States of America.

Preface

IT IS A HAZARDOUS UNDERTAKING TO WRITE ABOUT THE COUNCIL.
Bishops and experts who attended have the advantage of speaking about
something they have actually seen and heard. But they are bound to
secrecy. Their secrecy, however, can hardly be absolute if only because
of the new and different character of this Council. Its proceedings were
followed with respectful attention by public opinion everywhere, and
the Council itself aimed to be entirely open to the world.[1]

A journalist may speak quite freely about the Council. He is not
bound to secrecy,[2] but he has not been an eyewitness. Nevertheless, it is
to him that public opinion turns for information.

If he knows nothing about what really happened at the Council,
does he not run the risk of substituting his own theories about it for
complex facts unknown to himself? This tendency, which is only too
natural, is strengthened in this instance by the secret nature of a Council.
Consequently, the journalist is in danger of writing merely ideological
information, explaining everything categorically in terms of conserva-
tives and progressives, integralists and modernists, doctrinal and pastoral, curia and pastors, Italians and non-Italians, etc.

To the extent that the Council was the work of men, these tendencies
do exist, but the Catholic journalist should never forget that the Council
was something more than a human event. The Holy Spirit was at work
in this laborious search for truth, and the bishops were acting less as men
than as successors of the apostles, established by the Holy Spirit to
govern the Church of God. They were guided by someone who is above
them and who occasionally leads them where they had not expected to
go.

"To bring out the sacred character and mystery of the Council," John
XXIII told journalists on the occasion of the feast of their patron, St.

Francis de Sales, "the Catholic press must have an orientation and expression substantially different from methods based upon contingent interests and a purely human skill. It should resist suggestions that amplify useless controversies, or which fail to be charitably constructive and do not serve the Catholic community in its entirety."[3]

Unfortunately, it sometimes happens that the Catholic journalist imposes a strict discipline upon himself, refusing to apply the veneer of preconceived categorical distinctions to actual persons and things, or by declining to reveal what he has learned in secret, but the reader will not follow him in this austere path. Without discernment, he runs after sensational news, asserting that it is true simply because it pleases him, and because he has decided that things must surely have happened as he supposes.

The work of the Council was of long duration, and this creates another difficulty. The daily debates merely reveal one aspect of the truth being sought. The first session itself was only part of the whole. Divulging that aspect, day after day, amounts to conferring consistency or even a definitive value to what is simply an hypothesis or a part of truth.

There is still another drawback. When grave spiritual and moral questions conditioning the Church's life and the future of humanity become public knowledge, it makes public opinion not merely a witness of the preoccupations of the Church, which is appropriate, but somehow a judge of problems in matters that it is not qualified to decide.

Finally, if the journalist is asked to keep the historian's perspective in judging daily happenings, and, if he is a Christian, to view everything in the light of eternity, his criterion is nevertheless essentially daily and ephemeral, based upon appearance rather than substance. Cardinal Bea, speaking to journalists, warned them about this difference in valuation:

> Your profession leads you to speak of many things and to form opinions about them . . . and all this work must be done quickly, in a few hours, or in any case in a few days. You know, of course, that matters of faith under consideration in the Council are particularly difficult. . . . Let us remember that the Church is now in the twentieth century of her existence! Let us therefore think with her in terms of centuries and millennia. The value and the results of a Council can be adequately measured only by that standard, or even by the sole measure of eternity itself.[4]

All of these reasons should have held us back from writing about the Council. Nevertheless, we ignored them, and as the weeks and months have passed, we have been better able to appreciate the role played by the press in the course of the first session. This book aims to make that role clearly evident.

We shall proceed in line with the three fundamental conciliar objectives. The Council was primarily an internal renewal of the Catholic Church. By this very fact, it raises for all Christians the question of the true Church of Christ. Finally, the Council could not be really ecumenical if the bishops of the whole world, gathered around Peter, were not concerned about all men and all their problems. That is why the Pope and the bishops believe that the Council must be a contribution to world peace and justice.

The first section briefly reviews the history of the first session, from the origin of the Council, the opening address and the elaboration of the proceedings, to the principal orientations and great projects which were born in the final days of that session.

In the second section, concerning the Council and Christians, we report on the contacts between Rome and the non-Catholic denominations. Stress is laid on the relations between Rome and Moscow because of their importance, and also because we have devoted special attention to this particular problem for many years. We shall explain the nature of the dialogue that has begun to take place between Christians, and we shall examine the basis for the hope of reunion which the Council has inspired in them. In an appendix we record and comment upon two unpublished interviews granted by Russian observers to a Soviet journalist and his Polish colleague.

This book calls for a third section pertaining to the Council and the world. We have given a mere outline of this aspect in the conclusion which emphasizes the Council's contribution to world peace. But this requires a simultaneous consideration of many matters in many countries, touching on poverty, justice, peace, technical progress, demographic development and much else besides. The whole enormous task had just barely been undertaken by the Council.

We have also included in the Appendix an analysis of the repercussions of the Council in the Soviet press. Fully aware of the limits of this perspective, we believe, however, that our choice of this subject is not wholly arbitrary. In the political developments of recent months, and notably in the relations between the East and the Catholic Church, the important role played by the Council is quite apparent. To study Communist reactions, there were sources available to us which are not easily accessible to everyone. It was an advantage which led us to concentrate on this particular aspect rather than others. However, we are certainly not implying that the external effects of the Council have been limited to this single problem.

NOTES

[1] For bishops, article 26 of the regulations stipulates that "the Fathers are required to observe secrecy concerning discussions that take place in the Council and also with regard to each one's statements." Article 27 imposes the same obligation on procurators (of absent bishops or those unable to attend), experts, officials and other employees, binding them moreover by an oath.

For private experts, theologians, canonists or specialists to whom every bishop may have recourse, article 11 of the regulations provides that they are bound by oath to observe secrecy regarding the Council's acts and discussions. In his letter of January 6, 1963, addressed to the bishops, the Pope anticipates the association of new theologians with the proceedings occurring between conciliar sessions. This collaboration is to be "restricted to a limited number of persons who are capable of carefully observing secrecy concerning the Council."

Nevertheless, right from the start there was apparently a tacit acceptance of informal and unofficial communications derived from the Fathers and experts. Everyone, however, recognized the need for discretion. The acts of the Council and the content of the interventions obviously come under the rule of secrecy. Certain more delicate problems would require even stricter secrecy, although none arose in the course of the first session.

[2] All during the first session, the French newspaper, *La Croix,* published news about the Council which went far beyond the releases of the Council's press bureau. French bishops, however, were unanimous in their appreciation of this news, and Roman circles did not seem unduly surprised.

Officially, the press was accorded but little place in the Council. The booklet of the Commissions and Secretariats of the Council, listing the services of the General Secretariat, tersely mentions a third bureau *De Actis scribendis ac servandis* (the recording and conservation of the Acts), as if it were simply appended, giving the mere term *l'Ufficio stampa* (press office) and the name of its director, Msgr. Vallainc.

Msgr. Vallainc had seven priests assisting him as journalists, each of them in charge of the seven linguistic sections of this same bureau (Italian, Spanish, French, Portuguese, English, German and Polish). Until November 13, Msgr. Vallainc attended the conciliar sessions alone, with the responsibility of preparing a press release. This was a precarious and thankless task. He had to observe the rule of secrecy concerning the Council, while also giving a detailed description of each day's session. Journalists were forever complaining that they were not being kept well-informed. Others criticized the tendency of press releases to be ordinarily too favorable to the schemata. After November 13, Msgr. Vallainc had the help of two directors of the linguistic sections who, taking turns, also attended the Council. Under the supervision of Msgr. Vallainc, they prepared a text which was rapidly examined by Archbishop Felici, General Secretary of the Council, or, in his absence, by Archbishop Morcillo, the assistant secretary. The heads of the linguistic groups *freely* translated this basic text, which explains the occasional variations; some tended to be longer (Spanish, German) while others (French) abbreviated the Italian text.

It was customary, and even rather fashionable, to complain about the press bureau releases. History will be their judge. When personal factors that are always omitted from these releases are no longer of any interest, it will be recognized that they give a very accurate analysis of the conciliar debates. However, what may be advantageous to the historian can be a real drawback for the journalist who needs personalized, concrete, detailed information, and these are aspects which the press bureau's style excludes as a matter of principle.

[3] *Osservatore Romano,* January 29, 1963.

[4] *Documentation Catholique,* December 2, 1962, col. 1552.

Contents

pARt 1

The First Session

1

The Origin of the Council

POPE JOHN XXIII OFTEN SAID THAT THE IDEA OF A COUNCIL CAME
to him like a sudden inspiration of the Holy Spirit. Indeed, John XXIII,
elected pope on October 28, 1958, waited very little before proclaiming
to the world, on January 25, 1959, his great plan to convoke a Council.
Right from the start he was prepared to indicate the two great objectives
of the Council, seeking in the near future a renewal of the Church by
the affirmation of doctrine and the strengthening of discipline, and in a
more distant future the reunion of Christendom.[1]

The idea of a Council was certainly unexpected. Circumstances alone
bear witness to this. The Pope had asked the clergy and faithful of Rome
to be present at the Basilica of St. Paul's Outside-the-Walls on Sunday,
January 25, in order to pray with him . . .

for our brethren in the faith who, in a number of countries, are enduring
sufferings and outrages for the Sacred Heart of Jesus, and particularly for the
Catholics of China.[2]

We desire, therefore, that on next January 25th—the day when the Roman
liturgy commemorates the conversion of St. Paul, and on which, by a dear
and providential custom, the Octave of Prayer for the Unity of the Church is
brought to a close—the diocese of Rome gather with us in the Basilica which
houses the remains of the great Apostle of the Gentiles to manifest the solicitude and solidarity that are due to our Chinese brethren.

The public ceremony took place in accordance with this program. At
the end of the Mass, the celebrant, Abbot d'Amato of the monastery of
St. Paul's Outside-the-Walls, in a moment of recollected silence, read the
prayer which John XXIII had composed for the Church of Silence:

O Prince of Peace, grant that bishops and priests, Religious and layfolk,
be everywhere and always "careful to preserve the unity of the Spirit in the

3

bond of peace" (Eph. 4:3). May your omnipotent strength prevail over all human reckonings, so that pastors and flocks remain obedient to the voice of the only universal pastor, the Roman Pontiff, who feels in his heart the burden of that highest aspiration of your love: "Holy Father, keep in thy name those whom thou hast given me, that they may be one even as we are" (John 17:11).

After giving the blessing, the Pope went back into the abbey and told the Cardinals the great secret about his plan to convoke the Council.

Sudden Inspiration and Providential Preparation

During the audience which he granted me on February 27, 1959, the Holy Father assured me that the suddenly inspired idea of a Council was like heaven's response to his own anxious concern for unity. It was on Friday, the 23rd of January. John XXIII had decided to go to the Basilica of St. Paul's Outside-the-Walls on the 25th, to pray for the Church in China on the occasion of the closing of the Week of Prayer for unity. He wondered, however, what could really be done for the sake of unity. Is prayer sufficient? In the highest post of all, should he not take action? It was then that the sudden idea of a Council came to mind. This was not the result of long reflection, but rather the spontaneous flowering of an unhoped for springtime.

Two Bible texts filled the Pope's mind: *that they may be one* (John 17:11) and the Lord's concern about the harvests, *"lift up your eyes and behold that the fields are already white for the harvest"* (John 4:35).[3]

Peter remains always ready to fulfill his mission, taking into account the new possibilities offered by the modern world and the spiritual advantages to be derived from material progress. There are many political, economic and scientific Congresses held these days. Why not also bring together those who desire to exalt the faith and thus give it a new impulsion in the world? And so the idea of the Council was born.

While fully acknowledging the part of the Holy Spirit in the Pope's decision, we note that his own activity in the service of the Church had prepared Angelo Roncalli to take this initiative. As a young priest, under the direction of Bishop Radini-Tedeschi, he had studied the pastoral activity of St. Charles Borromeo. From an historical point of view, he could clearly see the beneficial effects of the reforms decreed by the

4

Council of Trent.[4] As the pastor he had always wanted to be, Angelo Roncalli consistently manifested a lively concern for the reform of the Church. He had this in mind just before the Conclave, as the letter which he wrote to the bishop of Bergamo attests. The Pope quotes this significant passage from it in a letter to Cardinal Alfrink, Archbishop of Utrecht, on the occasion of a televised program on Pentecost, 1960: "The soul takes courage in the hope that a new Pentecost will give the holy Church, through her new Head and the reorganization of the ecclesiastical organism, a new vigor for the triumph of truth, goodness and peace." And he adds, "What was then an ardent desire of Our heart was intended by Providence to be realized in part by Ourself."[5]

Consecrated a bishop on March 19, 1925, Angelo Roncalli was appointed Apostolic Visitor to Bulgaria. In November, 1943, he was sent as Apostolic Delegate to Greece and Turkey. He stayed in Istanbul until the end of 1944. This contact of twenty years with the East imposed a concern about unity upon the future Pope. Observing the faith and piety of the Orthodox people of Bulgaria and other Eastern countries, Archbishop Roncalli often wondered about the reasons for the separation. When he became Pope and the master of supreme decisions, John XXIII never once allowed the idea of unity to be forgotten.

From January 25, 1959, until October 11, 1962, the Pope spoke of the Council on countless occasions. There were the solemn Acts, like the Encyclical *Ad Petri Cathedram,* of June 29, 1959, soberly but precisely defining the purpose of the Council;[6] the creation of the preparatory Commissions, June 5, 1960; the Bull of Indiction of the Council, *Humanae Salutis,* dated December 25, 1961; and the message to Catholics of the whole world on September 11, 1962.

The historian or theologian who examines these Acts will find an astonishing continuity of thought and purpose in them. In announcing publication of the Bull *Humanae Salutis,* the newspaper *La Croix,* for instance, was in position to describe in advance, and in big type, the work and spirit of the Council. It said that the Council would enable the Church to contribute efficaciously to the solution of problems in today's world, and to strive for unity through doctrinal clarity and reciprocal charity.

In addition to these solemn Acts, John XXIII loved to speak about the Council on any pretext and any occasion. Once it happened that a chance remark fell to earth and was not gathered up by *L'Osservatore Romano*. However, birds from on high were not lacking to devour it! The journalists, in this instance, quickly laid hold of it and ensured its wide diffusion, but without any guarantees of authenticity or accuracy.

God gave John XXIII a charismatic gift, for he taught as much by his deeds as by his words. His actions were often symbolical gestures, like those of the ancient prophets, which help men understand the deep meaning of the words. Many examples can be cited.

The Pope, for instance, made known the name of the future Council—Vatican II—on December 7, 1959, in the Basilica of the Twelve Apostles. There were two reasons for this choice: the Council would be an assembly of the bishops as successors of the College of Apostles; it would labor for the reunion of the Churches. Significantly, the Basilica of the Holy Apostles is dedicated to the college of the Twelve, and contains the body of Cardinal Bessarion, the champion of unity during the Council of Florence. John XXIII did not forget to evoke the "universal spirit of that incomparable apostle of the Church's unity whom we love to see exultant in the supreme glory of the Saints."[7]

In the course of these informal comments, and in as many successive steps, the Pope gradually delineated the whole idea of the Council. For example, on April 19, 1960, he told the leaders of *Pax Christi*, "This event should unquestionably be an efficacious and important contribution to world peace."[8] The idea itself was new, at least for a large number of Catholics. In the eyes of too many Christians, the problems of war and peace depend only on political vicissitudes, even though moral attitudes and principles are constantly at stake in them.

Addressing the students of the *Russicum* on April 30, 1960, the Pope, in a prophetic vision, glimpsed the happy effects of the Council on the peoples of Russia, on condition that everything be well-prepared, with great charity and complete understanding of those peoples.

It is important to prepare everything well, with the greatest charity and perfect knowledge of the peoples, and also to take into account the sons of a very ancient tradition who now need to be understood and attracted by proofs of fraternity, kindness and peace. Without any doubt, the Lord will intervene with His grace and grant us great consolations, even if others are to enjoy the fruitful results in the future.[9]

Contemplating these ardent young men, he added, "The Church is firm and stable, bringing peace and guidance. The truth of the Lord abides forever, and to this truth the one, holy, Catholic and apostolic Church is anchored for the centuries."

First Reactions of the Cardinals

These remarks of the Pope are generally known, even if they are sometimes forgotten. What is less known, however, and in our opinion should be pointed out, are some of the typical reactions of the Cardinals. The Pope had asked them to express their thoughts and feelings to him.[10] Cardinals absent from Rome were consulted by a letter from Cardinal Tardini, dated January 29, 1959.[11] The first volume of the *Preparatory Acts and Documents of the Council* publishes a certain number of replies.[12] It is worth while perusing them. A few are simply polite acknowledgments;[13] others outline a program that was sometimes very near and sometimes very far from what the Council was to be.

Cardinal Fumasoni Biondi, who has since died, thought, for instance, that the principal purpose of the Council should be the fostering of a better knowledge of the catechism:

As a former Apostolic Delegate to India, Japan, and the United States of America, I have observed that Catholic education is provided in Catholic schools and institutions. In Korea, Japan, Australia, and especially in North America, a parish is not considered complete or satisfactory unless there is a Catholic school, at least at the elementary level. It is from these two sources, the parish and the school, that we derive our male and female vocations. In my opinion, this is the essential point for the religious reform that the world needs.[14]

Cardinal Fossati, of Turin, used harsh words to emphasize the evil doings of Marxism and Masonic liberalism, harmful errors that have even unsettled Christian doctrine. Obedience to the Magisterium is opposed, the holy Scriptures are criticized. "Men seek to adapt the wisdom of God to human knowledge, rather than the contrary, which would be logical and natural." This letter, highly interesting because it is complete, expresses the wish that the bishops of the Church of silence, and even those of Russia,[15] might participate in the Council.

7

Cardinal Gilroy, Archbishop of Sydney, destined to a high role in the Council, made certain suggestions to the Pope in his letter of March 18, 1959. He did not write about the Council, however—on this matter the bishops of Australia were not yet in agreement—but on the Synod of Rome. He recommended home-visiting to the Roman clergy: "It produces good results and we must not forget that Communists fear and detest this practice. The pastor who visits his people chases away the wolves of Communism."[16]

Cardinal Tien, Archbishop of Peking, who was then under treatment for his eyes in a clinic operated by the Society of the Divine Word at Siegburg, thanked the Pope for prayers said in behalf of China on the occasion of the solemn assembly at the Basilica of St. Paul.[17] But he did not mention the Council.

As the Pope had expressed his intention to publish the Oriental canon law before the Council, Cardinal Tappouni, in a letter of March 23, 1959, pointed out that it might be better to wait for the Council and not promulgate the Oriental Code until after "taking into account the general rules established by the Ecumenical Council." He went on to add:

Accordingly, our separated brethren will be unable to say that we want to simply confront them with deeds already done, or in other words, confront them with legislation already promulgated. As a matter of fact, our separated brethren do not possess the good dispositions which their brothers, the Eastern Catholics, must have, to accept new legislation so readily. On the contrary, they expect the Holy See to be very broad and liberal, at least in regard to disciplinary matters.[18]

Cardinal Ruffini, Archbishop of Palermo, expressed his joy in a letter, dated February 3, 1959, concerning the Pope's decision to convoke a Council:

It was a desire that I have been fostering for twenty years, and which I expressed long ago to your predecessor, Pius XII. If it is well prepared, the Council could consider subject-matter no less copious or less important than was examined by the Council of Trent. Such an event, which has already aroused universal interest, will indeed offer a providential occasion for an invitation to the separated Churches to finally return to obedience to the Vicar of Jesus Christ.[19]

Cardinal Urbani, the Pope's successor as Patriarch of Venice, really opened his heart. He brought a clear, quiet judgment to bear upon the present world situation, and drew appropriate conclusions from it concerning the purpose and procedure of the Council. He pointed out the tension between the two rival camps of free democracy and communist dictatorship, both of them powerful, the former through economy and finance, and the latter through productivity and a mastery of propaganda. The Church, transcending them both, should constitute not still another monolith, but a community of love, like a power station providing warmth and light. "Accordingly, the proclamation of the Council rings like the dawning of peace, and consequently of well-being and civilization."

A Council, according to Cardinal Urbani, could thus examine and discuss problems derived from the relations of Church and State, and from scientific, technical, industrial and commercial developments. It could consider the defense of family life, the school, public morality, technical means of communication and their application to pastoral activity, the reform of the parish internally (preaching and catechism instruction) and externally (relations with diocesan institutions, religious institutes, social movements); the problem of military exemption for Religious Orders, the Catholic laity "as an organization either dependent on, or convergent with the purposes of the Church, and as an active presence of Catholics with a Christian aim and outlook in the different institutions in which modern society now finds expression."

We believe that another feature of this letter should be stressed because it proves that the Cardinal of Venice understands the importance of the press in its relations with the Council.

In regard to this, it would be fitting for *L'Osservatore Romano,* the Catholic press and Catholic Action, to provide documentation and illustrations of past Councils and also of the coming Council, in order to create a fruitful waiting period and more solid interest. There was a time when the imperial and royal courts became impassioned about the Councils, especially in order to exert influence that was self-seeking and sometimes even harmful to the freedom of the Church. Today it is the press which constitutes the power of public opinion. We must not leave to others—our enemies—the initiative of providing news which might be malevolent or based upon self-interest.[20]

Cardinal Montini, Archbishop of Milan, had the most prompt re-

9

action. On February 2, 1959, he sent Cardinal Tardini a brief letter enclosing an article he had published in *Italia,* on January 27, 1959. It was a kind of prelude to the future *Letters from the Council* which he was to publish in the Catholic newspaper of Milan during the first session.

"This will be," the Cardinal wrote, "the greatest Council the Church has ever convened, both by its spiritual and numerical confluence and by the total and peaceful unity of her hierarchy. It will be the greatest by the catholicity of its dimensions, of real interest to the whole geographic and human world."

The Cardinal of Milan also perceived the blessings of the Council spreading over the world and society. "The Council will make Rome the spiritual capital of the world, its light radiating over the places and institutions in which men work for the union of the peoples, social peace, salvation of the poor, for progress, justice and freedom."[21]

The Turning-Point of September 11

Apart from the Pope's statements and the opinions which were expressed by cardinals and bishops concerning preparations for the Council, we depended for our news on the releases published by the press service attached to the general secretariat of the Central Preparatory Commission. This service published many news releases on the activities of the Commission and on the schemata under discussion. However, after using a certain amount of freedom in the beginning, Bishop Vallainc was reminded that the content of the schemata as well as the opinions of Commission members were to be kept entirely secret. Releases were then restricted to mere mention of the schemata under examination and a review of the Church's doctrine concerning them, in accordance with the latest encyclicals, canon law, etc.

The releases rarely made it possible to obtain an accurate idea about the schemata, and even less to know anything about the tendencies manifested during the preliminary examination. Nevertheless, the releases of the press service, such as they were, constituted an excellent *summa* of theological knowledge and a very complete inventory of the preparatory labor. And since this work itself was later contested by the Council, the releases represented an excellent basis for comparative study of the point of departure and the eventual point of terminus, especially for those who had no access to the enormous preparatory material.

In their general tone, these texts left the impression that the Council would be a reaffirmation of all dogma and morality, a review of all the institutions and laws of the Church. On reading them, one felt that the Fathers would simply affirm the faith and proclaim the law. The clergy and laity would then try to follow along as best they could. Many might find the going too hard, and the world, failing to see how this program concerned itself, would continue in its old way, far from God and from the Church.

Frequently I had a feeling of fear about this matter, which I believe was shared by many priests. Having often had occasion to speak to them about the preparation of the Council, I tried to re-assure them by showing that internal renewal of the Church, in its members and in its institutions, could not fail to have an exemplary value for the faithful, and eventually there would be beneficial results for all of society too. Or else I spoke about unity, even at the risk of giving too narrow a conception of the Council. This subject, however, seemed to be approached with greater breadth of view and a sounder appraisal of reality, largely through the efforts of the Secretariat for the Promotion of Christian Unity.

When we were too enthusiastic in speaking or writing about the Council, certain bishops who were well-informed in regard to the actual degree of preparation achieved, told us frankly, "Watch out for disillusionment!" And when we laid stress on spiritual preparation through prayer and penance, there were people who told us that this program was not new and held nothing exalting whatever. On September 10th, announcing to readers of *La Croix* the latest intervention of the Pope, we intended to prepare them for an appeal to prayer and interior renewal: "John XXIII," we wrote, "will issue a solemn appeal for prayer and penance. It is by these two means that the Christian dilates his soul to the full dimensions of the world and acquires true charity. In this way the union of hearts is achieved that will some day lead to a unity of minds."

The Pope's message, however, made no mention of this at all. There was hardly anything said about interior renewal, nor about the activity to which the preparatory schemata were almost exclusively devoted. On

11

the other hand, the Pope obligingly went on at length concerning the external activity of the Church which, of course, is also apostolic and tends toward the betterment of all mankind.

The message of September 11 elaborated the theme which would increasingly become the very heart and center of the Council: *Ecclesia lumen Gentium*. It showed that the Church, the spouse of Christ, *Salvator mundi*, savior of the world, would reveal itself through the Council as *Ecclesia mundi*, the Church of the world.[22]

After that message, John XXIII made reference to various aspects of this presence of the Church in today's world, speaking or writing in terms of freedom, peace and justice. And in *La Croix*, on September 12th, we wrote, "The Church claims a freedom that cannot be reduced to mere freedom of worship. Christ, who confided to her the mission of leading men to eternal salvation also gave her the power and means to fulfill this task. No state can legitimately deprive her of it. Moreover, truth and freedom are the foundation stones on which human civilization itself is built."

Seventeen years after the second world war, peace is not yet reestablished. The Council cannot be substituted for governments in this effort, but it will strongly proclaim the principles of that true peace to which peoples, families and individuals aspire.

Justice, in our day, is too often wronged. The Council will remind the 'haves'—whether states or individuals—of their obligation to share their wealth with the younger 'have-not' peoples. Rightly or wrongly, men have sometimes alluded to the Church of the rich. "Confronting the underdeveloped nations," John XXIII proclaimed, "the Church presents herself—and wants to be known—as the Church of all men, and more especially as the Church of the poor."

The Pope, as universal pastor, made the anguish of all human beings his very own. He wanted the Fathers of the Council to share these same feelings so that men of all the earth will know that they have a spiritual Mother who loves them, a God who is their Father, an only Savior, Master of all men, Jesus Christ.[23]

If we have been freely quoting from our own writings, it is because this analysis, since the close of the first session, shows that the address of September 11th prepared not only for the one of October 11th, but already defined the whole tone and spirit of the Council.

The Council, as the Pope let it be glimpsed, was very different from the kind of Council that the preparatory proceedings were planning for. All those who were familiar with this preparatory work had been struck by the dogmatic, narrow, scholastic character of the texts. Far from representing any progress, certain formulas on Revelation, the moral order, the problems of marriage, constituted a real regression in relation to the theology formulated by the Magisterium and especially by Pope Pius XII.

The bishops were reluctant to criticize these texts prematurely, because John XXIII, on many occasions, expressed great personal satisfaction with the preparatory work and the manner whereby it had been carried out. On the other hand, the Fathers reserved the right to express their own ideas and feelings during the course of the Council.

With the obligation of writing about the Council weighing upon us, we thought it well to ask the advice of friends in Rome. I spoke to a Roman cardinal about the difference in tone between the address of September 11th and what I knew about the schemata. He did not deny that the two documents were different in spirit. "It is for journalists," he added, "to help the Holy Father make the Council he desires."

"But what kind of Council does he want?" I asked.

"We'll probably know that on the opening day!" he replied.

All of us were tensely expectant, waiting for that day, and for the words which the Pope would utter on that occasion.

NOTES

[1] In undertaking the task of renewal in the Church, the Pope made the decision "to return to certain ancient forms of doctrinal affirmation and a wise ordering of ecclesiastical discipline which, in the Church's history during periods of renewal, produced results of extraordinary efficacy in the clarification of thought, the strengthening of religious unity, and the revival of that Christian fervor which we still recognize, even with reference to a happy life in this present world, as an abundant source *de rore caeli et de pinguedine terrae*—of dew from heaven, and fruitfulness of the earth" (Gen. 27:28). (Cf. Sermon at St. Paul's Outside-the-Walls, January 25, 1959.)

With regard to unity, the Pope expressed the hope that "the Council would also be an invitation to the faithful of the separated churches to follow us, obligingly, in this quest for unity and grace for which so many souls all over the world are yearning." (*Documentation Catholique*, March 29, 1959, quoting from *Acta Apostolicae Sedis.*)

Osservatore Romano, in the issues of January 26 and 27, had formulated the invitation to the separated churches in the following terms: "As far as the Ecumenical Council is concerned, the Holy Father believes that its purpose is not only to ensure the spiritual well-being of the Christian people, but also aims to be a call to the separated churches to seek the unity to which so many souls now aspire everywhere on earth."

2 During his first Consistory in December, 1958, when new Cardinals were named, the Pope spoke with anxious concern about the persecutions of which the Church was the victim in China, and the threats of schism there.

3 A fuller account, in greater detail, can be found in the Pope's address to the Synod of Rome. John XXIII revealed the same secret to many bishops. Also see the allocution to diocesan directors of Italian Catholic Action (August 9, 1959, published by *Osservatore Romano*, August 10 and 11).

4 In a sermon on November 4, 1962, on the occasion of the Coronation anniversary Mass celebrated in the Ambrosian Rite by Cardinal Montini, Archbishop of Milan, the Pope mentioned the conciliar and reforming activity of St. Charles Borromeo. He cited him as an example for all bishops. And what he said about him shows that John XXIII greatly counted upon the bishops for carrying out the reforms decided by the Council. "For the glory of St. Charles, it was a magnificent honor and a cause of exceptional merit to be found in the Church's service at the time of a Council whose sessions could no longer be prolonged and in circumstances permitting him to contribute to its final success in a providential manner. Moreover, he was able to devote about twenty years of his holy and sanctifying life (from 1565 to 1584) to the successful application of the Council's decisions and a restoration of the Church's life, by pastoral and apostolic visits and the convening of provincial Councils and diocesan Synods. This task inscribed his blessed name upon a whole era—the era of Saint Charles—which, thanks be to the Lord, still continues, giving us confidence in the future." (Cf. *Documentation Catholique*, December 2, 1962, n. 1389, col. 1510.)

5 Letter to Cardinal Alfrink (*Acta et Documenta Concilio oecumenico Vaticano II apparando*, Series I (*antepræparatoria*), *Volumen I: Acta summi pontificis Ioannis XXIII*, pp. 87–88). We shall quote papal texts and other documents according to this official edition, a magnificent volume printed by the *Polyglotte Vaticane*, cited hereafter as *Acta I*.

6 "The principal purpose of the Council will consist in fostering the development of the Catholic faith, the moral renewal of the Christian life of the faithful, the adaptation of ecclesiastical discipline to the needs and methods of our time. It will surely be an admirable spectacle of truth, unity and charity, and we have confidence that for those who are separated from this apostolic See, it will consequently be a gentle invitation to seek and find that unity for which Jesus Christ prayed so ardently to His Father." (Cf. *Documentation Catholique*, n. 1308, July 19, 1959, col. 907.)

7 *Acta I*, pp. 60–61 (*Osservatore Romano*, December 9 and 10, 1959). A third sign must be added. On that same day, the Vigil of the Immaculate Conception, the Pope placed the Council under the protection of the Mother of God, "our Queen and immaculate Mother."

8 *Acta I*, p. 81 (*Osservatore Romano*, April 22, 1960).

9 *Acta I*, p. 83 (*Osservatore Romano*, May 5, 1960). The verse of the psalm "*Veritas Domini manet in aeternum*" is one of the passages that the Pope loved to quote. In the troubled times of this world, it brings hope and security.

10 Sermon at St. Paul's Outside-the-Walls. "We desire from all who are present and from those far away, a cordial and confident word assuring Us of their dispositions, and graciously offering Us their suggestions for the realization of this triple objective." (Cf. *Documentation Catholique*, March 29, 1959, col. 388.)

11 A copy of the sermon at St. Paul's Outside-theWalls was included with Cardinal Tardini's brief letter.

12 The volume of the *Acts* seems to imply that all of the replies from the Cardinals were actually published, and therefore it was not a matter of selection. This part of the volume, titled *Appendix I*, has the following introduction: All of the Cardinals

received with joy and hope the first announcement concerning the Ecumenical Council, made by the Sovereign Pontiff, John XXIII, on January 25, 1959, at the Basilica in Ostia. Some of them, moreover, expressed their ideas in the letters that follow.

[13] For example, the letter of Cardinal Liénart, dated February 5, 1959:

Your Eminence:

I thank Your Eminence for having sent me, in the original Italian and in the French version, the words addressed by the Holy Father to their Eminences, the Cardinals, in the monastery of St. Paul's Outside-the-Walls, last January 25.

The great projects which His Holiness revealed on that memorable occasion have aroused enormous hope throughout the world. I am happy to bring my humble but ardent adherence and the assurance of my most devoted collaboration for their fulfillment.

I beg Your Eminence to accept the most respectful assurance that I am your humble and obedient servant.

(This was the only letter from a French Cardinal that was published in the Acta.—Ibid., p. 125.)

[14] Acta I, p. 118. In the new arrangement of the schemata, Schema XV, concerning the pastoral ministry, anticipates sections on the catechism and books of religious instruction, as well as a systematizing of catechetical training.

[15] Acta I, pp. 128–131. Because of his advanced age, Cardinal Fossati (born in 1876), who attended the Council, made no intervention. Original in Italian.

[16] Acta I, p. 145. The Cardinal also spoke forcefully about the reform of canon law. He wants the powers and duties of pontifical delegates to be strictly defined. Original in Latin.

[17] Acta I, p. 138. It is surprising that Cardinal Tien, in a letter dated February 21, 1959, referring to the ceremony at St. Paul's Outside-the-Walls, made no mention of the Ecumenical Council. Original in Latin.

[18] Acta I, pp. 146–148. Letter from Beirut, March 23, 1959, in French.

[19] Acta I, p. 124. The Cardinal expressed the hope that a journey to Rome (una capatina) would provide an occasion to converse with the Holy Father. He had, in fact, something to say on this subject, and he did so during a manifestation in honor of Pius XII on November 1, 1959. "Twenty years ago, I dared—and I was the least among priests—to suggest an Ecumenical Council as I knelt before Pius XII. It seemed to me that circumstances urgently required it and that matters for consideration and decision would be as abundant as they were at the Council of Trent. The venerated Pontiff did not reject this idea; he even made a note of it, as was his custom in regard to important questions. I know that he later mentioned this suggestion to some other prelate. . . . The conviction that a Council would be most useful grew in me during the summer of 1950 when I was granted an audience at Castel Gondolfo. I let my heart speak freely and told the Pope, 'Beatissimo Padre, I wanted to offer you my hearty congratulations. . . .'

" 'For the encyclical Humani Generis?' he said, interrupting me.

" 'Yes, Holy Father,' I replied timidly, 'I too wanted to congratulate you for that most famous document.'

" 'It was most necessary,' Pius XII continued in a resolute tone of voice, "and without it, no si salvava più niente—everything would be lost!'

"This last remark pierced me like a sword. I knew much about many errors and the more or less subversive theories in the area of faith and morals. But I could never have formulated such a disturbing conclusion. I must admit—I told myself—that the evil is far more serious than I supposed."

Father Daniel Stiernon commented on this letter in Unitas, as follows: "This frank statement of an Italian prelate, known for his doctrinal rigidity and his very definite position in regard to ecumenical matters, reveals to those who were still uninformed that attempts were made to persuade Pius XII to condemn what was called

15

neo-modernism and the new theology by a universal Synod. It also enables us to foresee the kind of pressures for reform that will be exercised in the conciliar assembly."

Unitas, on this occasion, also made reference to other anticipations of an eventual Council. On October 20, 1959, in a magistral panegyric evoking the memory of Pius XII, Cardinal Tardini said that it was this Pope's "great conception of the papacy" that led to "preparation for the Ecumenical Council, to which a select group of learned ecclesiastics had been devoting themselves for several years under his direction." (*Osservatore Romano,* October 26 and 27, 1959, p. 4.) Ten days later, in a press conference, he made this revelation again, confirming that "Pius XII had given thought to an eventual Council, and certain studies had been undertaken by a small number of learned churchmen whose efforts would be utilized." (*Osservatore Romano,* November 1, p. 2.) Doubtless this referred to the detailed schema of 200 pages written by Cardinal Costantini (1958), relevant to a Council on unity, which was given to the Pope at his request. (Cf. *Irenikon,* XXXII [1959], p. 309, and *Unitas,* nn. 48–49, [1959–1960], p. 14.)

Moreover, Father Lombardi, on the eve of the International Theology Congress in 1957, proposed the reopening of the first Vatican Council, because "this is the secret desire of the last generations of theologians."

[20] *Acta I,* pp. 134–136: Letter of February 16, 1959 (Original in Italian). It should be mentioned that Cardinal Urbani is a member of the Commission of Coordination created on December 6, 1962, and that he is especially concerned with problems pertaining to the apostolate of the laity and Catholic Action.

[21] *Acta I,* pp. 119–121.

[22] Homily of June 5, 1960, following the Vespers of Pentecost. "It is now a principle fixed in the minds of all believers belonging to the Holy Roman Church—because they are Catholics—to be and to remain citizens of the entire world, even as Jesus is the adored Savior of the entire world, *Salvator mundi.*" This message recommended universal openness in all religious and social relations, as a very appropriate exercise of catholicity. Cf. *Acta I,* p. 102.

[23] *La Croix,* September 13, 1962.

II

The Opening Address

The Blending of Heaven and Earth

Like everyone else on that gray morning, we were fairly brimming with desire and expectation. At six-thirty, the crowd of journalists was already gathering at the Arch of the Bells. Under the sad rain, they were all talking about the Russians, and nothing else. On the night before, the radio had announced their coming.[1] When the guards opened the grill for us about seven o'clock, there was a race around the apse of St. Peter's Basilica toward the Rezonico Gate. The journalists wedged as best they could into the stands set up on the sides of the galleries of St. Helena and St. Longinus. Some of them, however, had to be content with the *parterre* between the two galleries.

About eight o'clock, the first bishops arrived, all of them bent with age, and unable to take part in the procession. They brought to mind the Council of Nicaea, where confessors of the faith were present shortly after the persecutions. The observers arrived also; they were seated in front of the galleries of Saint Longinus and Saint Andrew, in the choir of St. Peter, so to speak, facing the Confession over the tomb.

Now the sun began lighting the vast Basilica, penetrating the windows of the cupola. The Swiss guards, looking exactly like those at the Council of Trent, walked around and showed people where to sit. The guards represent the last vestiges of the warlike Renaissance, together with the Roman patriciate proudly seated in the gallery of Saint Helena. Golden caissons lighted up in the vaulted arch above. And at eight-thirty the choristers broke into the *Credo*. It is the faith that brought us together here, enabling us to perceive the unseen, with the visible as our starting-point. Across from us, ambassadors were taking their places in the gallery of Saint Longinus. At eight-forty, the choir sang the *Magnificat*. I tried to imagine the procession moving through the vast Square, slowly progressing as the choirs alternated the *Ave Maris Stella* and *Ubi caritas et amor Deus ibi est*. "Truly a marvellous theme for the Council," I said to myself, "for where charity and love are found, God is truly present. May all disputes and quarrels be ended!"

The demonstrations surrounding President Segni brought my reflections to an abrupt finish. As the Fathers entered the aula, the Basilica of St. Peter looked more and more like the old prints of the Council of Trent and the pictures which history has left us of the earlier Councils. I had the impression that I was somehow picking up the thread of time exactly where they had left off, and I felt that what was happening in the Basilica that morning was the beginning of a new era for the Church.

I glanced over toward the observers, many of whom I knew. I noted especially the observer delegated by the Coptic Church of Alexandria, Michael Tadros, with whom I had such hopeful conversations at the Pan-Orthodox conference of Rhodes in early September, 1961, and then at New Delhi in November and December, 1961, at the third general assembly of the World Council of Churches. "We are Catholics," he told me, meaning that the Coptic Church believed the reality of the two natures in Christ.

St. Peter's was looking more and more like a swelling sea, with whiteness everywhere. The *Adoro te* was being sung. But why then? Archbishop Felici was seated at his table, busily examining lists and texts as a dignified secretary of the assembly. The procession moved along, and the loud-speakers brought us the echo of roars, indicating the passing of the Holy Father in the Square outside. Then the organ thundered, and the Pope made his entrance into the Basilica. There was much applause, even among the bishops. The observers moved forward to get a better view, and soon formed a kind of hedge in front of the Confession.

While the Pope was taking his place at the throne, there was a slight commotion as the processional acolytes and procurators tried to squeeze into a space that was much too small to accommodate them.

The Mass itself was unspectacular, and the liturgy, as everyone admitted, seemed inappropriate for this assembly on such a solemn occasion. A ceremonial guidebook had been officially prepared[2] and was especially intended for members of the diplomatic corps and bishops. But the General Secretariat also provided copies for journalists who cherished them as precious souvenirs. The liturgical prayers were printed in Latin and, where required, in Greek, with a vernacular translation. However, this ritual, which was carefully described by *Osservatore Romano* in an issue published on the evening of the 11th, and therefore after the ceremony, had in fact undergone substantial modifications. Some of the suppressions, as, for instance, the chanting of the Epistle and Gospel in Greek, can be explained by the desire to avoid prolonging a ceremony that already required five hours, not counting the time spent in preparation or in waiting. The Litanies of the Saints were shortened toward the end. And the prayer, *"Ut omnes errantes ad unitatem ecclesiae"* was not sung. But neither was the petition, *"Ut cuncto populo christiano pacem et unitatem largiri digneris:* Be pleased to grant peace and unity to the whole Christian people."

Other changes were even more significant. Although nobody was expecting it, and to everyone's great joy, a part of the Greek supplication was sung in Arabic and another in Slavonic. The Pope himself recited a prayer in Greek. The Greek Gospel selected for this occasion, as the guidebook indicated, was Matthew 16:18–19, which relates the privileges accorded to Peter by Jesus, *"And I say to thee, thou art Peter, and upon this rock I will build my Church, and the gates of hell shall not prevail against it."* However, the humble successor of Peter was unwilling to proclaim a Gospel to the Greeks that was not the same as the Gospel chosen for the Latins. He did not want to stand before the Eastern Christians asserting his rights and prerogatives. Consequently, the Gospel that was sung was not the passage originally selected, but rather the same as the Latin Gospel, Matthew 28:18–20, telling of the mission of the Apostles, which was so obviously appropriate for the Council: *"All power in heaven and on earth has been given to me. Go, therefore, and make disciples of all nations, baptizing them in the name of the Father, and of the Son, and of the Holy Spirit. . . ."*

Other happenings throughout the ceremony were meaningful signs, like the humble profession of faith made by the one who, because of his office, is however infallible, or the tone of ardent supplication when the Pope recited the prayer *Adsumus,* and his special emphasis apparent in the words, *"Simus in te unum et in nullo deviemus a vero:* May we be one in Thee and in no way depart from the truth."

The Charter of the Council

When everything was over, the Pope made his address. As the guidebook explained, it is customary for the Sovereign Pontiff to address the congregation during the Mass. But on this occasion the procedure was changed in order to ensure a better ceremonial arrangement.[3] As a matter of fact, the bishops and others in attendance, considered the ceremony as virtually finished. Someone sitting beside me remarked that it hardly seemed appropriate that a long sermon would still follow such a long ceremony.

The address, spoken in Latin and following an intensely religious service that had already lasted five hours, was hard to follow because of poor acoustics; thus it did not produce the impression it deserved. Minds were tired, and eyes had contemplated too many marvels. I watched members of the diplomatic corps distractedly trying to follow the Pope's text in copies given to them shortly before. It was amusing to see them turning the pages like schoolboys who seemed impatient for a lecture to be over and done with.

The Pope's address, however, revealed its full meaning to us when we had leisure to read and think about it in the translations prepared by the Vatican Press Office. This was a real privilege for us, because the bishops had only the Latin text and the Italian translation that had been published in the evening edition of *Osservatore Romano*.

Public opinion, for its part, had already been alerted by certain agency press dispatches and headlines regarding the "revolutionary" character of the papal address.

According to some reports, the Pope had made a condemnation of integralism in theological matters, and of pessimism in political matters. This was a caricature of an address which, although certainly bold, nevertheless maintained in all its parts a perfect balance between total fidelity to tradition and an equally considerable openness to the world.

The address of October 11th was the real charter of the Council. More than an agenda, it defined the spirit that was to prevail. More than a program, it provided real orientation. According to Cardinal Montini's audacious comment, it was the voice of a father—and of a prophet—the voice of a master who loves the world. We must always keep this opening address in mind, for it is the key that makes every-thing else understandable to us.[4]

For many people, it was a very dramatic address. To their great amazement, a Pope whom everyone considered conservative was propos-ing a program of innovation. And in a time of international tension, he spoke a language of hope, and publicly dared to assert his disagreement with the prophets of doom.

Whereas there were some who thought only in terms of retreating to defensive positions which the Council would then carefully consoli-date, the Pope placed the Council in the very heart and center of this present era. The Council's task, he said, would not be the repetition of doctrine as it was formulated in the past, but rather a presenting of eternal truth to men of our day, taking the modern mind into account as well as the progress achieved by contemporary research.

While some thought only in terms of condemning, the Pope was preaching mercy, for error bears the seed of its own condemnation within itself. To a poor world overwhelmed with evils and sufferings, the Council would manifest truth and charity, those real treasures of the Church which together constitute the foundation of peace.

Rather than withdrawing within herself, the Church would now have to go forward. The Council's task would involve making the Church's presence plainly apparent to the world, and its message mean-ingful to the mind and heart of the man engaged in the technological revolution of the twentieth century. Christian hope knows, indeed, that the Providence of God accomplishes its purposes even by means of human vexations. Something that is seemingly directed against the Church often turns to her advantage.

Consequently, there was no point in transforming the Council into a school in which excellent doctors of the faith would formulate Catholic truth in a most perfect manner. On this matter the decision was certain and sufficient, because, as the Pope said, for such an undertaking there would be no need for a Council at all. In the newspaper *La Croix,* on October 15th, it was mentioned that "some people considered this affirmation to be an allusion made by the Pope to schemata that were written too precisely in scholastic terms, and therefore incomprehensible to our time." The rest of the proceedings to which the Fathers had to apply themselves, and the spirit in which they conducted them, reveal more about this.[5]

Obviously, Pope John XXIII, burdened with the heavy responsibility of conserving the deposit of faith, possessed the ability to temper doctrinal severity with the gentleness of charity. Providence, which leads men *fortiter et suaviter,* with strength and graciousness, chose for the Council of the twentieth century a man and an assembly according to God's heart, who would give the world the message of truth, peace and reconciliation for which it waits and yearns.[6]

The Pope's Confidence and the Church of Silence

The press noted the resolutely optimistic tone of the opening address as another distinguishing feature. While reading the evening edition of *Osservatore Romano* on October 10th, I was curious about Mr. Manzini's editorial. A journalist knows by experience how difficult it is to write an editorial just prior to an event, when there are so many unknown factors to contend with.

Mr. Manzini's editorial was titled: "The Pope's Confidence," and this had a most striking effect on me. After the opening address, the article seemed so prophetic that I wondered if perhaps the Pope had personally suggested it to the director of *Osservatore Romano.* The resemblance between the two passages on the prophets of doom was particularly astonishing. The article in *Osservatore Romano,* published in the issue of October 11th (although available on the evening of the 10th), reported a statement of the Pope to the Central Commission:

It is certainly true that from time to time certain timid voices, in anxious whispers, wonder whether the world is not rushing toward very dramatic events. We have already expressed Our opinions on this matter on November 10, 1961,[7] in a radio broadcast to the world, to implore the blessing of a true and fruitful peace, and to pray, and induce others to pray, for it also. We then invited all those who govern to face up to their formidable responsibility. May truth and justice be strengthened, in the preservation of the essential freedoms and the inalienable values of every nation and every individual. We repeat again today our urgent invitation, and we say that our labor (of the Central Commission) aims to be humbly but resolutely a contribution to the expansion of a climate of confidence, hope, mutual collaboration and respect for the rights of the human person, redeemed by Christ, a preparation and defense of peace for the good of all mankind.[8]

In the address of October 11th, John XXIII spoke about pessimists in the following terms:

In modern times, these people only see prevarications and ruins. They tell you that our era, when compared with past ages, has greatly worsened. They behave as though they had learned nothing from history, which is however the mistress of life, and as though Christian thought and life and true religious freedom had fully triumphed in the time of previous ecumenical councils. Certainly, it seems necessary for Us to express our utter disagreement with these prophets of doom who are forever announcing catastrophes and almost the imminent end of the world.[9]

This point of view astonished the realists. Was it not pushing optimism too far? A Roman friend of mine explained that the Pope's opinion must be understood with reference to his immediate environment, in which certain people are so inclined to darken the situation and predict catastrophes that the Pope felt it imperative to react. However, John XXIII was not unaware of the political situation of the world, which was very serious indeed. The Cuban crisis occurring a few days later made this clearly apparent. The Pope then threw the full weight of his spiritual authority into the balance,[10] hoping to dispel the danger and preserve the peace, while also ensuring the successful continuation of the Council's proceedings.

On this important point the Pope's optimism was not groundless. The Council was truly free. It had been freely convoked and freely convened. The debates and discussions would continue freely also. In past centuries, kings and emperors exercised secret or open pressures upon a Council, and never before had any Council been able to meet in such favorable circumstances. Of course, the Church's freedom was not complete. In many parts of the world, in China, in Russia and some of the other people's democracies, bishops were prevented from coming to the Council. They were unable to respond to the Pope's call, and by a deplorable abuse of power they have remained excluded from this fraternal assembly of bishops of the whole world.

It was fitting for the Pope to lay emphasis on this, as he did, without provoking new tensions: "We confess to all of you that We are

23

deeply pained by the absence of so many bishops, who are most dear to Us. Either they are in prison because of their faithfulness to Christ, or else they are detained for other reasons. The remembrance of them impels Us to send up fervent prayers to God.''[11]

There were, in fact, six surviving bishops of the Soviet Union who could not attend the Council: the Ukrainian Metropolitan Slipyi (since liberated) and five Latin Rite bishops of the Baltic countries (of whom only one has been able to exercise his episcopal office). The absence of the three surviving bishops of ten Rumanian dioceses (one Latin Rite bishop under house arrest, and two bishops of the Rumanian Rite in prison) was also noted.

Only one of the two Bulgarian bishops attended the Council. Three bishops came from Czechoslovakia, although there are fifteen bishops living in that country. In Bohemia-Moravia, where not one of the six dioceses is governed by a bishop any longer, seven of the nine bishops are in prison. Only one was at the Council, His Excellency, Bishop Tomasek, who serves as a pastor in a Moravian village. Bishops Necsey and Lazik, Apostolic Administrators of Nitra and Trnava, respectively, were able to attend the Council. One other bishop stayed in the diocese which he governs as Vicar-capitular. And the three bishops who came to the Council were accompanied by a group of "peace priests," loyal to the regime, among whom was Canon Stehlik, appointed Vicar-capitular of Prague under government pressure following Archbishop Beran's arrest.

From Hungary, where sixteen bishops and one abbot nullius are living, only Bishop Hamvas of Casanad and Bishop Kovacs of Szombathely came to the Council, together with Msgr. Brezanoczy, Apostolic Administrator of the archdiocese of Eger, vacant since 1956. It was noted that this prelate was received by the Pope at the same time as the two bishops. Cardinal Mindszenty is still unable to leave the American Embassy in Budapest, where he resides, and two bishops are restricted to a village elsewhere. Five Hungarian bishops are unable to exercise their office.

Seventeen bishops from Poland attended the opening session on October 11th. Five others received their passports a few weeks later. But there are sixty-five bishops in Poland, and forty-three were unable to come to Rome. Four out of eight bishops in East Germany were at the Council.

Altogether, of the eighty-eight bishops of the Soviet Union and the satellite countries, only thirty-two took part in the first session of the Council.

Not one bishop could come to Rome from China, North Vietnam, or Albania. On the other hand, all of the Yugoslavian bishops were free to attend the Council. Twenty-seven of them did so, and only three, because of old age or sickness, remained behind in their country.

The Pope's discretion was inspired by his intent to avoid jeopardizing the universal effects of the Council which concerns all men everywhere, both in the East and the West. John XXIII wanted all those close to him, and in its own way the Council likewise, to share this attitude. On October 10th, a special evening edition of *Osservatore Romano,* devoted particularly to the Council, was published for local distribution in Rome. An article on the Church of Silence by Mr. Alessandrini, assistant director of the newspaper, had been previously announced. But the special edition did not contain this article. It was only the regular edition that published this homage to the suffering Church and set forth Catholic doctrine on the freedom of the Church.[12]

The Pope wanted the Council to observe the same discretion also, and it was his wish that the Fathers abstain in their discussions from all allusions to political matters, or to any countries or governments, whatever they might be. This became evident in the message to the world.

A Word about Different Translations

We feel compelled, at this point, to answer certain accusations made against the press and particularly against *La Croix.* The magazine, *Itinéraires,*[13] noting the differences between the Latin text and the French translation, used the occasion as a pretext for accusing journalists of doing poor work. The differences in question pertain to the passage considered as the boldest part of the whole address. The Pope defined the Council's task as a renewal of authentic doctrine

studied and expounded according to methods of research and presentation which modern scholarship employs. For the substance of ancient doctrine, contained in the deposit of faith, is one thing; and the formulation in which it is clothed, insofar as forms and proportions are concerned, and determined by the needs of a magisterium and a style that is especially pastoral, is something else again.[14]

Mr. Madiran, commenting on this version, had this to say:

One would think that the translator wanted to make this passage unintelligible. It finally founders, moreover, in meaningless gibberish. What is a formulation that determines forms and proportions according to the requirements of a style? Everybody asserted that it was admirable, although nobody understood a thing. And for good reason. Because the Pope did not say that at all. He spoke very differently, and he said a good deal more about it.[15]

Mr. Madiran went on to say,

What is really beyond explanation is that the whole French press went so far as to adopt a translation that was tendentious, exaggerated—and vague—whereas there was another French translation, published by *Osservatore Romano* which, though obviously done in haste and consequently containing a few approximations or omissions (like the conspicuous omission of the words *eodem tamen sensu eademque sententia*) at least provided us with an accurate, honest, intelligible and adequate version for a first reading.[16]

On still another point, Mr. Madiran felt he had found the journalist at fault. It pertains to the passage concerning the human person and the improving of the latter's condition, which are, as the text says, a matter of great importance (*negotium esse magni momenti*). The French translation reads: "We are convinced of the dignity of the human person, as of a supreme value." This translation is undoubtedly excessive. The term *supreme value* (or *highest worth*) is not appropriate (and is not found in the Italian translation). But is it fair or honest to level such a grave accusation of tendentiousness against a translation prepared under the supervision of the Vatican Secretariat of State? Mr. Madiran, in fact, wrote:

The *supreme value* conferred on the human person, a formula characteristic of atheistic humanism, was fraudulently interpolated in a papal address, apparently without arousing the least feeling of anomaly in any Catholic journalist. Perhaps they published this address in their newspapers and called it admirable in their comments about it, without even taking the trouble to read it. . . . Several explanatory hypotheses are possible. But not one of them is very enlightening. In any case, that is the level at which "information" is now given to the public by the reporters.[17]

How can such serious accusations be answered? First of all, it is difficult to understand why some people would comment only on one poorly translated passage of an address that was so rich in content. But it is particularly evident that Mr. Madiran is quite unaware of the conditions in which journalists do their work. The translation for which he blamed them was prepared by the Vatican Press Service, attached to the Secretariat of State. The latter had finished the task on the evening of October 10, and then used the press service of the Council to distribute a few copies to the press agencies and the radio and television networks, so that they could give a simultaneous translation during the ceremony on October 11.

The weekly periodical which Mr. Madiran would have preferred the journalists to consult for the translation was unavailable until a few days after the opening of the Council.[18] Mr. Madiran was doubtless right in pointing out the differences in translation between the Latin text and the French version. And the translation which he suggested is certainly more literal and more accurate.[19] However, the first French translation was obviously based upon the Italian text. But does that make it less reliable?

Without questioning the official character of the Latin text, we have every reason to suppose that the Pope wrote his address in Italian. The Latinists of the Press Service then produced the Latin text. It has often happened that in similar circumstances the Pope had to remind them to be more scrupulously faithful to his line of thought. We could therefore go on endlessly arguing as to what the Pope originally meant to say.[20]

A fortunate incident, however, which was perhaps purposely arranged, assured us that we can have confidence in the Italian text and consequently in the French version that was based upon it. In fact, on December 23, in his response to an address by Cardinal Tisserant, the Pope once again made mention of the Council's purpose. He quoted himself, but speaking in Italian he used the Italian translation that ap-

27

peared in *Osservatore Romano* on October 12th, page 3, and consequently in the very form that Mr. Madiran had criticized. The Pope
spoke about a forward stride in doctrinal teaching, *"in perfetta fedelta
alla autentica dottrina; ma questa studiata ed esposta attraverso le forme
della indagine e della formulazione litteraria del pensiero mo-
derno . . ."*[21] According to His Excellency, Archbishop Villot, speaking of the Council on the occasion of the seventieth anniversary of *La
Chronique Sociale,* this means that the Pope considered the wording as
suitably expressing the idea he had in mind. We could not improve on
his remark.[22]

New Garb for Ancient Doctrine

Mr. Madiran was also surprised that *La Croix* attached such importance to the text in question:

This passage doubtless produced a profound impression on the newspaper *La Croix,* which published it three times successively. The first time,
October 13th, on page 5; the second time, October 16th, on the same page;
and the third time, October 17th, it appeared on the first page, alleging
that Jean Guitton had considered it highly important (?).[23]

I do not know the meaning of Mr. Madiran's question mark. Jean
Pélissier, however, simply conveyed the opinion of French bishops
who had insisted that their admiration for the address be expressed in
La Croix. "French bishops," he wrote, "were impressed by an examination of the text of the opening address by His Holiness, John
XXIII, and especially the two following passages which, as Jean Guitton
remarked, fix the Council's form and emphasize its pre-eminently pastoral character."

Jean Guitton's opinion had been reported in *La Croix* by Jean
Pélissier in the issues of October 14 and 15, 1962. This address, Mr.
Guitton said, has historical significance. It indicates the Council's axis
and establishes its form, if not its matter.

How did he reach this conclusion? "The substance of ancient doctrine, contained in the deposit of faith, is one thing," the Pope had
said, "and the formulation in which it is clothed, is something else."

Mr. Guitton discerned in this passage a secret kinship with his own thinking, formulated some time before the Council in an interview granted to *La Croix:*

There is a lingual task to be done. Language is not truth, but rather truth's wrapping. We must determine whether, in the habitual, customary and traditional language by which we express eternal truths, there are not historical elements that are unnecessarily shocking or painfully offensive, and which are harshly alienating.

And he added, "These are also Cardinal Bea's opinions."[24]

This remark also received its full justification. During the reception for the observers by the Secretariat for the Promotion of Christian Unity, Professor Schlink of the Evangelical Church of Germany said, in fact, to Cardinal Bea:

During the past two years, Your Eminence often expressed in lectures the idea which is now heard again in the pontifical address opening the Council. In all our words and deeds truth is revealed which is absolutely binding. However, at the same time, we must distinguish between the substance of doctrine and the formulation of language in which it is garbed (*modus enuntiandi*). I am convinced that divided Christendom possesses more substance in common than may appear at first sight in its diverse formulations.[25]

To confirm his ideas and state their meaning precisely, the Pope, in his homily on St. Charles Borromeo, on November 4, spoke again about the new garb which the Council would have to find to present the ancient doctrine, complete and unchanging, to the modern world:

It is very natural that new times and circumstances would suggest different forms and attitudes to externally transmit the same doctrine and confer a new facing upon it. But the living substance is always the purity of the evangelical and apostolic truth, in perfect conformity with the teaching of Holy Church, which so often lends itself advantageously to the application of the maxim: *There is only one art but a thousand forms.* And more especially when it is a question of the good of souls or practical terms, that is to say, those solicitudes which Chapter 10 of St. John inspires and imposes: *". . . the shepherd of the sheep . . . calls his own sheep by name"* (John 10:2–3).[26]

29

NOTES

[1] Concerning the matter of Russian observers, *see* Part II of Chapter 2.

[2] A booklet of 80 pages: "The Second Ecumenical Vatican Council, the solemn opening ceremony in St. Peter's Basilica, October 11, 1962," with a translation and explanation of the ceremonies, Latin or Greek texts, and the vernacular translation of the latter.

[3] It would be interesting to compare the ceremony of October 11 with that of December 8, 1869, opening the First Vatican Council. Louis Veuillot gives us a detailed description of it in *Rome pendant le Concile*, I (Paris, 1872), beginning on page 10. Father Dehon wrote his own impressions in his *Diary*, published in 1962 by Msgr. Carbone (Léon Dehon, *Diaria del Concilio Vaticano I*, Polyglotte Vaticane): "The Blessed Sacrament is exposed on the high altar and when the prelates have adored it, they proceed to the Council hall. Then the Holy Father arrives. The crowd is unable to restrain its acclamations, in spite of the gravity and solemnity of the occasion. . . . The Holy Father adored the Blessed Sacrament, chanted prayers to the Holy Spirit and the Blessed Virgin, and went into the Council hall. The Cardinal Dean of the Sacred College sang the Mass of the Immaculate Conception. After the Mass, the Council heard a sermon by a bishop of the Capuchin Order, Archbishop Passavalli of Iconium. This devout Religious was born in Trent, and his function called to mind the last ecumenical council. For his text, he took David's saying, *'Euntes ibant et flebant mittentes semina sua, venientes autem venient cum exultatione portantes manipulos suos:* Although they go forth weeping, carrying the seed to be sown, they shall come back rejoicing, carrying their sheaves' (Ps. 125:6). He spoke of the sorrows of the present age and expressed the hopes that the Council was inspiring. The theme was well chosen, but the detailed developments were much too long . . ." Next came the ceremony of obedience, with the prayer *Adsumus*. The Gospel was taken from St. Luke, chapter 10: *Designavit Dominus*, which relates the appointing of the seventy-two disciples.

"Then the Holy Father had his allocution read to the Council. This allocution was also very good." (Father Dehon was apparently mistaken about this, for as most observers reported, it was Pope Pius IX himself who delivered the address in a voice broken with sobs.)

[4] Cardinal Montini, "Letters from the Council," in *Italia*, October 14, 1962.

[5] *La Croix*, October 14 and 15. The first session had in fact confirmed this interpretation.

[6] Here again the comparison with the address made by Pius IX is instructive. The situation of the Church and the Council was quite different. Father Dehon sums up that address as follows: "Our heart is exultant with joy in seeing this wonderful conciliar assembly, gathering under the auspices of the Immaculate Virgin, and in seeing all of you assembled here, more numerous than ever before, who share Our solicitude in the governing of the Church. You are gathered in Christ's name, to join with Us in witnessing for the Word of God, and to teach men the way of salvation, as also to pass judgment upon the opposing forces that are hidden beneath the name of science.

"You know how greatly the Church is attacked by powerful enemies who put forward the pretext of freedom. Respective rights are violated; the bonds of justice and authority are loosened. But the Church, as St. John Chrysostom remarked, is more powerful than all her enemies. Heaven and earth shall pass away, but the words of Christ will not pass away. And what are His words? *Thou art Peter and upon this rock I shall build my Church, and the gates of hell shall not prevail against it."* (Fr. Dehon, *Diary*, pp. 37–38.)

[7] After the events occasioned by the Berlin Wall, August 13, 1961, which had aroused international tension, we know that Khrushchev declared his agreement with

the Pope's address. *Osservatore Romano* then pointed out that this address should be taken in its entirety, and that the Pope had defined the conditions of peace in the light of the principles of natural and Christian morality.

[8] An address quoted without reference by *Osservatore Romano*, October 11.

[9] *Documentation Catholique*, November 4, 1962, col. 1380.

[10] History will some day relate the great service rendered by the Pope to the cause of peace by his intervention on October 25, at the height of the Cuban crisis. Journalists had been notified at ten o'clock in the morning that the Pope would speak at noon. We knew that it pertained to Cuba and an appeal for peace.

[11] *Documentation Catholique*, November 4, 1962, col. 1380.

[12] "The Church has always been persecuted," Alessandrini wrote, "but the persecution which strikes at Catholicism today in many countries of the world and so many millions of its sons, is the longest, the greatest, and most insidious that it has ever suffered since the far-off but still present days of Golgotha. And during all these years we have followed, and continue to follow, the drama of so many of our brothers, not with feelings of hatred or, as some affirm, in "a crusading spirit," but in order to make the world realize, and to prevent Christians from forgetting, the anxieties and sufferings of so many of their brothers. We sought to make it understood, insofar as this depended upon ourselves, that the granting of religious freedom, or respecting it and recognizing the right of Catholics not only to practice the rites of worship, but also to live according to their faith, does not mean that a privilege is accorded them, but rather that an elementary and fundamental human right is then respected."

[13] *Itinéraires*, December, 1962, the editorial "Autour du Concile," pp. 10–26, and February, 1963, pp. 100–106.

[14] *Itinéraires*, December, 1962, p. 14.

[15] *Ibid.*

[16] *Ibid.*, p. 16.

[17] *Ibid.*, p. 17.

[18] Georges Daix explained this very well to Mr. Madiran in a letter published in *Itinéraires*, February, 1963, pp. 100–103.

[19] *Itinéraires*, February, 1963, pp. 103–104, printed the French version and the translation suggested by Mr. Madiran in parallel columns.

[20] These discussions have been rather disconcerting to Protestants. One observer confided to me that he felt somewhat uneasy about interpretations of the Pope's address that were quite different, if not actually divergent. Catholics claim to have an infallible magisterium, but they do not hesitate to make very individual comments about its doctrinal declarations. Is this not a kind of second-degree Protestantism? The Protestants interpret Scripture with less freedom than Catholics ordinarily suppose, whereas Catholics quite freely interpret the pontifical declarations. What explanation can be given for this? All we can say is that they are neither dogmatic definitions nor *ex cathedra* teachings.

[21] *Osservatore Romano*, December 24–25, 1962.

[22] *La Croix*, January 13 and 14, 1963, reporting on the seventieth anniversary of *La Chronique Sociale* of Lyons, and summing up Bishop Villot's intervention.

[23] *Itinéraires*, December, 1962, p. 12. It was not only *La Croix* which attached great importance to this address. It was mentioned frequently by the Fathers in the conciliar assembly, but even more significantly by the Pope himself, who quoted it in a very important document concerning the rest of the proceedings. This was read during the general session of December 6. Wanting to remind the Council Fathers in what spirit the Commission of continuity and control had been working, the Pope again quoted this text in Latin. The heads of the Press Bureau's linguistic sections then hastened to insert the passage in their releases, using the same translation they had given out on October 11th, and therefore propagating the same divergences be-

tween the Latin and the modern translations. However, on the following day, *Osservatore Romano* reprinted the Italian version.

24 Jean Guitton's interview, *La Croix,* September 30 and October 1, 1962.

25 *Documentation Catholique,* November 4, 1962, col. 1426, which moreover reprints the *La Croix* translation of October 19, 1962.

26 *Documentation Catholique,* December 2, 1962, No. 1389, col. 1511. Curiously, *Documentation Catholique* mentions various forms and methods. The word *methods* corresponds to the Italian *attegiamenti,* which can certainly be translated as methods, but rather in the sense of pastoral method than any system of thought.

III

Organizing the Council

A Message to the World

THE OPENING ADDRESS OF OCTOBER 11 PRODUCED A PROFOUND sensation everywhere. The attention of both believers and unbelievers, all over the world, was now turned toward Rome. And sharing a sense of obligation toward the world, the Fathers also wanted to send forth a message of love and peace to all men. The first acts of the Council would be juridical in nature, or strictly theological, and consequently the bishops felt that they should tell the world in what spirit they had gathered together and for what reasons.

As early as September, Archbishop Guerry informs us,[1] certain bishops had written to the Cardinal Secretary of State to draw his attention to the great importance of a message from the Fathers of the Council to the world, as soon as the Council had opened, and before the theological discussions were under way.[2]

On Monday, October 15, *La Croix* announced that there would doubtless be a declaration of purpose, defining the ultimate objectives of the Council and its concern to bring the Church's response to the major problems of our time: peace, the defense of the human person, the fundamental equality of all men, and the third force.

Writing a text of that kind is a delicate matter, with regard to both content and tone. The bishops had arrived in Rome only a few days before and did not yet know one another. Nevertheless, the message would have to express the moral unanimity of the Fathers. A team of four French bishops prepared a draft within the perspective of the Council's task: the great design of God's love for the salvation of the world.[3] The message would reveal the Church's concern for the material and spiritual distress of the peoples, and their sufferings and aspirations. But this attention to human problems, and this opening to the needs of men, would appear as a requirement of faithfulness to the Gospel and Christ's love for men. Proclaiming the good news of salvation responds to the deepest needs of men and primarily the need for a Savior, Jesus Christ, "the only Savior."

Inspired by the lessons of the message of September 11 and also by the opening address of October 11, the Fathers wanted to declare to the whole world God's love for humanity. In the image of God, the Church must manifest her love in service. "We bring with us," the bishops said,

from all over the earth, the material and spiritual distress, the sufferings and aspirations of the peoples entrusted to our keeping. We are concerned about the problems that assail them. Our solicitude reaches out to embrace the humblest, the poorest and the weakest. Like Christ, we feel moved with compassion when we see these crowds suffering from hunger, poverty and ignorance. We feel a sense of solidarity with all those who, for lack of adequate mutual assistance, have not yet been able to attain to a truly human development.

Consequently, in our labors, we shall give an important place to all these earthly problems which bear upon the dignity of man and an authentic community of peoples. For "the love of Christ constrains us" and if anyone "sees his brother in need and closes his heart to him, how does the love of God abide in him?"

They laid stress upon two major considerations, the problem of peace and social justice.[4]

This proposed draft of French origin was submitted to the Cardinal Secretary of State, and then to the Conference of the presiding prelates, and, with their consent, to the conciliar Assembly at the beginning of the general session on Saturday, October 20.[5]

The Fathers were allowed a half-hour to examine the statement and give their opinion. Discussion was brief. One Father suggested inserting into the text a reference to Mary. His proposal was accepted in the form of an allusion to the gathering of the Apostles in the Upper Room: "Praying with one accord together with Mary, the Mother of Jesus, We, the successors of the Apostles, are gathered here in the unity of the apostolic Body of which Peter's successor is the head."

Bishop Fiordelli of Prato suggested including an allusion to the

"Church of Silence."[6] A Hungarian bishop, and then a Lithuanian bishop in exile, pointed out that the message, which ought to be a call to hope and brotherhood, should not contain anything polemical. On the recommendations of the presiding Cardinals, the text was therefore left as it was, without the suggested amendment.

Archbishop Felici then announced that the Assembly was summoned to vote on the matter. "Will the Fathers of the Council who accept the message please stand?" Almost unanimously, the Fathers rose to their feet.[7] "Only a few," Archbishop Guerry said, "remained seated, thus clearly showing that this proclamation of the message to all mankind was not a mere formality or an imposed act, but that it expressed the basic attitudes of the Fathers in general, and already foreshadowed the evangelical, pastoral and missionary significance that the proceedings of the Council would possess."[8]

Elections of the Conciliar Commissions

Friday evening, October 12, the French Ambassador to the Holy See, Guy de La Tournelle, held a splendid reception in honor of the French bishops at the Villa Bonaparte. The bishops were still feeling the effect of the opening address. One could see in their faces the joy of promises that would now be fulfilled. Full of hope and expectation, they spoke vivaciously about the first session that would take place on the following day, Saturday, October 13. This first general congregation was devoted to the election of members of the ten conciliar Commissions. Cardinal Liénart, who astonished everyone with his zeal and vivacity, confided to me on that evening that it seemed premature to proceed with the voting because the bishops did not yet know one another.

Saturday, October 13, Cardinal Liénart entered straight into history. Shortly before nine o'clock, the journalists had admired the long line of Fathers going to the Council, from which they, themselves, would now be excluded. That morning, however, held the promise of great joy for them, because the Pope, in spite of fatigue, wished to receive them in the Sistine Chapel,[9] thus according the same honor to the journalists as to members of the diplomatic corps who had been received in audience on Friday, October 12. Our amazement was great and bordered on stupefaction when, about 10:05 A.M., we saw the gates of Saint Peter opening and groups of bishops spreading over the immense Square, at the very moment when we were about to enter the bronze gate to attend the audience for journalists. It was a remarkable throng of bishops and reporters, the former coming down the steps and the latter going up them. There were more than 2,000 bishops, and over 1,000 journalists[10] and those in related occupations. In such a crowd, the secret was not kept for long. The surprise was really too much for everyone, and tongues were burning to speak out. On our way to the audience with the Holy Father, we knew quite exactly what had occurred.

The Role of the Episcopal Conferences

After the Mass celebrated by Archbishop Florit of Florence, the Secretariat distributed three booklets to the Fathers who had not already received them. The first contained the list of all the Fathers, the second listed bishops who were serving as members or consultants of the preparatory Commissions, and the third included ten sheets to be used as ballots for the election of 160 members of the ten conciliar Commissions, with sixteen members to be chosen for each Commission.

Archbishop Felici, Secretary General of the Council, asked the Fathers to proceed with the voting. It was then that Cardinal Liénart rose to speak. In the name of the French episcopate, he made "a motion to adjourn, alleging a need for prior consultation between members of the various episcopal conferences in order to permit the Fathers to have better knowledge of the candidates."

He pointed out that the proposed method did not seem practical. He felt it would be desirable if the Fathers of the Council would first confer together in order to select the most competent candidates. He mentioned that there are forty-seven episcopal conferences in the world, each with a secretariat in Rome for the duration of the Council, which facilitates the exchange of views between the different members of the episcopate. He said that bishops of certain countries where national conferences had not yet been organized could properly affiliate with the secretariats of other conferences. This method of procedure would make it possible to act more rapidly, and at the same time it would enable the Fathers to be fully informed when voting, and make for an atmosphere of greater confidence.

There was some applause. And then, after a moment of silence, Cardinal Frings, Archbishop of Cologne, in his own name and in the names of Cardinals Doepfner and Koenig, expressed the same opinion. Again, there was applause followed by general silence. The Assembly had clearly expressed its will. The presiding Cardinals and the General Secretariat took note of it. The session was adjourned, and the presiding Cardinals then met immediately to arrange the rest of the sessions. They were surprised by the turn the first general meeting had taken. Cardinal Liénart had not had the least intention of provoking an incident of any kind. When he asked for permission to speak, he had no way of knowing how the Assembly would react to his suggestion. The historian of the Second Vatican Council should make a note of the event, because on that Saturday, October 13, a new factor made its appearance in the Council: mention was made of the episcopal conferences, which would now be conscious of their responsibility and their authority. This concept of the collegiality of the bishops would be made increasingly manifest and specific during the Council.[11]

The journalist should consider the incident worth remembering as an irruption of freedom and spontaneity in the Council. In the evening, we could witness this ourselves when an Italian television program showed pictures of this historic session. The conciliar authorities had permitted television cameramen to remain inside St. Peter's to film the beginning of the first general session. We could not hear what the Fathers were saying, but their faces were so expressive that we had the feeling we were attending the Council. While Cardinal Liénart read his memorable declaration, the cameras managed to record the visible reactions of the Cardinals. This made it possible for us to see Cardinal Ottaviani's gesture of disappointment.

The press devoted a great deal of space to the first general meeting. Some thought it was a manifestation of independence on the part of the French bishops. Others facetiously commented that it was the first effect of the Franco-German alliance. A third group asserted that it was a revolt against the General Secretariat of the Council. There were certain people who claimed that it was the first evidence of a progressive tendency, and this was especially played up in the liberal press which made a point of reminding its readers that Cardinal Liénart, as the young Bishop of Lille, had intervened in favor of the strikers in 1930. It mentioned his attitude during the war in Algeria and his role as the head of the *Mission de France*. Everything was brought into the picture: labor unions, Abbé Davezies, and the worker priests.

As a matter of fact, things were more simple. It was merely a question of jointly finding the best procedural method, not only for the bishops of France, but of many other countries also, thus permitting them to confer together in seeking the best candidates to form the ten Conciliar Commissions.

From that moment there began a rather feverish preparation of lists for the various Commissions. The French bishops, anxious to ensure contact with the episcopal conferences of other countries, requested Msgr. Etchegaray, director of the pastoral secretariat of the episcopate, to establish connections with the various national conferences. Abbé Haubtmann, director of the secretariat of information, gathered the French journalists together to warn them against tendentious news items and sensational headlines. The French episcopate was determined to prevent the formation of partisan factions. It wanted the proceedings of the Council to be inspired by the pastoral spirit recommended by Pope John XXIII in his opening address.[12]

It was in this spirit that the French bishops reached agreement on the names to propose for the various commissions. They conferred with the other episcopates in the hope of preparing truly international lists which, as far as possible, would ensure that the various nations and continents would be represented by bishops whom the episcopal conferences considered most capable. Contacts with the Italian episcopate did not meet with success. With more than five hundred members, the Italian conference did not want to give its backing to an international list, preferring instead that the number of Italian candidates be in proportion to the number of their bishops. Furthermore, the names which they suggested for other countries were not always those which the national conferences had selected.

On Tuesday, October 16, the Council met again to proceed with the election. The voting began immediately, but the Fathers who had not yet made their choices were allowed a delay and could put off their voting until evening. The next assembly was set for Saturday, October 20, to allow for the counting of around 400,000 ballots.

The conciliar regulations anticipated an absolute majority in the first two rounds of balloting. A few perspicacious minds, and among them Cardinal Ottaviani, felt concerned that the Council might lose time that was precious. There was but little chance that all the candidates would obtain an absolute majority on the first ballot. In order to gain time, the presiding Cardinals asked the Pope to modify the regulation on this point. And when the session opened on Saturday, October 20, Felici informed the Fathers that the Pope, considering the large number of votes obtained by those of the candidates who had not attained an absolute majority, and wanting the proceedings of the Council to advance more rapidly, had decided to make an exception to article 39 of the regulation. Consequently, the sixteen Fathers who had obtained the largest number of votes were considered as elected for each Commission.

Members Designated by the Pope

The results indicated a clear success for the list suggested by the European episcopal conferences. Votes obtained by the Fathers ranged from 2,000 to 800. An absolute majority required about 1200.[13] As the Council was scheduled to begin the study of the schema on the liturgy on Tuesday, October 23, the Pope made known the eight members whom he had appointed to the Liturgical Commission at the session on Saturday, October 20. On October 27, he completed the other lists, but instead of naming only eight members, as the regulations anticipated, he named nine of them, without giving any explanation for this change. The Pope, who had raised the secretaries of the Roman Congregations to the episcopate, thereby making them Fathers of the Council, wanted their interventions at the general meetings to be infrequent and discreet. He decided, on the other hand, to appoint them to the corresponding Commissions, whose activities would benefit from their competence. By increasing the number of members of each Commission to twenty-five, the Pope added the name of Archbishop Dante, Secretary of the Congregation of Rites, to the list of members of the Liturgical Commission already published.

It has been said that the Holy Father's selection definitely modified the result of the conciliar elections. However, if there was a large number of Italian prelates among the appointed members, this was not detrimental to the other nations. On the contrary, the Pope wanted smaller and newer nations which, by the law of numbers, did not have any bishops in the various Commissions, to be represented in them also.[14] After a week of searching and discussing, choosing and balancing, the Council's real task could begin.

There is nothing surprising about these delays, rivalries or divisions. The struggle between the Gallicans and Ultramontanes had been even harsher during the First Vatican Council. In my spare moments, I enjoyed reading the diary of Father Dehon, the conciliar recorder, who was not favorable to the Gallicans. Five Committees had been organized for the First Vatican Council. The first of them, the Central Commission, which had to determine questions for discussions, had been named directly by the Pope. It included twelve Cardinals and fourteen bishops. Paris was not represented.

The other Committees were appointed to consider respectively: dogma, Church discipline, religious orders and the Eastern Churches. "The two factions," Father Dehon wrote, "put forth their principal efforts in connection with the election of the *de fide* Committee (on dogma). The list of candidates was prepared by groups from each nation. The voting took place on December 14. And the results were disastrous for the Gallicans. Bishop Pie was elected second on the list, but we did not see the names of the Archbishop of Paris, nor the Cardinal of Besançon, nor the Bishop of Orléans. After that election, *Univers* could rightly comment: 'The Council has now set its course.' "

Father Dehon went on to say, "But that day the opposition felt the need to organize. A list was made up for the balloting on the Church discipline committee, and the list was distributed at the entrance of the Council hall. But all this was in vain. It was not Bishop Dupanloup, but Bishops Plantier, Fillion and Sergent who were elected. The opposition tried again to win a majority on the committee for religious orders, but this met with failure too. It was Bishop Raess of Strasbourg and Bishop Saint-Marc of Rennes, who were chosen for France.

"After these elections, it could be truly said that the Council's course was set, but the whole activity of the opposition party, well organized and quite powerful, could be foreseen."[15]

An historian of Vatican I might suppose that it would have been preferable to constitute Commissions more representative of the Assembly, with a fair representation of both the majority and the minority.

This would perhaps have permitted the avoiding of certain difficulties. In contrast, it is evident how wise was the decision of the Fathers of the Second Vatican Council to confer within their various episcopal conferences in order to prepare lists that expressed the competence of the persons nominated as well as the universality of the Council.

Another wise measure was the clause in the rule stipulating that in addition to the sixteen members elected by the Assembly, eight members would be named by the Pope. This measure was intended less for correcting omissions or mistakes that are always possible in voting when such a large number of Fathers participate, than for expressing a judicious balance between the authority of the Holy Father and that of the Council.

NOTES

[1] *Pastoral Letter:* "The positive results of the first session of the Council." *Quinzaine diocésaine de Cambrai,* January 6, 1963, reproduced in *Documentation Catholique* (February 3, 1963), col. 175–190.

[2] The idea had been warmly approved by Cardinals Liénart, Doepfner, Suenens, Alfrink, Montini and Léger.

[3] We have reason to believe that the four bishops mentioned by Archbishop Guerry were Cardinal Liénart, Archbishop Guerry of Cambrai, Archbishop Garronne of Toulouse, and Bishop Ancel, Auxiliary Bishop of Lyons. The latter three prepared a French text that was then translated into Latin.

On Saturday, October 20, when it was necessary to publish an authorized French translation, these bishops no longer had the original one, and it had to be retranslated from the Latin. Bishop Pioger of Sées collaborated in this task.

[4] Text of the message, *Documentation Catholique,* November 4, 1962, col. 1407–1410. A text was also prepared by theologians, including Fr. Chenu, the theologian of Bishop Rolland of d'Antsirabé (Madagascar), and procurator of Bishop Girouard of Morondava (Madagascar) and Fr. Congar, an expert in conciliar matters. However, this document was written in terms of natural morality which, in other circumstances, would be normal for a dialogue with unbelievers, but there was no chance that it would be accepted by a Council. Moreover, it made no mention of the Savior. Consequently, it had to be laid aside in that form. Cf. Archbishop Guerry's Pastoral Letter, *Documentation Catholique,* February 3, 1963, col. 180.

[5] The press release says that the text of the message was proposed by the presiding Cardinals to the Fathers of the Council *with the approval of the Sovereign Pontiff.*

[6] The *Literatournaia Gazeta,* of December 8, 1962, in a report on the Council signed by Mtchedlov, the publication's special correspondent in Rome, points out that certain bishops would have preferred that persecutions in the Soviet Union be mentioned in the message to the world. But the Council refused to listen to them. For this reason, Mtchedlov added, the liberal and bourgeois press wanted to ignore the message, or even condemn it.

[7] Relying upon a press agency dispatch, we wrote that the bishops who remained seated were those who had been expelled from China. This false news was very saddening to these bishops. Four of them, expelled from China (Derouineau, Boisguerin, Pinault and Verineux), told us how painful it was for them when they

41

were confronted with a statement that was not only inaccurate, but even slanderous. On the other hand, Ukrainian bishops expressed an opposite reaction. Msgr. Malanchuk, Exarch of the Ukrainians in exile, insisted on telling us that fifteen bishops, bearing the suffering of their persecuted Church, wished to show the world that the dramatic situation in which their Church was involved was weighing upon their hearts and minds. They did not rise, because they felt the message did not adequately make this matter explicit.

[8] Pastoral letter, *Documentatian Catholique,* Feb. 3, 1963, col. 180.

[9] John XXIII won the hearts of the journalists by his simplicity. The Holy Father showed signs of fatigue, and when he had finished speaking, he had a few representatives of the press rapidly presented to him, and then left. Mr. Bergerre, president of the foreign press group in Rome, had invited the correspondent from *Tass* to be seated in the front row. This journalist had written a report on the opening session which had attracted attention. Italian newspapers expressed surprise that he had been given such a good seat. "Among the thousand journalists who crowded into the Sistine Chapel, there was the correspondent from the *Tass* Agency. I do not know how he arrived there, but at a certain moment I saw him comfortably settled in a fine red arm-chair, in the first row, only a few yards from the Pope's throne. Then I saw him conversing with Msgr. Angelo Dell' Acqua, representing the Secretariat of State, and when the audience was over, I saw him pushed around among the people who were trying to get near the Pope." (*Il Tempo,* October 14, 1962.)

In the front row, we noted Jean Marin, director of *Agence France Presse;* Charles Pichon, Don Rossi, directors of the *Pro Civitate Christiana* Center in Assisi, and, of course, the directors of *Osservatore Romano.* The Holy Father, on seeing me, pulled my cape and said, *"La Croix, l'Assomption!"* (naming the newspaper and the religious order).

[10] There were about 1200 accredited journalists. After the opening ceremonies, less than 200 remained to regularly follow the proceedings of the Council, by attending press conferences, meetings organized by the different national Press Centers, and especially by gathering information from reliable sources.

[11] *Osservatore Romano* published an outstanding article on the episcopal conferences with reference to this subject.

Msgr. Gouet, director of the Secretariat of the Episcopate, had established his offices at the French Seminary, where a large number of French bishops were staying. There were forty of them, including Cardinals Roques and Lefebvre. Twenty were lodged at St. Louis-le-Français, and fifteen others at the Procure de St. Sulpice, including Cardinals Liénart, Feltin and Gerlier. Cardinal Richaud was unable to attend the Council because of poor health.

The French Episcopal Conference with its various services was one of the most active at the Council. At all times it showed great interest in pastoral matters and a concern for universality which was appreciated by both Roman ecclesiastics and the national episcopates.

[12] There had been talk about an unfortunate headline in the French newspaper *France-Soir:* "French Bishops in Revolt at the Council." However, the newspaper's special correspondent had nothing to do with this. The bishops reacted vigorously. They were afraid that all their future activity would be jeopardized by sensational headlines. "If we do not react most strongly at the beginning of the Council, by a vigorous denunciation of this unpropitious kind of journalism, and by making Christians see the need for a Christian press, we shall be confronted with a most serious obstacle to the quiet and profound pursuit of the proceedings of our conciliar assembly, for as long as the Council lasts." It was Archbishop Guerry of Cambrai who wrote this in the *Quinzaine religieuse de Cambrai.* Cf. *Documentation Catholique,* November 18, 1962, col. 1457.

42

13 A list of elected Fathers can be found in *Documentation Catholique,* November 18, 1962, col. 1455 to 1468. Elected members are listed in the order of votes received.
14 *Documentation Catholique* (November 18, 1962), col. 1467–1468, drew up a most instructive list showing the allotment of members by countries, which is reproduced here. The figures in parentheses indicate first the members elected by the Council, and secondly those who were appointed by the Pope:
EUROPE (132). Italy: 44 (20–24); France: 20 (16–4); Spain: 18 (10–8); Germany: 12 (11–1); Belgium: 5 (4–1); Poland: 5 (3–2); Holland: 4(3–1); Yugoslavia: 4 (3–1); Switzerland: 4 (1–3); England: 4 (4–0); Austria: 3 (3–0); Ireland: 3 (2–1); Portugal: 2 (1–1); Luxemburg: 1 (1–0); Greece, Lithuania, Czechoslovakia: 1 (0–1).
AMERICA (66). United States: 22 (19–3); Canada: 10 (8–2); Brazil: 8 (7–1); Argentina: 4 (4–0); Mexico: 4 (3–1); Chile: 4 (3–1); Paraguay: 2 (2–0); Colombia: 2 (1–1); Bolivia: 2 (1–1); Ecuador, Guatemala, Panama, Peru, Uruguay, Venezuela: 1 (1–0); Dominican Republic, Cuba: 1 (0–1).
ASIA (36). India: 8 (6–2); Japan: 4 (2–2); Syria: 4 (2–2); Lebanon: 4 (0–4); China (Formosa): 3 (2–1); Philippines: 2 (2–0); Indonesia: 2 (1–1); Vietnam: 2 (0–2); Burma, Ceylon, Iraq, Jordan, Malaya, Pakistan, Thailand: 1 (0–1).
AFRICA (13). Congo (Leopoldville): 3 (2–1); Tanganyika: 2 (2–0); Madagascar: 2 (0–2); Cameroon, South Africa, Tunisia: 1 (1–0); Egypt, Ethiopia, Ivory Coast: 1 (0–1).
OCEANIA (3). Australia: 3 (2–1).
15 Léon Dehon, *"Diario del Concilio Vaticano I,"* a cura di Vincenzo Carbone (Polyglotte Vaticane, 1962), 217 pages, Chapter 10, *"Les grandes Commissions,"* pp. 62–64. This book is well worth reading. By way of comparison, the events of the First Vatican Council throw light on those of the Second. In regard to the latter, there has been talk and scandal because of opposing tendencies. But division was far more real during the First Vatican Council. Chapter 8 in Father Dehon's book is titled: "The Opposition and Its Causes." He begins with the remark, "It must be frankly admitted that there was an opposition party." And, as Louis Veuillot said, "Nobody would blame conscientious opposition, which is a natural, legitimate and often a very useful thing. The evil lies in systematic opposition, the spirit of opposition, and the stubborn and unrestrained determination to engage in opposition. That is what the Christian public would not have wanted to see at the Council . . ." (*Rome pendant le Concile,* II [Paris, 1872], 200–201).
"Where did this opposition originate?" Father Dehon asks. "From the Gallican and liberal spirit, and from German Josephism. As soon as it became known that infallibility would be considered in the conciliar proceedings, the party was formed and showed its colors. Msgr. Maret and Father Gratry represented the old Sorbonne. Döllinger was Luther's spiritual descendant. The article in the *Correspondant* on October 10 was a call to arms. It was said to have been inspired by Bishop Dupanloup, and was signed by the editors. Consequently, it involved the whole liberal school, which also could certainly be called the grandchild of the Reformation." These judgments are unfair. Father Dehon added, more reasonably: "I would not want to say that there were no faults on the other side." (*Diario, loc. cit.*)

IV

The Pope and the Council

"IN ROME WE HAVE FOUND A LOVING FATHER." This remark, which came from the heart, was made one day at the Council by Cardinal Gracias, Archbishop of Bombay. Every bishop could have said the same thing, because each had the feeling of being known and loved by the Pope as the pastor of a diocese, as a member of the episcopate of his country, and finally as belonging to the body of bishops assembled in the Council.

Audiences Granted to Bishops

The audiences granted by the Pope to the national episcopates at the end of exhausting days, while his health was increasingly threatened, were an effective element whose importance for the Council cannot be fully appreciated. The fraternal benevolence of the Pope toward the bishops helped to create a climate of confidence, charity, and freedom.

The Holy Father received the bishops in national groups during a series of audiences occurring between October 7 and November 27, the day when they had to be interrupted because of the Holy Father's illness. A list of the audiences follows here in chronological order. The dates mentioned, however, do not correspond to the days when the audiences took place, but rather to editions of *Osservatore Romano* which reported them in its official information column:

October 8–9:	Cardinal Wyszynski and sixteen Polish bishops.
October 10:	two Hungarian bishops and one prelate; two Yugoslav bishops.

October 13:	one Bulgarian bishop; three bishops from Czechoslovakia.
October 26:	four bishops from East Germany.
November 11:	the bishops of Korea and Thailand.
November 12–13:	the bishops of Australia and New Zealand.
November 14:	the Armenian bishops; Mexican bishops.
November 15:	the Chaldean bishops; the bishops from Belgium.
November 16:	the bishops of Ecuador, Pakistan and Cuba.
November 17:	the bishops of Japan and Ethiopia.
November 18:	Cardinal Urbani and the bishops of the Venetian dioceses.
November 19–20:	bishops of the United States, Greece and South Vietnam.
November 21:	the bishops of France, Burma, and the Maronite bishops.
November 22:	the bishops of Canada and East Africa.
November 23:	the bishops of Spain, Brazil, Malaya, Laos and Cambodia.
November 25:	the bishops of Peru and India.
November 26–27:	the bishops of Venezuela, Germany, Poland, Austria, England, Ireland; the Melkite bishops and Hungarian bishops.

It will be noted that the list begins with bishops of the Eastern countries, and that the Pope apparently intended to receive them a second time when his illness made it impossible. It was the Primate of Croatia, His Excellency Archbishop Seper of Zagreb, President of the Conference of Bishops of Yugoslavia, whose turn it was to be received, but who, at the start of the thirty-third general congregation, on December 4, came to the microphone to announce that the Fathers would forego these receptions, because they would doubtless be too great a burden for the Pope, although he wanted to continue them.

The unanimity of the Pope and the bishops was one of the blessings of a Council in which the question of episcopal collegiality arose so often, and in which an external observer might have felt that the bishops were only concerned to ensure their own authority. How could observers fail to marvel at such a fraternal exercise of the primacy, intended exclusively to serve the Church, but especially to those within the Church, its leaders, dedicated also to service? How could Eastern Christians, especially, fail to be impressed by the exercise of the conciliar function in the Catholic Church? The primacy, contrary to what was commonly asserted, had not suppressed the ancient conciliar form of teaching and government. The bishops of the monarchical Church were actually availing themselves of greater freedom than the bishops of certain autocephalous Churches in which the Patriarch and the Holy Synod have sometimes tended to usurp the place and function of the bishops.

The Pope and the Council's Agenda

The relations of the Pope and the Council constitute a delicate problem. The First Vatican Council defined the infallibility and primacy of the Pope over the whole Church. And yet, article 228 of the Code of Canon Law states that an Ecumenical Council possesses sovereign authority in the Church. Of course, this refers to a Council convoked by the Pope, and presided over by his legates. How could these two powers be exercised harmoniously?[1]

It is the Pope's prerogative to determine the Council's agenda. The Code of Canon Law provides for this explicitly[2] and the Pope, in the Bull of Indiction, dated December 25, 1961, indicated that among the schemata of doctrinal and disciplinary decrees, he would choose those that were submitted to the general assembly of the Council.[3] It sometimes seemed to us that certain Fathers had forgotten these texts. At no time, however, had the Pope established the Council's agenda in an explicit manner. In fact, when the bishops set out for Rome, they did not know what subject would be up for discussion when the proceedings began. Many believed that the order of the schemata, as published, implicitly constituted the agenda, including the sources of Revelation, custody of the deposit of faith, the moral order, chastity-virginity-marriage, the liturgy, the media of social communication, and unity (with the Eastern Orthodox Churches). This opinion was understandable, because these texts had not been printed without the Pope's consent, to say the least.

46

It is also true that the Pope knew of the majority's desire to begin with some practical subject like liturgical reform. And he was fully aware that many were hostile to the doctrinal schemata. Nevertheless, Cardinal Ottaviani insisted that the Council begin its work, according to tradition, with an examination of the dogmatic schemata. In these circumstances, the Pope left the choice of the first schema to the presiding Cardinals. "We have decided," Cardinal Liénart told the newspaper *La Croix,* "that the conciliar discussions should begin with the schema of the liturgy. Normally we would have begun with a doctrinal schema, but we have decided that an easier schema would enable the Council to get under way."[4] Cardinal Montini then wrote that this choice had been surprising to some people (he was thinking especially of the Italian bishops), but that it was a fortunate choice.[5]

The Role of the Presiding Cardinals

The Pope was represented at the Council by the presiding Cardinals.

According to the regulations, article 4, section 2, the presiding Cardinals, with the authority of the Sovereign Pontiff, are responsible for supervising the discussions of the Fathers and the whole procedure of the Council. This formidable responsibility and considerable power has not been abused by the presiding Cardinals. On the contrary, composed of ten Cardinals differing in mentality, character and national origin, this governing committee has sometimes seemed lacking in authority or assurance. However, when decisions were necessary, the presiding Cardinals made them.

On several occasions, at just the right moment, they proposed the termination of debate concerning some particular subject or even an entire schema. They used their right to supervise the debates with great moderation. Only rarely were the orators recalled to order or reminded of the subject under discussion, but there were many who were notified that they had spoken longer than the rules allowed. Among the latter, the most illustrious victim was Cardinal Ottaviani. On October 30, the Secretary of the Congregation of the Holy Office made an intervention on concelebration. He had been speaking for fifteen minutes. Cardinal Alfrink, who was then presiding, requested the Cardinal to conclude. And as the conclusion was long, Cardinal Alfrink cut short

47

the speech of Cardinal Ottaviani, who was displeased and upset about it. But Cardinal Alfrink did not feel that he was at fault in doing this. He had simply applied the regulation, and he was not personally responsible for the applause which approved his act of authority. In these circumstances, Cardinal Ottaviani did not attend the conciliar sessions for several days. There was no session between the 1st and 4th of November. The Cardinal did not appear on the 5th. The press suddenly became aware of the situation. Until that day, no newspaper had mentioned the incident. And the press then considered the matter as symptomatic of the opposition between the Cardinals of the Curia and the national episcopates, and belatedly attributed exaggerated importance to the incident.

The liberal attitude of the presiding Cardinals ensured complete freedom for the Council. Consequently, it was possible to learn by experience what could or could not be done. It became apparent that the Council needed an arbitrator and a supreme authority. If there had been no such power of arbitration, it seems that in several important circumstances the Council would have bogged down, or would have divided into majority and minority factions, with all the deplorable consequences of such a division. The authority of the Pope, acknowledged by all the Fathers, always made his decisions acceptable to everyone, if not gladly or with heartfelt enthusiasm, at least with loyal and total submission.

The Interventions of the Pope

John XXIII, who did not attend the Council, thus conforming to an ancient tradition and leaving full freedom to the Fathers, made use of a closed television circuit to follow the debates with passionate interest until the day when illness made it impossible for him to do so. One day, when the discussions on the sources of Revelation had brought the Council to a standstill, he told the French bishops that he felt he was like the patriarch Jacob, who kept silent while his children quarrelled: *Ipse autem tacitus rem considerabat* (Gen. 27:11).

But silence did not mean indifference, and respect for the Council's freedom did not exclude interventions for purposes of guidance or resetting the course to be followed. "Your Holiness," said Cardinal Tisserant in his Christmas address, "intervened whenever the interpretation of rules or the aims and goals of the Council required a loving word of guidance from the venerable Head of the Church."[6]

The two most important interventions were certainly the return of the schema on the sources of Revelation to a mixed Commission, and the publication of the rule concerning work undertaken between the conciliar sessions. However, there were other deeds, decisions and interventions which were instrumental in giving direction and orientation to the Council. A glance at the following list is informative in this respect:[7]

October 11: the opening address, the real charter of the Council. In the evening, an allocution to the people.

October 12: an address to members of the diplomatic corps concerning their responsibilities for preserving the peace of the world.

October 13: an address to journalists, stressing their duties in regard to the Church, the Council, and to truth generally. In the evening, an address to observers, on the need to glorify God for each day.

October 15: nomination of four Under-Secretaries (instead of the two required by the regulations): their Excellencies, Morcillo, Archbishop of Saragossa; Krol, Archbishop of Philadelphia; Villot, Archbishop-coadjutor of Lyons; and Kempf, Bishop of Limburg.

October 18: nomination of a fifth Under-Secretary, Msgr. Nabaa, Melkite Archbishop of Beirut.

October 20: modification of the rule governing elections. The first sixteen of the list for each Commission are elected (instead of two ballotings for an absolute majority). Nomination of the eight members of the Liturgical Commission.

October 22: the Secretariat for the Promotion of Christian Unity was raised to the rank of a Commission.

October 25: an anguished appeal for peace during the Cuban crisis.

October 29: the nomination of members of nine other Commissions (nine instead of the eight provided for by the rules). The Pope's

49

reply to the good wishes of the Fathers on the occasion of the fourth anniversary of his election on October 28, 1958.

November 4: an address on Saint Charles Borromeo, pastor and reformer.

November 5: nomination of the members of the administrative tribunal.

November 6: authority given to the presiding Cardinals to propose to the assembly that discussion of a chapter be terminated when the *pro* and *con* arguments seem to be exhausted. Decision to end the first session on December 8.

November 12: the decision that the second session would begin on May 12 and continue until June 29, 1963.

November 13: insertion of the name of St. Joseph in the Canon of the Mass.

November 21: return of the schema on the sources of Revelation to a mixed Commission.

November 24: nomination of the members of the mixed Commission.

November 26: Pope's reply to the good wishes of the Fathers on the occasion of his 81st birthday (November 25).

November 27: postponement of the second session until September 8, 1963.

December 2: the Pope, although sick, appeared on the balcony and spoke to the crowds gathered below.

December 5: abridgement of the schemata. Recitation of the *Angelus* with the Fathers, in St. Peter's Square, and an allocution. Signing of the norms for the continuation of conciliar tasks and proceedings (communicated to the Fathers on the 6th).

December 7: visit to the general Congregation. Allocution and recitation of the *Angelus*.

December 8: closing address.

December 9: canonization address.

December 12: nomination of the members of the Central Commission of control.

January 6: letter to the bishops on the remaining tasks and proceedings.

The Secretariat of the Council

The Pope was also connected with the Council by the Secretariat for Extraordinary Affairs, whose function was to examine new questions proposed by the Fathers, and then submit them to the Sovereign Pontiff. Composed of seven Cardinals, this Secretariat was under the presidency of Cardinal Cicognani, the Secretary of State. The resolutions or injunctions of this organism consequently expressed the will or opinion of the Sovereign Pontiff. The Secretariat for Extraordinary Affairs was often the superior court in which the presiding Cardinals discussed the Council's wishes and preferences, acting together as an agent or attorney for the Fathers.

Finally, mention should be made of the Secretariat General. Archbishop Felici carried out his heavy and delicate functions with exemplary efficiency, together with devotion and loyalty to persons and institutions, and this won everyone's admiration. His smile, good humor, and unflagging zeal have already become part of the history of the Second Vatican Council. Archbishop Felici imbued the five sub-secretaries of this Secretariat General with the same spirit. The Pope had appointed them during the first days of the Council, choosing them on the basis of the five predominant linguistic groups: French, English, German, Spanish, Arabic (Italian being represented by the Secretary General).

The Fathers of the Council could turn to each of the sub-secretaries as to a brother in the episcopate, to express their wishes or their complaints, or to seek counsel or explanation. His Excellency, Archbishop Villot, whose ten years of activity in directing the Secretariat of the episcopate had prepared him for this task, was a particularly devoted and efficient secretary. Those who observed him in his relations with the presiding Cardinals, the Fathers of the Council, and the experts and observers, are full of admiration for the tireless effort which he put forth and the perspicacity with which he supervised all undertakings by constantly directing them towards the Council's ultimate objectives.

The presiding Cardinals, the Secretariat for Extraordinary Affairs, and the Secretariat General were intermediaries between the Pope and the Council, whereby possible disputes were pacified, the most audacious projects were examined and modified, and the Council's general orientation was constantly reaffirmed.

Above Tendencies and Opinions

There is one final point that should be emphasized: The Pope allowed full freedom of expression to all the various tendencies of the Council. Nobody tried to conceal or deny conflicting opinions. However, the usual classifications do not always correspond to reality.

Cardinal Liénart characterized the two principal tendencies quite perfectly:

There are two tendencies which have been constantly contrasted. There are those whose special concern is to avoid errors and to maintain and affirm doctrine, and others whose primary purpose is to offer this doctrine to the world, giving it perhaps a less scholarly garb, but more readily assimilable. These two tendencies exist, of course, and it is surely understandable, since they represent two responsibilities of the Church, and it is not surprising that some of us are more concerned about one aspect while many feel deeply about the other. Division can only occur if these two tendencies are opposed, instead of perceiving them as complementary. Basically, the problem which we must solve together is to find a way to give full expression to all of our doctrine, faithfully and without attenuation, so that it will be of "interest" to the world, for we are all convinced that the Church has a message for men of today.[8]

Archbishop Guerry, for his part, protested against the opposition between teachers and pastors. The separation of doctrinal and pastoral functions is an error. There should not be bishops faithfully defending and safeguarding doctrine on one side, and on the other, the pastors solely intent on fulfilling their pastoral mission.[9]

Bishop Ancel applied a beautiful and profound formula to the Council, saying that the Fathers accepted one another with their differences, and loved one another in their complementary oneness.[10] Archbishop Florit, of Florence, in a letter addressed to the faithful in the final days of the first session, reacted against a certain manner of interpreting the Council in terms of parliamentary debates. He wrote:

Rather than a confrontation of tendencies and opinions, it seems to me that we should speak of an *encounter* which enriches and gladdens everyone, like probing deeply into the adorable word of God. For centuries this word holds all plenitude within itself, and in its transcendence it harmonizes and synthesizes in a vital and mystical unity everything which, in our limited human language, schematic and logical, may sometimes seem opposed.[11]

The diversity of tendencies, according to Cardinal Montini, is attributable not only to personal differences of temperament and outlook, but also to the very complexity of the problems being considered by the Council.

Unity and catholicity (*in the sense of universality*), antiquity and modernity, rigidity and development, interior values and exterior relations, the search for the essential and concern for particularity, the vision of things in their sources and the perception of the resulting consequences—all constitute different perspectives of a judgment or conclusion which can be brought to bear upon a religious problem, and they show to what extent a discussion can be complicated and intense because of the great love for truth that imbues those who take part.[12]

Jean Guitton, in a poetical image, characterized the two tendencies.

I hear two voices in the Council: the voice of the Fathers who are profoundly and primarily concerned about the conservation of the deposit of faith in all of its integrity. And that of the Fathers who, while possessing the same concern just as profoundly, have the pastoral desire to proclaim this truth in all its purity, but in language that is comprehensible and desirable for men of today. In my opinion, the first tendency represents the vertical axis of the cross of Jesus Christ, the axis of unity, integrity and truth. The second tendency is the horizontal axis of the cross, the axis of openness, universality and dynamism. We must be simultaneously faithful to both of these axes which cross each other at the high level of the heart.[13]

From this point of view, what can be said about the conflict between the bishops and the Curia? The press has often mentioned it, judging everything with reference to this particular question and laying stress upon the determination of the bishops to resist any further domination by the Roman Curia. In the course of the first session, there was no discussion pertaining to the relations of the bishops with the Curia. If there was occasional antagonism, it is because most of the bishops questioned the quality and orientation of the preparatory work. As the ten Cardinals of the Curia, being presidents of the ten preparatory Commissions, were responsible for these writings, the Roman Curia found itself involved in the same controversy. And in the way in which it tried to justify itself, it did not always improve its position in the matter.

In the new arrangement of the schemata, the relations between the bishops and the Roman Curia are part of schema 10 (the powers of bishops, the procedure of the Congregations in their relations with the bishops). The news bulletin issued by the press service of the Central Preparatory Commission, in its report on the proceedings of the Commission of bishops and diocesan government, laid stress upon the bond between the Roman Curia and the Sovereign Pontiff.

The Roman Pontiff, by virtue of the primacy given to him by Jesus Christ, may extend or limit episcopal jurisdiction which, itself, is derived immediately from Our Lord. Because of this power, which is used exclusively for the welfare and benefit of the Church, the Sovereign Pontiff may arrogate to himself all cases considered major, because they are the most important, or because their solution is more difficult, or whenever they concern people of prominence. However, this does not mean that, with the passing of time, these cases cannot entail changes which make a revision possible. Propositions in this respect were already made at the first Vatican Council, with the sole purpose of helping bishops to carry out their duties and govern their dioceses more easily, with regard to both spiritual and material matters, with legislative, judicial and coercive power, according to canonical rules.[14]

The bishops in no way question the universal jurisdiction of the Pope, nor the legitimacy of the central government of the Church. They only want the Curia to always consider its powers as *delegated*. The service which it renders to the Church with devotion and impartiality arouses the admiration of all those who can closely observe it at work. It is also a service which concerns real persons: bishops, priests and layfolk, who comprise the Church in the humble, concrete cases that are brought before the Curia for consideration and solution.

Between the Curia and the bishops, as between those who are called teachers and pastors, the Pope had no need to choose. They all constitute the Church, and he is the father of them all. Without denying the existence of two different tendencies, John XXIII did not want the press to make excessive mention of it, and he certainly disliked any suggestion that the Council could be described in terms of contrasting tendencies. A journalist, writing about the Council, had said: "They do not agree!" And the Pope commented rather indignantly, "On the contrary," he said, "there was complete harmony in the Council, and it could not possibly have been greater because the same flame engulfed all of them, for they were all seeking the best ways to extend and diffuse ever more widely the incomparable grace of Our Lord."[15]

The Pope believed that his role as father required that he be a personal source and center of unity. With this in mind, he always reminded the Fathers of the need for charity and concord. He succeeded in obtaining unanimity, not for every particular resolution of course, but in the principal orientation and general decisions. At the Council, Pope John was the bishop of peace and charity. To his brothers in the episcopate, he showed that the Church which presides in the capital of the Romans still deserves the high praises of the martyr bishop, Ignatius of Antioch: holy and venerable Church, worthy of blessing, worthy of praise, worthy of prosperity, worthy in her purity and foremost in the bond of love.[16]

NOTES

[1] In his letter *Mirabilis ille,* dated January 6, 1963, the Pope mentions, in canonical terms and in view of the experience of the first session, the relations between the bishops and the Sovereign Pontiff: "The Council receives its general orientation from the Pope who convoked it, as is normal, but at the same time it appertains to the bishops to ensure its free development. It will be necessary for the Pope to confirm the decrees in an official and definitive form, and they will then receive their value and force of law from his apostolic authority. However, it is incumbent upon the bishops to propose, discuss and prepare in the desired form the various determinations and, finally, to place their signatures upon them together with the Roman Pontiff." (Cf. *Documentation Catholique,* March 3, 1963, col. 291.)

[2] Canon 222, section 2. It is the Pope's prerogative to establish the agenda of questions for consideration.

[3] *Documentation Catholique,* January 21, 1962, col. 102.

[4] Interview by Jean Pélissier, *La Croix,* December 8, 1962.

[5] Cardinal Montini, "Letter from the Council," *l'Italia.*

[6] *Osservatore Romano,* December 24–25, 1962. Italian original.

[7] We have reference here only to public acts. Doubtless there were other decisions communicated to bureaus or persons concerned with particular matters. Let us at least mention the Pope's decision to call to the Council the superiors of religious orders with at least a thousand members under perpetual vows. Their presence was most fortunate. The results will become apparent when the Council's decisions are applied in the life of the Church. Superiors of Orders and Congregations who attend the entire series of conciliar sessions will be better informed regarding orientations to give to their communities, and they will know the kind of apostolate and the spirit and outlook best suited to their religious.

Mention should also be made of the counsel given to delegates and apostolic nuncios, as well as to secretaries of the Roman Congregations, advising them not to speak during the conciliar sessions, so as to allow the Fathers to discuss matters freely, and more epecially those from far countries, directly representing the college of bishops.

8 Interview by Jean Pélissier, *La Croix,* December 8, 1962.

9 Archbishop Guerry, interview by Jean Pélissier, *La Croix,* December 1, 1962. Addressing the *Tourisme et Pastorale Congress* at the *Domus Pacis,* Archbishop Felici also mentioned a certain point of view that opposed the doctrinal and pastoral aspects of the ministry. The only thing factual, however, is the following: "All (the bishops) were concerned to discover which truths should be emphasized and which methods would be most efficacious in proposing them to the faithful." All of this occurred in complete freedom. "It is within these perspectives," the Secretary of the Council also said, "that particularly heated discussions should be considered, for they were always inspired by the spirit of charity, even with reference to the schema on the sources of Revelation. It is the study of truth that enabled the Council to give better expression to its pastoral orientation." (*Osservatore Romano,* February 23, 1963.)

10 *Documentation Catholique,* December 16, 1962, col. 1614.

11 *Documentation Catholique,* February 3, 1963, col. 193.

12 "Letter from the Council," in *l'Italia,* November 18, 1962.

13 Interview by Jean Pélissier, *La Croix,* January 22, 1963.

14 *La Croix,* March 6, 1962, and the news bulletin of the press service of the Secretariat of the Central Preparatory Commission, February 21, 1962.

15 *Osservatore Romano,* February 9, 1963.

16 Ignatius of Antioch, *Letter to the Romans.*

V
The Liturgy

THE DISCUSSION OF THE SCHEMA *De Sacra Liturgia* TOOK PLACE in the Council from October 22 through November 13. The Fathers met in general congregation at least fifteen times for this examination. Three hundred and twenty-nine oral interventions occurred during these sessions. Six hundred and twenty-five written interventions were presented to the Secretariat of the Council.

The Spirit and Content of the Schema

Of the seven projects proposed to the Fathers before the Council, the schema on the liturgy was generally considered the best. It was in line with the Council's purpose and the pastoral needs of the Church. It consecrated the efforts undertaken in recent years by various movements and centers of liturgical study emphasizing the pastoral ministry. As a conciliar document, it marked the birth of a new style which Canon Martimort characterized in lapidary terms:

A new theological language, a new ecclesiastical style has been created, and we find it only in the schema of the liturgy. Formerly, the style of theology was scholastic, and we find this in all the other schemata. But the style used in the schema of the liturgy is biblical and patristic, wholly oriented toward the pastoral mission of the Church. This style will be understood by the people and will profoundly impress and influence all men. It is a style commonly in use among the Orthodox, the Protestants and even among pagans.[1]

The *De Sacra Liturgia* includes a preamble and eight chapters. The first chapter, which contains a third of the subject matter for discussion, is essential not only for the liturgy itself, but for the whole orientation of the Council. That is why the Fathers spent so much time on this section. After the general discussion, which took place during six general congregations, the Fathers returned to this same section on several occasions when voting on various proposed amendments. There was a vote on the first chapter as a whole on December 7th, during the last general congregation. Although it was not like voting in the solemn form of a Constitution, the Council intended to give definitive consecration to Chapter One. Msgr. Felici explained to the assembly the meaning of the vote and the manner of voting. It was, in fact, the first time that the Fathers voted not only by *placet* (yes) or *non-placet* (no), but rather by *placet juxta modum*. It was a vote that was essentially affirmative, emerging from many shades of opinion and reservations. For the sake of precision, if the votes were not explained to the Secretariat by December 31st, they were considered as positive. And to avoid any equivocation, the Under-Secretaries of the Council explained, one by one, and each in his own language, the significance and conditions of voting.

The first chapter was adopted by an immense majority, indeed we might even say unanimously. Of 2,118 votes cast, there were 1,922 *placet*, 11 *non-placet*, and 180 *placet juxta modum*, with 5 that were null. The majority was so great that the Secretary General informed the Fathers who had voted *placet juxta modum* that there was no need for them to transmit their remarks because the vote had been decisive.[2]

"The Constitution *De sacra liturgia* was in luck!" That is how Fr. Vagaggini, an expert at the Council and Vice Rector of the Pontifical Atheneum of Saint Anselm, expressed his feelings in an article written in *L'Osservatore Romano* on December 8, 1962.[3]

He mentioned "luck" because at certain moments the opposing Fathers, like a violent squall, seemed to be swooping down upon the schema to sweep it all away. And when Fr. Antonelli, promoter of the faith, was substituted for Fr. Bugnini, as reporter, it did not seem at first a good omen for the defenders of the schema.

In all this we perceive the secret of the Council. From the early stages of research, all opinions were freely expressed, the faith being preserved in its integrity. As long as argument or dispute remains at the level of men, passion can of course make its appearance, but when the hour for decisions rings out, the Holy Spirit blows and dispels the tempests. Anyone who had tried to decide what would happen to the

58

liturgical reforms after hearing the discussions that took place during the first general congregations would certainly agree that it looked like reform was a dead letter.

Cardinals and bishops in large numbers, with impressive authority and quiet assurance, had pleaded for Latin, calling it the language of the Church and a sign of unity. They insisted that the Roman See alone was competent to undertake reform of liturgical books. On these two points—decentralization and the use of modern languages—the reform seemed hopelessly compromised.

Nevertheless, while the debates of the Council in all other matters merely revealed certain tendencies and made it possible to perceive general orientations, in the question of the liturgy the general principles of liturgical renewal received the consecration of a definitive vote. Three specific gains should be emphasized:

1. The definition of competent authority in the matter of liturgical reform.

2. The difficulties of using Latin as a liturgical language.

3. The adaptation of the liturgy to cultures and mentalities other than Latin or Western.

Competent Authority in Liturgical Matters

Paragraph 22 of chapter 1, after declaring that the only competent authority for liturgical reform is the Holy See and the bishop, specifies further that by legal concession this right can also be granted to a supra-diocesan, territorial episcopal authority. In chapters regulating concrete applications of the reform, it is to this authority that the adaptation and execution of the general principles will be entrusted.

This provision, according to Fr. Vagaggini, is a real innovation because it establishes the bases for decentralization in liturgical matters, not in favor of each bishop locally, which would lead to excessive segmentation, but rather a supra-diocesan territorial authority.

To designate this authority, the text makes deliberate use of a general formula. It mentions "various territorial and competent assemblies of bishops, legitimately constituted." These assemblies will function as a provincial council or as a regional or national episcopal Conference. Actually, neither the Commission nor the Fathers could go further in clarifying the formula because they did not want to exclude any necessary or desirable possibilities. Moreover, they were determined to leave the door open to the Council when the question of legislating on episcopal conferences came under discussion.

Latin and the Modern Languages

To really understand the full scope and consequence of the debate, we should remember that the Pope, on February 22, 1962, had solemnly promulgated the Constitution *Veterum Sapientia* concerning the study of Latin.[4] A particular prescription of this Constitution required responsible ecclesiastical authorities to exercise great care and vigilance so that none of their subordinates "intent on innovation, engage in writing against the use of the Latin tongue, whether in the teaching of the sacred disciplines or the sacred rites of the liturgy—or attempt to diminish the firm will of the Holy See in this matter."

This statement was very alarming to many Catholics. In Holland, especially, emotions ran high.[5] Certain Roman commentators let it be known that this prescription was in fact an advance decision regulating the question of the use of modern languages in the liturgy by a clear refusal. But these fears proved to be without justification. The Pope had always said that he was leaving the whole matter of liturgical reform to the Council. And events demonstrated that the Fathers discussed everything in absolute freedom.

There was talk about a real battle concerning the use of Latin. There was, indeed, a very heated confrontation! One of the Fathers went so far as to say that moving a single inch away from Latin was tantamount to a proportionate deviation from unity and the Catholic faith itself!

A release issued by the Press Bureau, which was often accused of partiality, set forth in calm and detached language that characterized the work done by this organism, the respective advantages of both Latin and the modern languages.

The Fathers have discussed the matter of liturgical languages. There are reasons militating in favor of Latin. The use of Latin does not possess a traditional value alone, but exercises a real unifying function. Moreover, because of its logical precision, its concrete and juridical character, Latin is particularly capable of expressing theological and dogmatical concepts. We may also note its psychological and ascetical value. The Latin language imposes a logical and rational discipline which prevents yielding to sentimentalism and romanticism, leading instead to sobriety and realism in both expression and action.

On the other hand, we cannot question the importance of the reasons set forth in recommending the use of modern languages. The first and most important reason is that they can make the rites accessible to the whole community of the faithful, thus favoring their active participation in the celebration. The use of modern languages, moreover, visibly shows forth the universality of Christianity, capable, without losing its immutability, of assuming the values and traditions of all peoples, in all places and for all times, in this present day and through all the centuries to come.

The Fathers of the Council are discussing these questions, each bringing the treasure of his own knowledge and experience. It is not a matter of confrontation, but rather a fraternal quest in common. The various points of view are freely manifested with the sole purpose of finding a liturgical practice which is better able to achieve, at the catechetical and pastoral level, the ends and goals which the Church intends in her divine mission, the saving of souls.[6]

This press release gives the impression that two contending parties were alone in dividing the assembly between them. Actually, however, there were not only two tendencies, but three. One group insisted that there should be absolutely no concessions made to the vernacular tongues![7] At the other extreme, some of the Fathers hoped for a quasi-general use of living languages. Finally, there were those who wanted to maintain the principle of Latin, but they were also willing to open the door to vernacular tongues. The vast majority of the Fathers shared this middle opinion, and this was the opinion chosen by the schema.[8] It represented the way of prudence and apostolic audacity in a harmonious blending. The Second Vatican Council, officially introducing bilingualism into the life of the Latin liturgy, took an historic decision.

Adaptation of the Liturgy

The Council, which intended to be both pastoral and missionary, had to demonstrate the capacity of the Christian message to adapt itself to all mentalities, and the aptitude of its form of worship to express itself in all cultures everywhere.

Should the Catholic Church continue to impose the Latin liturgy on the nations she is seeking to evangelize, even at the risk of always seeming foreign to the masses of people, and in mission lands merely forming a minority that is limited in its influence and restricted in its scope of action? Or instead, shedding the garb which seemed to be crushing her missionary zeal, will she devise new expressions of worship by immersing these peoples in the bath of God's word and the sacraments?

New peoples appear one after the other upon the scene of history to proclaim to the world a word or message that we do not yet know. Christians, who are a minority in the world of our time, are also seeking a liturgy and a form of worship that will be for the Church like a word that is new, proving that the source of the Spirit has never run dry nor has that creative genius been exhausted which, in the first centuries, brought forth so many liturgical forms in a rich variety of rites, in a great diversity of languages and cultures.

Why would not the Holy Spirit perform tomorrow what He accomplished yesterday? He is the same Spirit who is forever renewing the face of the earth.

The Council must not obstruct the workings of the Holy Spirit, but open wide the gates on the road of history. The Fathers understood this well. They declared:

The Church when neither law nor the common good is at stake, does not want to impose rigid uniformity, not even in liturgical matters. On the contrary, the Church highly esteems and encourages the gifts and spiritual qualities of the different peoples and nations. She considers with benevolence everything which, in the customs of the peoples, is not indissolubly linked with superstition or error, and if possible, she protects and maintains these things. Sometimes she even incorporates them into her liturgy if this can be done harmoniously with the principles of a true and authentic liturgical spirit.[9]

Fr. Vagaggini rightly notes that the principle of adaptation, commended so insistently by the popes since Benedict XV in the general field of missions, is now explicitly and solemnly extended to the liturgy. Prudently, no doubt, but also with freedom and truly apostolic audacity, the Council has opened the way toward a possible slow but profound adaptation of the Roman Rite to the local needs of peoples who, in the development of their own civilization and culture, owe little or nothing to the Roman or Western tradition.

The Chalice in Communion and Concelebration

It would be premature to formulate conclusions concerning particular liturgical changes. Highly diverse opinions had been expressed, and numerous amendments had been proposed in such great number that one bishop said that of the whole structure of the schema hardly anything remained. While waiting for the balloting, however, and the promulgation of the Constitution *De Sacra Liturgia,* it was possible to predict one thing for certain and another that seemed probable.

The certainty: The general principles formulated in the first chapter received the consecration of a conciliar vote. Consequently, they will be applied to the particular chapters which pertain to the sacrifice of the Mass, the sacraments and sacramentals, the divine office, the liturgical year, and sacred objects, music and art.

The probability: It is foreseeable that the text of the schema will be approved in substance. The great majority who approved the general principles, in their spirit more than in their wording, seem determined also to give approval to the particular applications, inspired by the same spirit.

The general principle, providing for greater use of living languages, especially in the readings, admonitions, certain prayers and chants, if authorized by the competent episcopal Assembly, is applicable to the Mass also. This implies the possibility of important changes.

Communion under two species (bread *and* wine), which has been the subject of so much discussion, is only mentioned once in the schema: "If there is no danger to the faith, communion under both species may be granted to both clergy and laity in certain specific cases."

Communion of both species has always been practiced in the Eastern Churches, although the rite itself was attenuated. The faithful no longer receive the chalice itself, which would be impractical whenever communicants were numerous, but they are given a parcel of consecrated bread dipped into the consecrated wine. The disciples of John Huss, a radical reformer of the fifteenth century, had demanded the use of the chalice for the faithful. But the Council of Constance refused this demand, declaring that the Church had the right to regulate the administration of the sacraments, provided that their substance be respected. The Protestant Reformation again renewed this question, declaring that to be faithful to the Lord's command, Christians should receive both the bread and the chalice in communion. They quoted Our Lord's warning, *"If you do not eat of my flesh and if you do not drink of my blood . . ."* The Council of Trent (1562) decreed that the faithful communicating under one kind only were deprived of no grace necessary to salvation.[10]

If the practice of communion under both species is authorized again, this will not become a general measure. Restoration of communion under both species in specific circumstances, as in an Ordination Mass, a Nuptial Mass, or the renewal of baptismal vows, will be a visible proof of the Church's fidelity to Holy Scripture and the celebration of the Eucharist, even in its outward form. And this return to the original tradition will constitute, as is often the case, a step forward in the ecumenical encounter.

Concelebration is treated in a more fully developed manner in the schema. This practice, which is still common in the Churches of the East, only subsists in the Latin Church in a vestigial form at the Mass for the consecration of a bishop or the ordination of priests. The Council seems to favor extending this usage to Holy Thursday, which would assemble a large number of priests around the bishop, and to other gatherings of the clergy. It seems that the Fathers substituted more theological motivations for the practical reasons of convenience which the schema had set forth. Wherever many priests happen to be gathered together, concelebration expresses the unity of the sacrifice far better than the multiplication of Masses. One of the guiding principles of liturgical reform can find its application in connection with this practice. The liturgy is both communal and hierarchical. Consequently, whenever possible, the communal form of worship is to be preferred to the individual and almost private form.[11] It is true, of course, that the Mass is always, by its very nature, a public and social act of the Church.

With regard to the obligation of reading the Breviary, various opinions were expressed. But the opposition between Cardinals of the Curia and pastoral bishops of the dioceses did not occur in this instance. There were voices of the Curia suggesting audacious reforms, whereas pastoral bishops rose to defend the *status quo*. Cardinal Wyszynski reminded the Fathers that the recitation of the Breviary was for very many priests during the years of agony a source of consolation and strength. By these prayers recited in Latin, they felt they were in communion, not only spiritually but almost physically, with all the priests of the world saying the same prayers.

All the Fathers agreed in saying that to be supernaturally fruitful, the pastoral action of the priest must find its source in prayer. However, being aware of the ever increasing burden of responsibility that overwhelms the priest in today's world, the bishops, who themselves have the pastoral responsibility of caring for their priests, want to avoid imposing too heavy a burden, creating for many souls a situation that can be agonizing. They also want this prayer to be said in truth, and not in the manner of hypocritical formalism. It was necessary, therefore, that the Council seriously consider the extent and importance of the Breviary obligation. But it does not seem that agreement was reached, except perhaps on general principles. Consequently, certain principles were formulated, leaving freedom and the choice of practical applications to the episcopal conferences.[12]

A Fixed Date for the Feast of Easter

The Council devoted a great deal of time to the problem of the calendar, and especially to the feast of Easter. The schema recommended that Easter be celebrated on a fixed day, and that an agreement be reached with other Christian Churches and civil society on this question. The Catholic Church is not opposed to the establishment of a perpetual calendar, provided that the week of seven days be maintained.

The question of a perpetual calendar is not new. In the United Nations the matter was discussed on various occasions. What is new, however, is that the Catholic Church now seems determined, in conjunction with other Christian Churches and the civil authorities, to seek a satisfactory solution. There are two reasons for this attitude, one of them "ecumenical" and the other secular.

The Church, in fact, notes that the calendar of civil life, tending toward increasing stability, seems to be diverging more and more from the paschal calendar that regulates liturgical life. The civil life and liturgical life no longer fully correspond. The Church hopes to eliminate this hiatus, in order to continue, as in past ages, to imbue the rhythm of time with a Christian spirit derived from the paschal cycle.

The reasons for this reform were clearly set forth by Cardinal Feltin:

1. Celebration of Easter on a fixed date would facilitate the pastoral ministry in the parishes and would make the organization of diocesan life more convenient and satisfactory.

2. This reform would increase and enhance the feast of Easter in civil life. Easter, in fact, has lost much of its importance during recent years, and Holy Week also, which liturgically prepares for Easter and constitutes but one observance together. And yet, in some countries, the public authorities determine the scholastic Easter vacation period without any reference to the date of the feast. These inconsistencies would not occur if Easter were always celebrated on a fixed day of the year.

3. The proposal would also facilitate the activities of teachers, the regularity of scholastic work, and consequently the family spirit.

However, the problem concerns the various Christian Churches first of all. But they themselves are divided on the question of selecting the proper date for Easter. As a matter of fact, the Eastern Churches never followed the example of the Roman Church when Pope Gregory XIII undertook the reform of the old Julian calendar centuries ago.[13] There is no one who does not deplore this division or who would not want to find a remedy. That is why the matter of a fixed date for Easter cannot be the task of the Council alone. It has been suggested that an organism be created which would be in touch with the Christian Churches through the intermediary functions of the Secretariat for the Promotion of Christian Unity, and with international organizations through the Vatican Secretariat of State.

Several solutions have been proposed, first of all, the universal calendar which provides for years of fifty-two weeks, always beginning on Sunday, while the last day of the year (or in leap-years the last two days) would be nameless.

Msgr. Bafile, Nuncio at Bonn,[14] pointed out that this system, whose advantages were obvious for civil society, would however create difficulties for the Church. He considered the cycle of the week as a fundamental religious fact. Jews, Moslems and Christians all observe it scrupulously. But the new calendar under consideration, while maintaining the week of seven days, would really break the natural rhythm. The second year of the universal calendar, normally beginning on a Monday, would instead begin on a Sunday, and December 31st, a Sunday in fact, would be a nameless day. Bishop Bafile would prefer, for his part, that there be years of fifty-two weeks, with the insertion of a supplementary week each time that there be an extra seven days.

Chapters pertaining to sacred objects, music and art were not fully discussed. The new freedom for diverse cultural expressions, affirmed in the general principles, allows for a field of privileged application in this respect. If the West, in past centuries, found its own ways to express the sacred, why should not the new nations of modern times, often possessing the heritage of ancient civilizations, also find ways that are appropriate for them? "There are some people," according to the Bishop of Allahabad, in India, "who seem to think that there is no religious art except what is found on the Left Bank in Paris, thus implying that religious art found in the mission fields is simply Western, and even the worst of Western art."

Poverty in Worship

There was one tendency that deserves special mention. Several Fathers expressed the desire that the Church, in her worship, show contempt for wealth and manifest the countenance of poverty. Bishop Larrain of Talca, in Chile, who transformed his palace into a home for the poor, made a very moving and wonderful intervention. "Men," he said, "recognize the face of God more easily in poverty." Worship must be beautiful, of course, and worthy of God, but not with the splendor that wealth confers. It must instead be the splendor of truth.

Poverty is the distinguishing characteristic of the Incarnation. In fact, what is the liturgy if not the continued mystery of the Incarnation, the mystery of a God who, according to St. Paul's profound saying, emptied himself to accept the form of a servant? It is regrettable that the pedagogical means available to the liturgy for making God known are sometimes turned aside from their true end for the sake of human vanity. The Church, which deplores the apostasy of the masses, as John XXIII remarked, must now appear as the Church of the poor, not only in words but especially in deeds.

Bishop Gouyon, of Bayonne, spoke in the same vein, expressing the pastoral anxiety of many bishops. Is there no danger, he asked, that excessive use of wealth in worship may not be an object of astonishment and sometimes even of scandal? That wealth, in times past, may have attracted the people, although Saint Bernard long ago reproached the monks of Cluny because of the excessive splendor in their forms of worship.

In our day, many people who do not really know the Church see only the aspect of display and pomp when they watch a television program showing the celebration of Mass. As a consequence, these same manifestations become a kind of counter-witness, whereas an act of worship more fully inspired by poverty would be a witness and way to unity. Bishops need to remember that they are not princes, but pastors. They are not lords, but servants. Except for objects directly associated with the act of worship, a simplification and a greater degree of poverty are desirable. Everything that is used exclusively for the sake of magnificence and vanity should be suppressed, because these things, of themselves, are contrary to the very object and purpose of the liturgy, which is the revelation and manifestation of God.[15]

Saint Joseph in the Canon of the Mass

The discussion of the schema on the liturgy included some very exciting hours. Toward the end, however, some of the sessions were rather dull. Debating particular details, the Council risked the loss of time and the possibility of forgetting the general plan. On November 13th, utilizing the faculty which the Pope had accorded them, the presiding Cardinals suggested to the Assembly that the discussion be ended. This proposal was unanimously accepted. During the same session, a communication from Cardinal Cicognani, Secretary of State, made it known that the Holy Father, anticipating the desire expressed by many Fathers, had decided to insert the name of Saint Joseph in the Canon of the Mass, immediately after that of the Virgin Mary. This insertion, in the mind of the Holy Father, was to be in remembrance of the Second Vatican Council, in honor of the Council's patron. The Holy Father's decision was to become effective on December 8th. Meanwhile, the Congregation of Rites would prepare the necessary acts.

This decision of the Pope was received with mixed reactions, and comments about it were many and varied. Above all else, as we wrote at the time, this was an act of pious devotion to Saint Joseph by the Holy Father. Saint Joseph is the patron of the universal Church, and the Pope also designated him as the patron of the Council.

It would serve no purpose to overlook the reactions of the observers on this subject. The Orthodox, being very attached to tradition, hesitate to make any changes in liturgical rites or venerable prayers like the Canon of the Mass. We know, for instance, that a revision of liturgical books of the Russian Orthodox Church in 1656 led to the schism of the Old Believers, who remained faithful to the ancient "faith."

Protestants are now rediscovering the place of the Virgin Mary in the Gospel and in the economy of salvation. But they greatly hope that the Catholic Church will not extend or increase the particular honors paid to the saints, as if under the effect of a chain reaction.[16]

The decision was an act of the Holy See, certainly in connection with the Council, but it was not an act of the Council itself. It was for the happy outcome of the Council that the Holy Father wanted, in a gesture of piety to which he associated the whole Church, that Saint Joseph be invoked every morning by all the priests of the world and all the faithful attending Mass. The effects of this prayer can only be benevolent.[17]

NOTES

[1] Reported by the KIPA agency, October 30, 1962.

Canon Martimort was an expert at the Council. *Osservatore Romano,* on September 28, published a list of two hundred and one conciliar experts, named by order of precedence. These included theologians, canonists, specialists in pastoral theology, sociology, Latin, etc. During the sessions of the Council, there were other nominations of experts, but no proclamation was made about them in order to avoid any striving for expert status. Some of these nominations made up for omissions that are hard to explain. At the end of the first session, a pamphlet was published containing the names of members of the various organisms of the Council, the Commissions, and a new list of *periti.* The latter then numbered three hundred and six persons. (Cf. *Documentation Catholique,* No. 1387, November 4, 1962, col. 1406–08, and No. 1391, January 6, 1963, col. 62–64.) This means that one hundred *periti* had been nominated during the course of the Council.

The work of the theologians was less apparent than in previous Councils, but not less efficacious. Of course, they did not do any speaking while the Council was in session, except for the reporters speaking in the name of the Commissions, but it often happened that a particular intervention by a bishop faithfully reproduced the proposed declaration that was provided by some theologian.

Moreover, theologians played an active role in connection with the episcopal conferences that often requested comment and guidance concerning schemata that were then under discussion. Finally, the various Commissions appealed to specialists who were well-informed about the questions being debated. Although the theologians did not possess a deliberative or consultative voice, they certainly had a definite role in the preparing of amendments.

[2] Cardinal Montini was especially pleased with the approbation which the Council gave to the schema on the liturgy. This discussion made it possible to define and specify the Council's orientation. It rewarded those who, during many years, had worked in the liturgical movement, not for the sake of spiritual estheticism, or scholarly archaism, or because of devotional fantasies, but solely in order to bring forth the essential values of the prayer of the Church, and to ensure a purer expression of that prayer, resulting in greater pastoral efficacy. ("Letter from the Council," *l'Italia*, November 18, 1962, after a first vote of orientation on the general principles of the liturgy, November 14th, which gave the following results: 2,162 in favor, 26 against, and 7 null.)

[3] *Documentation Catholique*, January 6, 1963, reproduced this important article, col. 71–78. It was the first time that *Osservatore Romano* published an article quoting excerpts from a schema. Our own comments are largely tributary to that article.

[4] The Constitution published in *Osservatore Romano*, February 24, 1962, contains two parts:

1. Considerations on the value of Latin, "a universal language, unchangeable and not a vulgar tongue." (Pius XI)

2. Practical prescriptions in eight articles.

While it is true that these measures are justified in order to ensure and guarantee the exactitude of the theological training of priests, it is also true that it would be dangerous to imply or suggest that Christian doctrine can only be expressed in the Latin language. Nothing could be more detrimental in a time when the world expects from the Church assembled in Council a real manifestation of universality, as well as an openness towards all cultures and every language. The young nations are jealous of their own culture and suspicious of any enterprise that consists in channelling the Gospel into the mould of Latin culture and language.

The identifying of Latin culture and language with the Church is occasionally offensive to many. Two commentaries on the Constitution that appeared in *Osservatore Romano*, for instance, the first by Cardinal Bacci, on February 26, 1962, and the second by Cardinal Pizzardo, March 1st, are not above reproach in this respect. The first ended his article with two verses of Ovid (Fast. II, 683, 684), "To other nations was given a land with exact frontiers. But for Rome, the space of the city is coterminous with that of the whole world." Cardinal Pizzardo, in his commentary, quotes the phrase, *"Simul stant, simul cadant!"* "Together they stand . . . together they fall." This is inadmissible. The destiny of the Church is not bound up with the destiny of any human language, no matter how noble, and regardless of the intimacy of the bond that unites it to the Church, or its administration, intellectual life or theology.

[5] A group of Dutch laymen sent an open letter to the Episcopate asking for explanations of the commentaries which the Constitution had occasioned.

Refusing to accept these Roman commentaries in their literal sense, the authors of the letter to the Dutch hierarchy stated that "many people were disappointed and troubled in mind because they were led to believe that the growing desire within the Church for wider use of modern languages had been rejected and that nothing should be expected from the Council regarding this matter. To suggest particularly that the decisions of the Constitution anticipated those of the Council, and simply passed over the latter's head, seems to be dangerous procedure and derives from a very negative attitude."

6 Reported by the Press Bureau, October 26, 1962.

7 At the very most, they might have consented to the use of modern languages in the administration of the sacraments and in certain other ceremonies, but they were absolutely opposed to any use of living languages in the liturgy of the Mass.

8 The text of article 16, adopted on December 7, 1962, reads as follows:

1. The use of the Latin language, with particular prerogatives remaining in force, will be continued in the Latin Rites.

2. However, since it may often be profitable for the laity to have the Mass, the administration of the sacraments or other parts of the liturgy in the "vernacular" tongue, we accord a greater usage of the latter, more especially in the readings, the admonitions, and in certain prayers and chants, while adhering strictly to the regulations which, accordingly, will be defined each time in the following chapters.

3. It appertains to the territorial authority, mentioned in article 22, section 2, to establish the mode and usage of a vulgar tongue, respecting the norms previously set forth, and after having consulted, when necessary, the bishops of neighboring regions who speak the same language. Decisions taken must then be approved or confirmed by the Apostolic See. (*Osservatore Romano*, December 8, 1962.)

9 Constitution *De Sacra Liturgia*, first chapter, article 37. It should be noted that the last paragraph was added by the Council. This proves that the Council enlarged rather than shortened the schema, thus acting in the spirit of the Commission that prepared it.

10 The Press Bureau released a documentary note on Communion under two species, which was published by *Documentation Catholique*, No. 1389, December 2, 1962, col. 1545–46.

11 Constitution *De Sacra Liturgia*, first chapter, article 27. Every time, according to this article, the rites provide for a common celebration with attendance and active participation by the laity, this form should be preferred to any individual and semi-private celebration. The Council added a further statement to this article: "This especially pertains to the celebration of the Mass, because of the essentially public and social nature of the Mass, and to the administration of the sacraments."

12 Jean Pélissier reported in *La Croix*, November 13, the interventions of Archbishop Garrone of Toulouse, and Archbishop Yago of Abidjan. "The bishop's mind," the first of them said, "is full of concern. There is certainly no question of meddling with anything as important and venerable as the Divine Office, but pastors cannot ignore the concrete conditions of life and the pastoral task of their priests. Nor is there any love of innovation in this concern. It is simply a matter of wanting priestly prayer to be made in truth. Let it be made to render copious thanks to God, but not in formalism nor, occasionally, in a language that is but poorly understood."

Yago said, in substance, "It is not a matter of shortening prayer, but rather of finding the time to pray better. In this era when so many are rightly concerned about ensuring a greater and more active participation of the laity in the prayer of the Church, why should we not pursue the same goal with regard to priestly prayer, and first of all by inspiring and facilitating a greater taste for it?"

13 This reform consisted in catching up with the ten days of delay which the Julian calendar had lost in relation to the solar cycle. The date was therefore advanced from October 4, 1582, to the 15th of October. But the Eastern Orthodox Church did not accept this reform. Even now, a double calendar is used in the Greek Churches, the Julian calendar for the paschal cycle and the Gregorian calendar for the fixed feasts. In the Russian Church, however, only the Julian calendar is in use, although there is a delay of thirteen days in relation to the civil calendar which was immediately adopted by the October Revolution. This explains why the anniversary of that Revolution (October 25, 1917) is celebrated on November 7th.

[14] Bishop Bafile intervened in this question because of his particular competency. It has already been noted that the Pope had requested the nuncios and the secretaries of Roman Congregations not to intervene in the debating. A second derogation was the intervention of Archbishop Parente, assessor of the Holy Office, during the discussion of the schema on the two sources. Moreover, he specified that he was then speaking in his capacity as the Archbishop of Ptolemais "in the desert."

[15] In a letter on the Council, published by *la Semaine catholique du diocèse d'Agen* (January 11, 1963), His Excellency, Archbishop Johan, tells this anecdote:

"A bishop, whose stand regarding the simplification of liturgical insignia was notorious, was approached one day by a cynic who said to him, 'Show me your pectoral cross.' The bishop then opened up his *manteletta* and revealed, on his chest, a very simple cross of wood." This was Bishop Gouyon.

[16] It is necessary, of course, to remember the freedom prevailing in Protestantism in order to fully appreciate this. Karl Barth, for instance, in an interview published in *Réalités*, February, 1963, was asked the question:

"The Pope has just added the name of Saint Joseph to the prayers of the Canon of the Mass. Is this decision not likely to irritate many Protestants?"

Karl Barth answered, "It does not annoy me. Since Rome believes in the intercession of the Saints, why should Saint Joseph be overlooked? Personally, I love Saint Joseph a great deal. Recently I spoke about this to an American Jesuit. I am as hostile to the further development of Mariology as I am favorable to a development of 'Josephology.' Because Joseph, in my opinion, in his relation to Christ, played the same role as the Church should exercise. The Roman Church, I know, prefers to compare her role to that of Mary, which was more glorious. She brings the Gospel message to the world in the same way that Mary gave us the Christ. But the comparison is fallacious. The Church cannot give birth to the Redeemer, but she can and must serve Him with discreet and humble zeal. This was specifically the role of Joseph, who always remained in the background, leaving all the glory to Jesus. This must also be the role of the Church if we want the world to rediscover the splendor of the Word of God."

[17] On November 18th, Cardinal Montini wrote in his letter to the faithful of Milan concerning the insertion of Saint Joseph's name in the Canon of the Mass, "The veneration of this Saint who was all humility and silence now receives a greater honor. It establishes in the Church and in souls the image of incomparable, evangelical authenticity. . . . This decision was a surprise prepared by the Pope for the Council." The Cardinal issued an analogous decree for the Church of Milan and the Ambrosian Rite, in order to express the bond of unanimity with the universal Church.

VI

Divine Revelation

THERE WAS MORE THAN ONE HIGH POINT AND MORE THAN ONE
decisive day at the Council. On Thursday, November 14th, the Council
undertook the discussion of the schema on the sources of Revelation,
and on Tuesday, the 20th, the Pope decided to send the schema to a
mixed Commission, for further consideration.

A Controversial Schema

As early as Tuesday, November 13th, there was a certain agitation
apparent in the Rome of the Council. The Fathers were concerned about
the direction that discussion of the schema might take. It was publicly
rumored that this text, drawn up according to scholastic methods and
orientated toward the condemnation of errors or the refutation of certain doctrines favored by theological schools of thought, was far from
assured of winning the votes of the majority of Fathers. Certain episcopal conferences were unanimously hostile to it.[1] And then there
appeared a phenomenon which has occurred, we believe, at all the Councils recorded in history. Counterprojects were circulating, and especially
one of German origin which had received the approval of the presidents
of various episcopal conferences of Austria, Belgium, France, Germany,
and Holland.

"As it seems impossible," according to the preamble of this text,
"that the Council will discuss all the schemata and engage in voting on
all of them, it may be necessary to omit some, shorten others and com-
bine them." That is why the presidents of the episcopal conferences of
Austria, Belgium, France, Germany, and Holland suggested the following outlines as a starting-point for the discussion, summing up the sub-

ject matter of the first two schemata in a more positive and more pastoral tone.

This text was not an improvisation. It reflected Karl Rahner's theology quite faithfully, and was titled: "On the Revelation of God and Man in Jesus Christ." It comprised three chapters:

I. The divine vocation of Man.
 1. The end of this vocation.
 2. The meaning of this vocation.
 3. The mode of this vocation.
 4. The sublimity of this vocation.
II. The hidden presence of God in the history of the human race.
 1. The grace of God, forever present.
 2. Man's capacity for grace and revelation.
 3. Evangelical preparation in human history.
 4. Evangelical preparation in the economy of the Old Testament.
III. The presence of God revealed in the Church's preaching.
 1. The Lord Jesus present in the Church.
 2. The Revelation contained in Holy Scripture.
 3. Holy Scripture transmitted by the Church.

The text also suggested a preamble, declaring that the unity of the world facilitates and encourages a new scope and zeal in the preaching of the Gospel. The Gospel is the message of eternal salvation. It concerns the whole of man and consequently, it also contains light for the solution of the problems of this world. The Council aims to bring the Good News of the Gospel to the entire world, like a candle placed in a candelabra.

The schema of the theological Commission was titled: *"On the Sources of Revelation,"* comprising five chapters.
1. The double source of Revelation.
2. Inspiration, inerrancy, literary style.
3. The Old Testament.
4. The New Testament.
5. Holy Scripture in the Church.

The first chapter pertains to the double source of divine Revelation, Scripture and Tradition, and the relations between them. This question was raised by the Reformation at the beginning of the sixteenth century. The Council of Trent left it an open question, although it defined the value of Tradition against the Protestants who advocated the principle of *"the Bible only!"* (the Bible is the sole rule of faith).[2]

The chapter devoted to the New Testament defends the historical value of the Gospels and the truth of the episodes related about Christ's life against the errors of those who question the historical facts of Christ's childhood, His miracles and His resurrection.[3]

Chapter 5, concerning Scripture in the Church, describes the role of God's word for priests, the faithful, exegetes and theologians. Together with formal encouragements, there are also certain reticences and suspicions which are said to be based partly upon the difficulties of the sacred text, and partly on the boldness of certain exegetes.[4]

Cardinal Ottaviani spoke to a meeting of members of the theological Commission on Tuesday evening. He was severely critical of the text that was circulated among the Council Fathers. "Such a procedure," he said, "only serves to disturb and confuse the minds of many, and it does not respect the regulations governing conciliar proceedings which call for a prior preparation and discussion of the schemata by Commissions that were set up by the Pope for that purpose."[5]

The Cardinal was correct in his criticism. However, when earlier Councils took place, there was also a circulation of texts which sometimes lacked the reliable origin which could otherwise be claimed for the text in question. At the Council of Trent, for instance, the papal legates complained about this practice. But the Pope, while withholding his approval, put his faith in the Holy Spirit who assists the bishops when they proceed to the vote.

Different Points of View

On Wednesday morning, in presenting the schema to the Fathers of the Council, Cardinal Ottaviani declared that the teaching of doctrine is also a pastoral act. But there should be distinction of literary style and presentation, because a papal encyclical is one thing, a bishop's pastoral letter is something else, and finally, a dogmatic constitution of the Council is something else again.[6]

Msgr. Garofalo read the rest of the Cardinal's report. "The Council's first task," he said, "is to defend and promote Catholic doctrine in the most accurate formulation. Doctrine does not innovate, but develops." The report then explains the schema in its various parts, emphasizing the work that was done in its preparation. Members and consultants of different countries and universities participated in its elaboration, keeping in mind that a dogmatic constitution promulgated by the Council should not be written in the style of an encyclical, nor a homily, nor a pastoral letter, but rather as a text that is immutable, although perfectible in its presentation.[7]

Cardinal Liénart spoke first. He expressed a severe *"Non placet."* The text of the schema is inadequate, he said, falling short of the definitions of the Council of Trent. It is Christ, the Word of God, who is primary in Revelation. The schema is cold, scholastic, and barely reveals the munificence of the divine revelations mentioned in the Letter to the Hebrews:

> God, who at sundry times and in divers manners spoke in times past to the fathers by the prophets, last of all in these days has spoken to us by his Son, whom he appointed heir of all things, by whom also he made the world; who, being the brightness of his glory and the image of his substance, and upholding all things by the word of his power, has effected man's purgation from sin and taken his seat at the right hand of the Majesty on high. . . ." (Heb. 1:1–3).

Cardinal Frings, Archbishop of Cologne, was no less severe:

> It is true, of course, that teaching is also a pastoral function, but there are several different methods of teaching. In the schema, we do not hear the maternal voice of the Church, but rather the voice of professors. On several points, for example, the two sources of Revelation, inerrancy, and inspiration, the schema seeks to nullify disputes between schools of thought, which is contrary to the customary procedure of Councils.

Cardinals Ruffini of Palermo and Siri of Genoa defended the importance, usefulness, and rectitude of the schema. Cardinal Quiroga y Palacios, Archbishop of Santiago de Compostela, spoke in the same vein, but with greater reticence.

Cardinal Léger, Archbishop of Montreal, was incisive. He deplored the excessive assurance with which the schema attempted to settle questions that are still a subject of controversy between theologians. It was inadmissible that there be mistrust while speaking of Holy Scripture.

Consequently, he requested that the schema be re-examined from start to finish.

Cardinal Koenig, Archbishop of Vienna, expressed less substantial reservations, whereas Cardinals Alfrink, Archbishop of Utrecht, Suenens, Archbishop of Malines-Brussels, and Ritter, Archbishop of Saint Louis (U.S.A.), stated their absolute disagreement unsparingly.

The opposition of Cardinal Bea, who was a professor of Sacred Scripture during his entire life, and is now responsible, under the Pope's authority, for the destiny of ecumenism in the Catholic Church, greatly impressed the Assembly. "The schema," he said, "does not correspond to the purposes which the Pope determined for the Council, which should reflect a concern for the pastoral ministry and unity."

Patriarch Maximos IV, as was his custom, spoke in French. He wanted to know what dangers the schema was attacking. This remark was not whimsical. Other bishops were totally in the dark concerning the basis of the quarrel. No doubt problems may arise in some country or other, and this may entail a particular danger, but the same problems do not arise elsewhere because of a lack of maturity in theological development. However, if Holy Scripture or Revelation were really in any serious danger, it is simply inconceivable that the bishops assembled in Council would not have immediately perceived it.

The attack was harsh.[8] What can account for such an earnest and nearly unanimous opposition on that first day? Not everything has been said by way of explanation when the words *pastoral* and *ecumenical* have been emphasized. The Fathers who expressed their disagreement with the suggested text felt that it canonized certain theories as opposed to others, and that it hardened positions connected with the Council of Trent, more especially in this era of ecumenism when everyone is advocating a dialogue between Christians and the avoidance of any further deepening of the chasm that divides us.

Scripture and Tradition

As an example, let us consider the relationship of Scripture and Tradition. The writers of the schema favored a specific theory which lays stress upon the duality of the sources, affirming that Revelation is partly contained in Scripture and partly in Tradition. However, another theory emphasizes the unity of all Revelation, declaring that it is transmitted in substance integrally in Scripture and integrally in Tradition also.

The schema states that certain truths are transmitted only by Tradition. Yet we have seen the Church's magisterium take recourse to scriptural proofs for such recent definitions as those of the Immaculate Conception and the Assumption, which, at first sight, do not seem to be contained in Scripture.

A large number of bishops were surprised at the flat disagreement with the schema expressed by certain Cardinals who were, however, members of the Central Commission. After all, had not the Central Commission given its *placet* to this text? In defense of the dissenting Cardinals, it must be explained that the schema had been presented to the Central Commission during the session of September, 1961, and was examined in the two sessions of September 19th and 20th. Many members of the Central Commission had voiced reservations regarding this schema, and gave a merely conditional assent to the text by voting *"placet juxta modum."* This formula expresses agreement, with reservations concerning requested changes. The Commission responsible for revision no doubt made corrections that were formal rather than fundamental. This explains why members of the Central Commission found themselves in disagreement with a text which they had previously examined, but which furthermore, they did not have the time to review in its corrected or amended form.

The False Opposition between Teachers and Pastors

If the discussion of the following days did not cast light on the real object of the schema, it did however facilitate the specific orientation of the Council. Two points, especially, received great emphasis. First of all, the concern for an ecumenical dialogue was voiced in a remarkable intervention by Bishop de Smedt of Bruges, made in the name of the Secretariat for the Promotion of Christian Unity. Further mention of this is found in the chapter devoted to the ecumenical dialogue. In the second place, there were some who increasingly tended to contrast and oppose teaching and pastoral functions, implying that doctors of the faith were more concerned about integrity of doctrine, while others apparently were rather indifferent to doctrine as such and interested above all in pastoral tasks. The French bishops, all of whom sided with the "pastoral party," recognized the danger and error of categorical distinctions that exclude one another.

Archbishop Guerry, in the name of the French episcopate, declared that there should be absolutely no opposition between doctrinal and pastoral concerns:

> As pastors, the bishops know very well that their primary function is the teaching of doctrine, neither veiling nor minimizing any of its exigencies. But they hope to discover and specify the best way of setting forth that doctrine so that it will be better understood and more desired. They also hope to conform their own pastoral minds to that doctrine itself, and by their very lives, lead the flock entrusted to them, and witness for the truth in charity.

La Croix, published an interview with Archbishop Guerry concerning this same subject, on the 2nd and 3rd of December. He said:

> Separation between doctrinal and pastoral functions is inadmissible. It is an error. It weighed upon the Council like an equivocation, threatening to culminate in the division of the conciliar Fathers into two groups, with one faction faithfully defending and safeguarding the Church's doctrine, and another faction, comprising the pastors, concerned above all else with fulfilling their pastoral mission . . .[9]

The discussion of the schema continued on following days without bringing new light or new arguments in favor of the opposed theses. Rather than reporting in detail the arguments of the Fathers, which were summed up in press releases, or quoting their interventions, which must be kept secret, we prefer to mention two comments of the Pope. The first of these, at the beginning of the discussion, was addressed to the general audience on Wednesday, November 14th, just at the end of the first general congregation that was devoted to this schema. The Pope had been following the debates and seemed to speak more confidentially to the vast crowd of people than he would to the bishops:

> We must not suppose that everything can be said in four words. There must be reciprocal benevolence, listening to one another, formulating one's own thoughts on these important questions and expressing in them in such a

way that they result in a doctrine, an encouragement, an exaltation of Christ in Himself, in His grace, and in His activity.[10]

The Pope's second remark was made in confidence to the French bishops during the memorable audience granted to them by the Holy Father on Monday evening, November 19th, when the discussion was brought to an end, although nothing definite had been decided. Replying to the address made by Cardinal Liénart, the Pope referred to the tasks of the Council. "There is controversy," he said, "and that is good in itself and necessary. But it should be carried on with fraternal feeling, and then everything will proceed very well. As for myself, I am an optimist." In this quarrel between brothers, the Pope thought of himself in the role of the patriarch Jacob, witnessing the disputing of his children, *"Ipse autem rem tacitus considerabat:* He watched what was happening and kept silent."

Return of the Schema to a Mixed Commission

It seemed more and more useless to continue the discussion of the schema. The best thing was to count the pros and cons. Consequently, it was necessary to proceed with the voting. But in the circumstances a majority of two-thirds was required to reject a schema, because the discussion had been normally proposed according to the rules. The voting took place on Tuesday amid obvious confusion and nervous tension. The excessively long discussions had strained the atmosphere. When the voting was over, Archbishop Felici, contrary to the usual procedures, made no mention of the results. He merely announced that the majority of two-thirds, necessary for sending the schema back, had not been attained. Accordingly, as the press release reported, the examination of the chapters of the schema under discussion would be continued.

The Secretariat of the Council certainly did not think that the result of the vote could remain secret. But the presiding Cardinals wanted to inform the Pope first of all.[11] By evening, the press agencies and newspapers knew the exact results: 1,368 Fathers were in favor of sending the schema back, and 822 voted for continuing the discussion. The majority felt understandably bitter about this. Wednesday morning, on their way to the Council, the Fathers still thought they would be taking up discussion of the schema again, chapter by chapter. But before proceedings were even under way, Archbishop Felici, by order of the Cardinal Secretary of State, read a communication concerning the previous day's vote:

Taking into account the fact that the opinions expressed during the interventions of recent days indicate a rather laborious and prolonged discussion concerning the schema of the two sources of Revelation, it has appeared useful to revise the schema by a special Commission, before continuing the examination. According to the Holy Father's desire, this Commission will be composed of several Cardinals, as well as members of the theological Commission and the Secretariat for the Promotion of Christian Unity. The Commission's task will entail a revision of the schema on the sources of Revelation, by making it shorter, and giving greater emphasis to the general principles of Catholic doctrine already deliberated by the Council of Trent and the First Vatican Council.

This decision brought great relief to the Council. *La Croix* did not hesitate to put the news in big headlines: *"The Council Breathes New Air,"* and the newspaper, *Le Monde,* proclaimed: *"The Pope Intervenes to Free the Council from Deadlock."* We had written in *La Croix* that the Pope made his decision because of the endless discussion and Tuesday's voting. It was a necessary decision. "He entrusted the examination of the schema on the sources of Revelation to a mixed Commission composed of members of the Theological Commission and the Secretariat for the Promotion of Christian Unity."[12]

There is no one who fails to see the significance of this measure. For one thing, it takes into account the legitimate reticence and hesitation manifested by the majority of the Council with regard to the schema. Moreover, the Pope made it perfectly clear that the Council would define nothing until after hearing the reasonable requests of Christians who, although not forming part of the visible body of the Catholic Church, share with Catholics their faith in Christ and the honor of the Christian name. In fact, the Secretariat for the Promotion of Christian Unity, as we know, is attentive to their desires and somehow lends its voice to speak in their behalf to the Council. Finally, the supporters of the schema still had every possibility of defending their point of view, since they were well represented in the new Commission.[13]

Cardinal Bea expressed his satisfaction with the work of this Commission in an interview granted to the Lutheran daily *Kristeligt Dagblad* of Copenhagen, in January, 1963. Bea said that the mixed Commission had completed its task and, in spite of divergences, there was now general agreement about everything except the question of the relationship between Scripture and Tradition. Some think that certain truths of faith are based upon Tradition alone, whereas others (including Cardinal Bea) maintain that every truth of faith is contained in Holy Scripture, even if this requires, in certain cases, a development and explanation to discover them.

The mixed Commission met again on February 23 and 25, and also on March 1 and 3, 1963. It agreed upon the definitive text to be submitted to the Council. According to the press release, the new text was elaborated in conformity with the decisions of the first session, in the light of directions given to the Commission by the Holy Father, and in accordance with principles set forth in the opening address to the Council.

Cardinal Ottaviani and Father Tromp Explain
Their Points of View

In principle, the Theological Commission, jointly and separately, was responsible for the doctrinal schemata.[14] In fact, two persons, Cardinal Ottaviani, President, and Fr. Tromp, Secretary of the Commission, a Dutch Jesuit, professor at the Gregorian University and consultant to the Congregation of the Holy Office, were especially singled out for explanations.

Cardinal Ottaviani defended his attitude in an interview that was broadcast by German radio stations. The talk was then published by *France Catholique,* and finally by many French newspapers and publications interested in the Council. The question was asked unsparingly:

In public opinion, Your Eminence is regarded as the leader of a typically conservative group of conciliar Fathers. People say that you are too rigid and antipathetic with regard to the results of theological research, etc. This tendency was perhaps apparent especially during the debate on the schema of the sources of Revelation. What is your position?

The answer was more vague:

My personal position is that of a man who, by his very functions, has the duty of guarding intact the deposit of faith, and who, at the same time, must permit full freedom to the progress that is necessary for a better enlightening, deepening, and presentation of Catholic doctrine. Let us never forget that everything that is new is not for that reason true or good. Today, there are new opinions in theology which, if not wholly false, are at least questionable. In such circumstances, it is a truly positive action to defend the teachings of Holy Scripture and Tradition in order to prevent any darkening of the truths of faith on the pretext of seeking progress and adaptation.

Father Tromp explained his position in an interview published in the newspaper of Nijmegen, *De Gelderlander Pers,* on December 18, 1962. Fr. Tromp said:

There is now a great fermentation of ideas that are still premature. And a dogmatic constitution cannot adopt premature ideas or those which have not yet been accepted by theologians of world repute. Must we use a different language in speaking to the Second Vatican Council than was used for Trent and the First Vatican Council? My answer would be that we must speak the same language, but with another tone. Whatever the Council of Trent defined four centuries ago is still the norm of truth for ourselves, and it will remain so for our successors. Using the language of our day simply means that we have recourse to a language that will be quite old-fashioned twenty-five years from now. Changes in traditional terminology, for instance, in whatever concerns Revelation or the faith, could result in considerable confusion of mind and produce more evil than good.

When asked about the ecumenical dialogue, Fr. Tromp replied that this dialogue can only be carried on by a clear and unequivocal presentation of Catholic doctrine. It will be the task of the bishops and theologians to explain to others, according to each case, whatever the Council has taught to everyone. We must not use language that is pleasing to our separated brethren, but rather one that they can understand. This is not easy, for Protestantism has many faces. But even to our separated brethren, the Church must speak her own language. It is not possible for her to speak simultaneously in accordance with seven different mentalities.

Fr. Tromp denied that the theological schemata expressed the point of view of only one school of thought. He maintained that there are various stages in the preparation and examination of the texts.

Asked about the relations of the preparatory theological Commission with the Secretariat for the Promotion of Christian Unity, Fr. Tromp said:

> You are now touching upon a delicate question which I consider secret. The Theological Commission, and it alone, was responsible for dogmatic constitutions. Other Commissions, by the Pope's decision, were obliged to submit their texts to the Theological Commission every time that a dogmatic question was under consideration. That is why a mixed Commission was inconceivable. But this does not mean that the Theological Commission would be unwilling to be informed about the opinion of the Secretariat for Unity and take it into account. The thirteenth subcommission of the Secretariat, which was to take up the matter of Tradition and Scripture, unfortunately submitted its report much too late, that is to say, five months after the constitution of the schema on the sources of Revelation had been examined by the Central Commission.[15]

Regarding the mixed Commission, instituted by the Pope to free the schema from the deadlock, Fr. Thomp said, *"They will not prepare a new schema."* Conformably with the Pope's desire, the old schema will be shortened and corrected. Fr. Tromp finally expressed the hope that the contending positions would come together and that a better understanding would follow, because, as a matter of fact," they were less distant from each other than was commonly thought."[16]

A Defense of a Thesis at the Biblical Institute

The discussion on the sources of Revelation was followed by a kind of epilogue on Thursday, November 21, the day after the Pope had decided to send the text back to a mixed Commission. We have reference to the defense of thesis by Fr. Lohfink, professor of Sacred Scripture in the Jesuit faculty of theology at Frankfurt, on the literary analysis of chapters 5 through 11 of Deuteronomy.

The subject had no bearing on the Council. But the errors mentioned by the schema and the exegetical dangers which it complacently pointed out were plainly and often attributed to the Biblical Institute in Rome. Nevertheless, the presence of so many Cardinals, bishops, and experts signified encouragement and approval of the teachers and scholars who were often and unfairly criticized during recent years. Fr. Lohfink's thesis was consequently a worthy homage rendered to the Biblical Institute and the work of the exegetes. Twelve Cardinals were present on this occasion: Their Eminences, Pizzardo, president,[17] Tisserant, Gerlier, Doepfner, Frings, Bea, Gilroy, Alfrink, Ritter, Léger, Confalonieri and Testa. Cardinals Montini and Koenig had excused themselves. There were also one hundred and fifty bishops and three thousand other persons, including the General of the Jesuits and several Superiors General of religious orders, as well as many experts and such observers as Professor Cullman, Msgr. Cassian, Msgr. Sarkissian, and the Ambassadors of Austria, Germany, etc.

During the discussion of the schema, there was a great deal of talk in Rome concerning the attacks against the Biblical Institute since 1961 by Msgr. Romeo and Msgr. Spadafora.[18]

Bishop Weber had given a lecture at the Biblical Institute in Rome on the "Value and Limitations of Biblical Sciences."[19] The Bishop of Strasburg briefly related the dispute concerning Fr. Jean Steinmann's *Life of Jesus,* which was the subject of the *monitum* of the Holy Office on June 20, 1961, and was placed on the Index, on June 26 of that same year. Bishop Weber declared:

The "judgmens and opinions" which seriously endanger the exact truth and objective of Holy Scripture, mentioned by the *monitum,* are generally inspired by the exegetical method that is now the most widespread, called *Formgeschichte,* which is the history of both forms and the formation of evangelical documents, and sometimes also called the method of *Form-und-Traditionsgeschichte,* being the history of forms and Tradition. As these names indicate, the method is applied to studying the progressive formation of the evangelical narratives, by classifying them according to literary categories, according to their form, and by establishing the role of primitive Christian Tradition in their elaboration.

Bishop Weber then spoke of the origins of this method and its present development, pointing out what is acceptable and what is not. Noting that the area of evangelical studies is not yet wholly cleared,

85

he hopes that the hierarchy will put their trust in the exegetes. It is a good thing to have recourse to the method, but one must be aware of its limitations. Professors and students should avoid any expression that would create the impression that the New Testament is purely a myth, a series of legends, or a construction of the Christian community, even if the latter had been assisted by the Holy Spirit. If the Church were not closely linked to Christ, the Son of God, and did not faithfully transmit His message, what value would her teaching possess? And if it was her duty to learn more about the message of Jesus (John 14:26 and 16:13), and then adapt it in some statement or other, we must remember that the Church did not create it.

Cardinal Bea, for his part, felt that it would be timely to make available to the bishops who had requested it, a brief essay on the historicity of the Gospels which he had prepared about two years previously when the quarrel was just beginning, and which he had since completed.

The Cardinal examined the historical character of the synoptic Gospels, first from the perspective of human history, and then as writings inspired by the word of God. In the first part, he inquires into the history of forms and literary styles. In the second part, he investigates the relations between inspiration and methods of writing history. Finally, he formulates a few practical rules for interpretation, taking into account both the laws of history and Catholic affirmations on the inspiration and inerrancy of the word of God.

To really understand a sacred author, it is important to know what he intended to say, and why he placed some particular episode in a particular context, or why he mentioned some detail or other and wrote about it in this manner or that. The answer is found in comparing the Gospels, determining the literary style and its laws, and studying the various modes of expression. These rules are applicable not only to the Gospels, but to the documents which the evangelists integrated into their narratives. Delicate work of this kind surely requires much patience and reflection but it is a most necessary and meritorious task.

The Church encourages exegetes to undertake and pursue this task. As the pillar and ground of truth, she guides the exegetes in their studies and, if necessary, prevents them from going astray. In their turn, the exegetes render service to the Church by achieving an increasingly complete knowledge of the word of God.

NOTES

[1] The French bishops met together in consultation concerning the schema when the discussion was already under way. There were 80 against the schema, and 30 in favor of it, with the reservation that substantial and profound modifications be applied. Only one of them found the schema wholly acceptable. However, this does not mean that the French bishops approved the schema circulated by the five presidents of the episcopal conferences.

[2] The Council of Trent clearly stated that its purpose was to ensure the preservation within the Church, of the Gospel which, originally promised by the prophets in the holy Scriptures, was first promulgated by the mouth of Our Lord Jesus Christ, the Son of God, and then by His apostles whom he commanded to "preach it to all creatures as being the source of all saving truth and every moral precept." As these truths are contained in the "secret books and unwritten traditions which, received by the apostles from the mouth of Our Lord, or transmitted as if from hand to hand by the apostles, under the direction of the Holy Spirit, have come down to us," the Council receives and venerates the holy Books "as well as the traditions concerning faith or morals, as coming from the very mouth of Our Lord or prescribed by the Holy Spirit and preserved in the Catholic Church by a continuous succession." (Cf. *"The Catholic Faith,"* doctrinal texts of the Magisterium of the Church, translated into French and presented by Gervais Dumeige, S.J., p. 98.) The Council of Trent therefore left this discussion free and open. It does not mention two sources, but only one: the Gospel, and its double transmission. This theory is often upheld by many Catholic theologians. It would be unsuitable for the Second Vatican Council to limit this freedom surreptitiously, thus creating difficulties in theological research at a time when the Pope himself prefers to keep the doors open.

One theologian directed our attention to the fact that the theory underlying the wording of chapter one creates an unnecessary difficulty for Protestants. It discourages the important movement which, among themselves, has been rediscovering Tradition. Several observers were simply shocked and dismayed when reading the first pages of the *schema.* Of course, this reaction cannot serve as a theological criterion for the Council, but, in the circumstances, it corresponds to the fact that the writer was advancing a particular human theory rather than expressing a dogma.

[3] Cf. the appendix at the end of this chapter.

[4] Cardinal Montini, in his "Letter from the Council," which he published at regular intervals in the newspaper *l'Italia* (Milan), enumerates the problems which arose as soon as discussion of the schema was begun. "Everybody can readily understand that this matter is fundamental for our religion and, consequently, it is but natural that the Council should mention it. But only those who are well-informed about theological developments, the progress of biblical studies and the tense character of controversies regarding these questions among Catholics and others also, can measure the apprehensions, hopes, and fears which the new subject has brought to the conciliar Assembly. Certain questions arise: Was it really necessary to consider and discuss this subject? How can it be linked to the affirmations of the Council of Trent and Vatican I concerning the same matter? Was this problem not settled by the encyclicals *Pascendi,* of Saint Pius X, and *Humani Generis,* of Pius XII? Are not the pontifical documents on this subject sufficient to determine the speculative and practical attitude of Catholics with regard to Scripture? Should the new study trends that are perturbing the schools in scriptural matters be objects of dogmatic definition or decisions of the ordinary magisterium? Do the unquestionable dangers which certain new methods of scriptural interpretation face and the grave errors which may be hidden in their roots, require the direct and solemn intervention of the Council? Had it not been decided to wholly avoid pronouncing anathemas and dogmatic definitions? How then was this subject

included in the Council's program, since the latter was meant to be especially pastoral?" This enumeration itself reveals the Cardinal's secret apprehension.

5 The Secretariat of the Council had not received communication of a text of which 2,000 copies had been circulated.

6 Cardinal Ottaviani merely introduced his report. He requested Msgr. Garofalo to read the rest of it. It is known, of course, that the Cardinal's eyesight is not good, and he is often obliged to have certain things read by others.

7 Press release of Wednesday, November 14th.

8 *Osservatore Romano,* dated the 15th, which had been circulated on the evening of the 14th, published a note addressed to journalists to inform them about the special difficulty of the subject and to warn them against superficial information. We ourselves were sensitive to this argument, and rather than give any particular details on that day, we preferred publishing general considerations on the schema, its content, and the difficulties which it entailed. The text of the Press Bureau's release declared, "The Press Bureau of the Second Vatican Council, after the experience of these first months of conciliar proceedings, is glad to express to accredited journalists its satisfaction with the way in which they have tried to inform public opinion concerning the progress of these great sessions.

"The schema which the conciliar Fathers have begun to examine today is lofty, complex, and delicate. It requires considerable conceptual clarity and the precise formulation of terms in order to divulge knowledge of it while avoiding dangerous and upsetting obscurities or ambiguities.

"In a spirit of profound awareness and esteem, the Press Bureau of the Council invites all accredited journalists to confront this difficult subject with the care, prudence and discretion that it requires. Qualified explanations will be given to them each time that it becomes necessary."

9 Referring to the questions of Mr. Pélissier, Archbishop Guerry dispelled several errors that threatened to become widespread because of certain news reports concerning the Council:

First of all, it is not doctrine itself that needs adaptation, but rather its presentation and formulation.

Next, it is absolutely not a question of minimizing doctrine. We do not accept any compromise in this area. The truth must be set forth in its integrity and purity. We would be betraying our mission by accommodation or silencing of any truth, under the pretext that it would be too hard a saying or too difficult to grasp. The example of the Catholic laity who always insist upon the teaching of all doctrine, applying it to the whole of life, is eloquent evidence of this demand for light and action.

It would be simpler, as some think, to repeat the formulas of the theological manuals. But is this the easiest way? On the contrary, for the pastor it is the most difficult, requiring not a new theology, but arduous efforts of thought, reflection, and the study of traditional doctrine, as also a personal assimilation of the living truth, in order to translate it to his people in terms that enlighten and influence them.

Moreover, we feel that a pastoral mission of this kind requires an openness to the needs of our time. We believe that the best way to safeguard doctrine is to open up new fields of penetration and diffusion, as the Sovereign Pontiff explicitly requested in the opening address of the Council: "The Church must look out upon the present, perceiving the new conditions and forms of life introduced into the modern world, which have opened up new paths to the Catholic apostolate."

Think of all the elaboration required for a theology of earthly realities and human values: the body, love, work, money, art, technology and science.

Consider all the doctrine pertaining to international social problems and ecumenism. A pastoral ministry that must lay hold of all these great human problems requires a most demanding effort of reflection on the part of both pastors and teachers.

That is how the French episcopate conceives of its pastoral mission in the modern world. Let us add that it commits itself with ardent faith in the power of the word of God, in the might of the Resurrection, as Saint Paul said, and the efficacy of theological charity and the supernatural means of the Church. (Msgr. Guerry, *La Croix,* December 2–3, 1962.)

10 These improvised comments of the Pope did not appear in *Osservatore Romano.*

11 Cardinal Frings, however, requested Archbishop Felici, at the end of the session, to communicate the exact result of the vote to the Fathers.

12 The members of this Commission were appointed on November 25th. The schema was called *De Divina Revelatione* (On Divine Revelation) and no longer *De Fontibus Revelationis,* which was the title of the original schema when it was taken for granted that controversial matters had already been settled.

13 The *KIPA* Agency, on March 2, 1963, informed us that fourteen Cardinals had sent a letter to the Pope on November 24, 1962. They thanked the Pope for having sent back the schema *De Fontibus* to the mixed Commission, but laid stress, nevertheless, on the importance of Tradition and the magisterium of the Church. The letter made reference to the norms of Tradition, including the *sensus ecclesiae,* the universal *consensus,* and the analogy of faith. Moreover, it pointed out certain errors regarding the inspiration of holy Scripture and literary styles.

Originally there were nineteen signatures, but five Cardinals later withdrew their names, so that finally there were fourteen who signed the letter: Their Eminences, Cardinals Bacci, Marella, Pizzardo, Urbani, Taglia, Ruffini, Siri (of Italy); Browne (Ireland); Agagianian (Armenian); de Barros Camara (Brazil); McIntyre (U.S.A.); Santos (Philippines); Godfrey (England); Bueno y Monreal (Spain).

14 Cardinal Ottaviani and several Fathers who were favorable to the schema constantly reminded everyone that the schema was not the work of only a few persons, but was prepared by a Commission comprising theologians of various schools of thought and different nations. As a matter of fact, however, there were very few exegetes in that Commission, and only two of them at first. There was not a single representative of the Biblical School of Jerusalem nor the Pontifical Biblical Institute of Rome. This latter omission was later corrected by the nomination of Fr. Vogt on February 26, 1961, when the work was already far advanced.

15 It is surprising, indeed, that the positions of the schema on several important matters are directly contrary to the *votum* written by the Secretariat for the Promotion of Christian Unity, and another prepared by the Pontifical Biblical Institute.

16 See the analysis of the Dutch newspaper's article in *Echo der Zeit,* January 20, 1963, by Bishop Jean Brosch of Aix-la-Chapelle.

17 Cardinal Pizzardo presided in his capacity as Grand Chancellor of the Gregorian University, of which the Biblical Institute is a part (Faculty of Sacred Scripture and Ancient Oriental Studies).

18 Msgr. Spadafora, professor of exegesis at the Pontifical University of the Lateran, a former student of Msgr. Romeo, who was a member of the pre-conciliar Commission for studies and seminaries, had distributed to all the Fathers of the Council a pamphlet titled *Rationalism, Catholic Exegesis and Magisterium,* in which he said that the full scope and origin of all errors of modern Catholic exegesis can be found in the *"Formgeschichte"* method which is in flagrant contradiction with Catholic doctrine, so that the Council ought to consider "whether it might now be appropriate, or even necessary, to expressly condemn and denounce this system." (Cf. *KIPA-Council,* November 16, 1962.)

19 The text is published in *Documentation Catholique,* February 3, 1963, col. 203–212.

VII
The Media of Social Communication

A T THE SAME TIME ARCHBISHOP FELICI ANNOUNCED THE FATE
of the schema on the sources of Revelation, he informed the Fathers that
the Council would broach the schema on the means of social communication on Friday, November 23.[1] This included the press, radio, motion
pictures, television and theatre, pageants and spectacles of all kinds.

The text of this schema was divided into four parts:

1. The doctrine of the Church on the media of communication.
2. The apostolate of the Church by the media of communication.
3. The discipline and guidance of the Church.
4. Particular regulations concerning the various media of communication: the press, motion pictures, radio and television, other media.

From a subject that was wholly theological, the Fathers went on to
consider a subject that was practical and moral. Some people will feel
that these matters pertain more properly to the competency of the State,
and to laws governing such techniques, than to the Church. However,
the Church has a fundamental reason for being interested in the media
of social communication quite apart from the fact that many aspects of
the schema pertain directly to morality, as, for instance, respect for the
moral order by the media of information, freedom of information and
the right to information, the manner of discussing or reporting moral
evil and freedom of art, etc.

The Encyclical *Miranda Prorsus* of Pius XII, dated September 8,
1957, sets forth Catholic doctrine in regard to these matters, declaring
that the Church's solicitude for audio-visual techniques is derived from
the very mission which Christ entrusted to the Church. These techniques,

in fact, exercise a powerful influence upon the thought and action of both individuals and groups. And the Church is responsible for man and for whatever fashions his manner of thinking and feeling.

On the other hand, the Church is continuously a bearer of news, for she received from her divine Founder the command to transmit the Glad Tidings of eternal salvation to all men, a message of incomparable abundance and power, which all men of all nations and all times must know and welcome.[2]

The Special Field of the Apostolate of the Laity

Discussion of the schema was conducted briskly. Begun on Friday, November 23, it was completed on Monday.[3] The French bishops took an important part in this discussion. René Stourm, the new Archbishop of Sens, had been designated as the reporter by the Commission of the Council. The preparatory secretariat, responsible for the text, had three objectives in view: the right and duty of the Church to teach by technical media; the right and duty to instruct the faithful to make use of them; the right and duty to organize them. And this organization must be undertaken on the international, national, and diocesan levels.

According to Archbishop Stourm:

The Church must be aware of the movement of history. A new order is being built by the media of social communication which suppresses obstacles between nations and renders them permeable. These media will make them pagan or Christian, as the Church utilizes such media or not. In the Middle Ages, men were instructed by theological disputation. Today, however, this is achieved by modern technical means.[4]

In the course of the discussion there soon appeared a certain unanimity of the Fathers in emphasizing the pre-eminent role of the laity in this field. The media of social communication offer laymen a magnificent field of apostolate for the realization of the *consecratio mundi,* the consecration of the world. According to Pius XII, this constitutes the apostolic task of the laity. The press release laid stress on this, emphasizing the need for laymen, imbued with a Christian spirit, to become fully aware of the possibilities for action in each of the areas or fields that have some part in the formation of public opinion. This

91

activity of laymen must be developed in the technical work proper to journalists, stage directors and artists as well as among readers and spectators.

A more intensive activity was desired for the spiritual and technical training of an ever larger number of laymen in order that their competency might equal their apostolic zeal, and consequently enable them to bring the influence of Christian ideas to bear more strongly upon both the press and theatre.

Mention should also be made of the appeal addressed to the Fathers by the bishops who are responsible for the evangelization of new countries, in the hope that concrete assistance in men and equipment will be made available to the young nations that are now entering into our technological civilization.[5]

Bishop Gouyon of Bayonne, a former journalist, came to the defense of newspapermen:

Opinion is often too harsh against them. We ourselves do not sufficiently realize the difficulties of their task. We are too quick to reproach them for inaccuracies or vagueness, forgetting the pace at which they must work. Does it not happen to ourselves that we seek for some exact formulation which we cannot always find, although we possess time that is lacking to journalists?

He also stressed the importance of written news:

The words of the radio and the pictures of television quickly vanish, whereas writen words remain. We read and re-read the newspaper, especially the daily newspaper, and this reading, continually renewed, acts like a drop of water falling upon the rock. Slowly but surely it hollows out a groove and forms a mental outlook.[6]

In a Pastoral Perspective

In his diocese of Versailles, Bishop Renard is concerned to make the best use of the resources of the Catholic press for evangelization. The Christian press tends to Christianize public opinion. It is a kind of forerunner of Catholic Action. Only too often the pastoral activity of priests and the apostolic efforts of the Catholic Action movements end in failure because the seed falls into poor ground. It is for the press to improve it by forging a favorable mentality and creating a receptive climate.

Bishop Renard expounded these principles to the Council: "The Church," he said, "now finds itself in a world of public opinion, whose influence upon men is great, especially by means of the daily newspaper."

The Church is making a magnificent apostolic effort these days, including catechetical instruction, missions, parochial schools and Catholic Action. But this effort is often limited, or even destroyed, by an all-powerful secular press.

It is therefore necessary that the Church, by her priests and militant laymen, bring all the resources made available by modern civilization into the service of the kingdom of God. *Everything can be useful in this apostolate.* The man who holds to a single method should be feared more than the man of a single book. Recourse to many methods, jointly and severally, useful and necessary, will enable the apostolate of both priests and laymen to correspond more fully to the freedom of the Holy Spirit who blows where he wishes, and to reach men of very different temperaments through evangelization, while also benefitting from the practical and technical possibilities of a particular era.

The Bishop of Versailles then concluded with a hope: "May the Council encourage all those who are engaged in a pastoral task of information, and those who, in the press, judge events in the light of the faith, as well as those who have dedicated themselves to the Catholic press, specifically." He asked all Catholics to support and circulate Catholic newspapers, the weeklies, and more especially the dailies. St. Paul spoke of the essential end and purpose of the apostolate and the variety of means to be used: "Provided that Christ may be proclaimed in all things."[7]

Archbishop Duval of Algiers spoke of the Christian press, referring to his painful but fruitful experience of recent years and in the terms of the new situation of Christians in his diocese. The Catholic press is not only responsible for Christians, but like the Church, it bears a missionary responsibility with regard to all mankind. What is the best way to make non-Christians hear and understand our message? We can achieve this if we speak or write in terms of conscience and natural morality.

Moreover, by taking an interest in all human problems and making men realize that a fully satisfying solution of these problems can only be found in a Christian perspective, the voice of the Church echoes throughout the world like the voice of human conscience.

A Permanent Commission

At the end of the session of Monday, November 26, the presiding Cardinals suggested that the discussion should be ended. On Tuesday, the 27th, Archbishop Felici presented a resolution to the Council that tended to make the results of the discussion concrete and specific:

In order to proceed with the final formulation of the schema on the media of social communication, the following points are now proposed for the voting of the Fathers:

1. The schema is substantially approved. It is most opportune that the Church, in the exercise of her conciliar magisterium, be concerned about a subject of such importance at the pastoral level.

2. Keeping in mind the observations made by the Fathers, the competent Commission receives the mandate to extract from the schema the essential doctrinal principles and the more general pastoral directions, in order to give them a formulation which, while conserving the entire substance, will be shorter, and which can finally be submitted to the voting of the Fathers.

3. By an express order of the Council, whatever is pertinent to practice and execution, must be written in the form of pastoral instructions, and this will be done by the service mentioned in paragraph 57 of the schema, with the collaboration of experts of various countries.[8]

The proposition received 2,138 votes against 15. And there were 7 that were null. Paragraph 57, to which the proposition made reference, reads as follows: "The Fathers of the Council, adopting the resolution expressed by the Preparatory Commission of the Council with regard to the press and theatre, request the Sovereign Pontiff to extend the competency of the Pontifical Commission for Radio, Motion Pictures and Television to all the media of social communication, including the press."

The Commission in question, whose competency will be extended to the press, was established by Pius XII in 1948. In January, 1952, it was transformed into a Pontifical Commission for Motion Pictures, with the task of studying the problems of the motion picture industry in relation to faith and morals. This competency was then extended to radio and television when the statutes of the Commission were approved on December 16, 1954. Pope John XXIII, by the motu proprio *Boni Pastoris,* issued on February 22, 1959, attributed new competencies to the Commission and decreed that it would possess a permanent character as an Office of the Holy See for the examination, development, and direction of various activities in the fields of motion pictures, radio, and television. The Congregations of the Roman Curia and the other Offices of the Holy See must hereafter consult this Commission before making any decisions or authorizations in these different sectors. The Commission is attached to the Secretariat of State, which indicates its importance and connects it directly with the Holy Father.[9]

It was certain that the second session would ratify the revised schema and especially article 57. Consequently, through the intermediary function of this Commission, the problems of the press will in future be the direct concern of the Pope insofar as they pertain to questions of faith and morals.

NOTES

[1] This term is new, and it has not been sufficiently noted. Until now it was customary to speak of the techniques of diffusion, audio-visual methods and mass media. But none of these terms was adequate. The first of these, *techniques of diffusion,* emphasizes excessively the technical rather than the human aspect of diffusion. *Audio-visual* methods exclude the press. And *mass media* could possibly imply an impersonal approach because of the stress upon people in general. The term chosen by the Secretariat, however, covering the press, radio, theater and other media is most satisfactory and should be used in ecclesiastical documents as also in the terminology of spoken language among Catholics generally. It really expresses the instrumental role of these various techniques: the *means* considered as the nature of the activity, *communication* in its various forms; and the word *social* which indicates that the press, radio, etc., always aim at men in groups or whole communities. It is a term which includes all the advantages of other expressions, without their unsatisfactory connotations.

[2] On this subject the encyclicals *Miranda Prorsus* (September 8, 1957) and *Vigilanti Cura* (June 21, 1936), as also the addresses of His Holiness, Pius XII, (June 21, 1955 and October 28, 1955) are worth reading. The word *Miranda* expresses the Church's admiration for these techniques. The schema also shares this same admiration, beginning with the words *"Inter mirifica . . ."* (among the marvellous discoveries of technology . . .).

[3] In the review, *Journalistes catholiques* (issue of January-February 1963), Father Gabel commented about this rapidity. He said, "Any discussion can be quickly concluded, either because everyone is in agreement, or because there is but little to discuss, or because the schema is proposed at a precise moment like a kind of intermission performance. But it was surely because the Fathers of the Council were in

agreement concerning the importance and the nature of the means of social communication and the conditions of their best utilization. All of them had strong, clear and simple ideas on this subject, a kind of intuition which has often been crystallized in formulas since the days of Leo XIII and Pius X, and which have come down to us in our time. The journalist should not complain about this rapid and solemn assent given to all that constitutes his work and his professional concern, as also to everything that represents his share of the apostolate within the Church."

[4] The text of Archbishop Stourm's report was published *in extenso* by the *KIPA* agency, November 27, 1962. *Documentation Catholique,* on December 16, 1962, quoted long excerpts from it.

[5] Press release of November 24, 1962. Referring to Africa, Bishop Perraudin pointed out that tradition was essentially oral. Nevertheless, the press, particularly the Catholic press, is progressing there. It greatly needs competent help and collaboration, as also in the fields of radio and television. The Church has, and must have, her place in radio broadcasts and television programs, either in the government networks or in broadcasting stations of her own, according as different situations and various countries allow, and here again this requires help in both money and men. The ecclesiastical organisms necessary for this activity should be subject to the collective authority of the bishops of each particular region. This request was repeated by a Nigerian bishop, Msgr. Nwedo, who made an appeal to better equipped countries to come to the aid of countries that have recently become independent, in order that the Church may make her message heard in them more effectively and extensively.

[6] *La Croix,* November 27, 1962.

[7] Cf. *La Semaine religieuse du diocèse de Versailles,* December 7, 1962.

[8] Press release, November 27.

[9] Cf. *l'Annuario Pontificio,* 1963, page 1520.

VIII
Unity

O N NOVEMBER 27TH, THE COUNCIL BEGAN EXAMINATION OF the schema on unity, entitled *Ut omnes unum sint*. The discussions continued during three general congregations on November 27, 28 and 29. This rapid examination enabled the Council, at the very start, to eliminate an equivocal aspect. The text, in fact, in spite of its general title, only pertained to the Eastern Churches. But properly there cannot be two different theologies of ecumenism, one of them defining the relations between the Catholic Church and the Churches of the East, and the other pertaining to the Catholic Church and the various Churches or sects of Reformation origin. At the very heart of the ecumenical movement is the Church's theology and her constitution, and this theology can only be one.

The ways and means of ecumenism may, however, be different. This explains why the question of unity was considered by the pre-conciliar Commission of the Eastern Churches and also by the Secretariat for the Promotion of Christian Unity. Moreover, the schema on the Church, likewise, includes a chapter on ecumenism. There are, consequently, at least three different places in which there is reference to ecumenism, and not in the same terms. In fact, the tendencies and concerns of these three Commissions, and the men who compose them, are not the same.

The News of Unity with the Orthodox

The schema, *"That they all may be one"* is meant to be a homage of the Catholic Church to the venerable Churches of the East. Indeed, if we except the principal divergence on the primacy and infallibility of the Pope, we have everything in common, because the minor differences

97

regarding the *Filioque,* Purgatory or Mariology can be reduced, for the most part, to differences in theological formulation.[1]

The text is divided into three parts:

The first pertains to the unity founded on Peter, who is Vicar of Christ only within the visible Church. In the order of grace, he is like all the faithful, subject to the sacraments. But, as head of the visible Church, he exercises authority over the economy of grace and judges matters of faith, either alone or with the college of bishops.

The schema gives a historical account of the separations that occurred in the long life of the Church, emphasizing that it was always a separation from the central See. Often enough, good faith subsists and the separation may only be external, but for the separated Christians it entails the loss of advantages which result from the exercise of the magisterium. Finally, vestiges of the unity and the ancient common heritage still subsist in the separated Churches.

The second part examines the various ways to foster unity—not the Church's unity, of course, which already exists—but of Christians generally, or the Church considered as a social body which must still effectuate the unity, even externally, of all baptized Christians:

Supernatural means: like prayer, or the novena preparatory to Pentecost, established by Leo XIII to foster Christian unity, and the Week of Unity, and finally, prayer to Mary, in which the East and the West are united. It was, in fact, from the East that we learned the praises of Mary.

Theological means: we must remember that theological methods may be varied. There is an Eastern theology. It is important that we keep this in mind, and that we approach it by a return to our common tradition. The schema rejects every polemical or apologetical method.

Liturgical means: in this respect, it seems that the Council wants to proclaim its unchanging veneration, now and forever, for the Eastern rites. Never again could there be a restriction of the rights and privileges of the Eastern Churches. On the contrary, the Council will be an occasion for affirming more seriously, and if necessary, for increasing them. The rites may be many, and many the languages also, but there is only one heart praying to God, and only one voice rising to the Father, though there be many voices of sons united in the same faith and the same love.

Psychological means: a sincere and mutual love, the avoidance of all proselytism, the spirit of repentance and reparation for the sins committed by all of us against unity, and common action for the defense of the faith. This last point is most important. Nevertheless, we must exercise caution in our use of language, so that we do not confirm the suspicions of those who are tempted to accuse the Council of merely seeking to establish a common front against atheism and materialism. The common action of Christians and all other believers must take place in a positive manner, as in the defense of the moral, human, and social values that are universally acknowledged.

Practical means: it is for the bishops to stimulate ecumenical activity, and to foster the training of experts in Eastern theology, the recruiting of teachers and students, etc.

The last part of the schema examines the juridical and practical norms whereby unity can be established. There is a historical form commonly called *Uniatism,* which provides for Churches keeping their own rites and particular customs while also recognizing the Roman primacy. However, this form has not given full satisfaction, doubtless because it put a Uniate Church of the same Eastern rite, and with a parallel hierarchy, alongside every separated Church. We wrote in the special issue of *Osservatore Romano* on the very day that the Council first convened:

This Roman undertaking aroused considerable opposition among Eastern Christians who seemed to feel that the Uniates were simply wolves in sheeps' clothing. They regarded the whole Uniate enterprise as a kind of piracy undertaken by evil shepherds attempting to seize the flocks of others. The origin of this regrettable mistake will be found in the impossibility, for Eastern Christians, of considering the Roman Catholic Church as anything more than the historic Latin Church of the West. But if the Eastern Christians have somehow lost the authentic idea of a universal Church, it is partly our own fault. From their point of view, the true expression and countenance of Catholicity is no longer apparent in the Roman Church.

The schema specifies the conditions and modes whereby unity could be achieved either with persons or with groups; it calls for a general profession of faith, emphasizing primarily the unity of the Church.[2] The next to the last paragraph lays stress upon the validity of the sacraments in the Eastern Churches, and notably the sacrament of Holy Orders. This means that if unity is eventually achieved, the Eastern clergy will be received into the Catholic Church, each according to his particular Order, as bishops, priests and deacons.

Finally, the last paragraph clearly states that the present legislation of the Church is neither definitive nor unchangeable. "According to circumstances, and if the Holy See considers it useful, ecclesiastical discipline and hierarchical order may receive a new form which corresponds more perfectly to new conditions and gives greater recognition to the dignity and importance of the Eastern Churches."

The Dignity of the Eastern Churches

Bishop Edelby, an auxiliary of Patriarch Maximos IV, addressed the French bishops on the subject of the schema. He severely criticized the first eleven paragraphs, which set forth the Catholic doctrine of unity and the causes of the separation. In this schema there are too many offensive terms, too many psychological errors, together with an obvious measure of good will. And there are too many historical inaccuracies, too. For instance, has the Catholic Church always really been seeking unity?

With regard to the last paragraph of the schema, Bishop Edelby asked why the separated Eastern Christians must first come back to the Church before they can be respected and revered, especially if the Church's legislation can be changed now. What they would like would be fewer promises and a better performance, together with the place of love reserved for absent brethren.[3]

The valiant and active Greek Melkite Church has generously devoted itself in the cause of the Churches of the East. Sometimes it is criticized because it seems to act and speak as if it constituted the whole Eastern Church, whereas there are several Eastern Churches of various rites and different importance, including the Maronite, Syrian, Armenian, Chaldean and Coptic Churches. It is true, of course, that among the Eastern Churches in union with Rome the Melkites occupy a special place. Their Church did not result from a union or return of a group or part of a separated Church. With the heritage of its own tradition, its own rights and privileges, and with a patriarchal succession that has been uninterrupted since Saint Peter in Antioch, it re-established union with the Roman Catholic Church between the sixteenth and eighteenth centuries.[4]

It is for this reason that Patriarch Maximos spoke with such self-assurance at the Council. During the session of November 27th, speaking in French as was his custom, he said, "The Churches of the East are apostolic Churches, that is to say, they were founded by the Apostles. They are not daughter Churches, for they existed from the beginning."

This voice was particularly impressive because the Patriarch and the Church which he governs are ready and willing to be sacrificed in the cause of unity, and to yield their place to those Eastern Christians who are still separated from Rome, on the day when unity is finally achieved.[5] Maximos IV declared, "As Catholics united to Rome, it is our vocation to be the redemptive victim of unity." One day, in his residence at Ain-Trez, in Lebanon, the Patriarch told us, "We are Catholics as much as anyone, and we are ready to shed our blood for the Catholic faith. But we are not and can never be Latins."

Msgr. Nabaa, Greek Melkite Archbishop of Beirut and Gibail, Assistant General Secretary of the Council, expressed regret concerning certain terms used in the schema, and the omission in the enumeration of the means to be used in seeking unity, of any reference to common action in charity to arrive at truth. He also emphasized the need to make reparation for past mistakes and sins committed against unity by both the East and the West.

Bishop Edelby, giving expression to the feeling he had already manifested outside the general Congregation, was hostile to the dogmatic preamble of the schema. However, he accepted the provisions for fostering reunion, provided that certain changes be made. "The Catholic Church," he insisted, "has not done as much for unity as the schema seems to imply." He also demanded that the Eastern Churches, even though separated from Rome, be recognized as *Churches,* because of their apostolic origin.

Bishop Zoghby, Greek Catholic patriarchal vicar for Egypt, also spoke in French. He said:

The Eastern Church which has always recognized the Roman primacy,

101

although not in a clear and explicit manner, has never been a part of the Latin Church. It does not derive its existence from her. Its dogmatic and disciplinary development is independent of the Latin Church. Consequently, the Eastern Church is an original source, like the Latin Church in the West. Dogma is substantially the same in both Churches, but there are differences in theology. This difference in their traditions, concepts and discipline is reflected in the difference of the rites.

The difference in liturgy has always been recognized by Rome. "We must carry out this principle to its logical conclusion and acknowledge the legitimate differences in discipline and theology," Bishop Zoghby declared; and these aspects, in fact, are fundamentally linked together. Bishop Zoghby then showed, for instance, that the Eastern and Western conceptions of Christmas are not at all the same. The feast of the Nativity of Christ, like that of the Epiphany, is for Eastern Christians a celebration of the divinization of human nature. The West, however, has emphasized the concrete fact that Christ was born of the Virgin Mary. In the course of history, the Eastern Church and the Western Church have evolved in the way that their own historical destinies have led them, the Orthodox Churches becoming increasingly autonomous, while the Catholic Church moved toward excessive centralization. Catholics and Orthodox can only unite when they achieve equilibrium in mutual harmony.

Bishop Zoghby concluded:

The Catholic Church of our day assembled here in this Council, which God has blessed, appears to be universal and ecumenical with regard to territorial representation. But it longs for the day when Orthodoxy, with its two hundred million members, will also be represented in proportion to the patrimony which the Fathers of its Church, its great Doctors, and holy monks have bequeathed to Christendom, a patrimony which still enriches and sustains the Churches of both the East and the West. Some have said that this Council is not a Council of reunion. And that is true. But so long as Christains are divided, no Council inspired by the Spirit of Jesus Christ can be indifferent to reunion.

The venerable Maronite Church, which has always remained in communion with Rome, a claim to inestimable glory if we consider the vicissitudes of its history, is now the most important Eastern Catholic Church from the standpoint of numerical membership.[6] However, it has been said that this Church could have made its presence felt more effectively at the Council. Maronite representatives usually intervened only to modify one or another affirmation of Eastern ecclesiastical autonomy whenever it seemed that the affirmation was excessive, not so much with regard to the Fathers who had spoken, but rather because so many persons who, until then, had no direct contact with the Eastern Churches, might have misunderstood.

It cannot be said that the Churches of the East have come to know each other better because of the Council, since they have all existed side by side for many centuries, and sometimes there has even been inter-penetration. Nevertheless, with regard to the old Latin Churches of the West and the younger Churches of Africa and Asia, they are aware that their witness will be all the stronger, and their experience more mean-ingful, according as they appear united themselves, not only in the faith but also in their witnessing and their service.

The Ancient Institution of the Patriarchates

Mention was often made of the Patriarchs in the discussion of the schema on unity, although the term itself merely appears there in pass-ing. The preparatory Commission for the Eastern Churches had, in fact, prepared a particular schema on the Patriarchs. It would seem that it might have been better to discuss these two schemas together, since the patriarchal structure is essential to the Churches of the East. However, this does not mean that the patriarchal institution exists by divine right. Originally, the title of Patriarch was given to the heads of certain apostolic Churches, like Antioch, founded by Peter, or Alexandria, as-sociated with Mark, the disciple of Peter.

The ecumenical patriarchate of Constantinople, ranking first among the Eastern patriarchates, is not directly of apostolic origin. It lays claim to Saint Andrew, whose apostolate according to tradition was exercised in Pontus; but it would be more exact for this See to invoke the name of Saint John who made the Churches of Asia Minor illustrious.[7] The apostolic origin of Jerusalem, of course, is unquestionable; yet it was not recognized as a patriarchate until the Council of Chalcedon in 451.

The patriarchate of Moscow, now the most important patriarchate with respect to the number of the faithful and the political power of the country in which it is established, is of recent origin. It dates from 1589 and was suppressed between 1721 and 1917 by the secular authorities.

The Bishop of Rome, in this perspective, is considered as the Patriarch of the West.[8] But the Popes have always felt that their prerogatives as patriarchs of the West were distinct from the rights and powers appertaining to the universal primacy. This was strongly affirmed in the letters of Leo the Great, for example. And John XXIII referred to this historic doctrine in the encyclical commemorating the fifteenth centenary of the death of Saint Leo.[9]

Rome has always affirmed that the primacy existed from the beginning together with episcopal collegiality. The patriarchates and the autocephalous Churches are the result of a historical development, but the primacy is of divine institution.

Beyond doubt, beginning with the tenth century, the Church of Rome has been practically identical with the Latin Church. Its theology and canon law are almost exclusively Latin. The task of the Council will be to distinguish whatever is purely Latin or Western from that which is truly universal, and whatever is essential to the primacy from anything that is merely accessory. It will also be the Council's task to determine the rights and privileges of the patriarchal or autonomous Churches. The reunion decree of the Council of Florence (1439) proclaimed the universal primacy of the Bishop of Rome as well as the rights and privileges of the Churches of the East. However, these rights and privileges were not clearly specified, and it is quite possible that they were interpreted very differently in the East and the West.[10]

Cardinal Bea was among those who preferred that the question of the patriarchates be examined at the same time as the schema on unity with the Eastern Churches. Intervening toward the end of the discussion, he, nevertheless, praised the general tenor of the text and the good intentions it revealed. But he felt that any decision would be premature and inopportune in a matter that pertains to ecumenism as a whole. The presiding Cardinals agreed with him and suggested that the debate be ended, and this was approved by the Assembly.

On Friday, November 30, before undertaking the discussion of the schema on the Church, the presiding Cardinals suggested that the Assembly vote on a resolution which recommended the combining of various documents pertaining to ecumenism into one text, and a full discussion of the subject at a later time. The resolution was worded:

The examination of the decree on the unity of the Church being terminated, the Fathers of the Council approve it as a document in which the common truths of the faith are set forth, and as a mark of attention and good will towards our separated brethren of the East. However, according to the observations and propositions formulated in the Council chamber, this decree shall form a single document with the decree on ecumenism and the chapter on the same subject contained in the schema of dogmatic constitution, on the Church.[11]

The Fathers approved the proposition by a tremendous majority. 2,112 votes were cast, and there were 2,068 in favor, with only 36 against. Eight of the ballots were null. But not all of the Fathers were immediately aware of the full meaning of their vote. As a matter of fact, in the discussion on the Church there were many of them who again brought up the question of ecumenism, although they had just previously voted to detach that chapter from the schema under discussion!

NOTES

[1] Cf. our own article, *"Les divergences doctrinales entre l'Eglise catholique et les Eglises orthodoxes,"* which appeared in the *Nouvelle Revue théologique* (June, 1954), 631–654. We examined the principal differences, one by one, including the Catholic doctrine of Purgatory, the Immaculate Conception, the *epiklesis,* the *Filioque,* ecclesiology, and the primacy and infallibility of the Pope.

Certain articles in *La Croix* have been criticized for theological minimalism, especially with regard to the *Filioque.* However, the Council of Florence declared that the Greek formula, "The Holy Spirit proceeds from the Father through the Son" and the Latin formula, "The Holy Spirit proceeds from the Father and the Son" were both accepted by the Catholic Church. (Cf. Denzinger, *Enchiridion symbolorum,* n. 691.)

[2] For Christians in good faith, no abjuration would be necessary. But an express abjuration of error would be required of individuals who had themselves left the Church and then desired to return.

[3] His Excellency, Msgr. Vuccino, Titular Archbishop of Aprus, made a notable intervention on November 27, 1962, concerning the schema on the unity of the Church. "It is not without serious concern," he said, "that we wonder how a purely juridical description of the Church's unity can contribute to the dialogue with our Orthodox and Protestant brethren. . . . Let us rather speak to them in that evangelical language which they love and understand. Tell them that Peter's primacy is specially a diaconate, a pastoral function, a service which the leader of the apostles received from Christ, not to exercise power or to dominate others, but rather to feed the flock of Christ; for, in fact, the juridical power of Peter was instituted for the sake of this pastoral function."

[4] The history of the relations of the Greek Melkite Church with the Roman

Catholic Church is quite complex from 1583 until 1724. It was between these two dates that unity between the Melkite Church and the Catholic Church was re-established. In 1583, Patriarch Michael VII of Antioch made a profession of Catholic faith. In 1724, Patriarch Cyril was expelled by the Orthodox and took refuge in Lebanon.

5 In December, 1962, an important book was published by Desclée de Brouwer for the patriarchate of the Melkite Church, a volume of 206 pages, with the French title, *Voix de l'Eglise en Orient* (The Voice of the Church in the East), including selected writings of Patriarch Maximos IV and other Melkite bishops. The table of contents clearly reveals the interesting subject matter that is especially significant in these days of the Council and the ecumenical movement. The chapters include: the Vocation and Destiny of the Christian East; the Coming Council and Christian Unity; the Defense of the Rights of the Christian East; Against the Latinization of the East; Liturgy and the Vernacular Languages; and Excerpts from the Writings of Patriarch Maximos IV.

Mention should also be made of a recent book by A. Simonet, *l'Orient chrétien au seuil de l'unité* (Editions Grands Lacs, Namur), a volume of 264 pages, which is both a history and good contemporary reporting, written in an ecumenical perspective.

6 The best book on this Church was written by Pierre Dib, Bishop of Cairo, honorary professor of the University of Strasburg: *Histoire de l'Eglise Maronite* (Editions La Sagesse, 1962), 356 pages.

7 The 28th canon of the Council of Chalcedon attributes to Constantinople, the "New Rome," the first place after the Old Rome. Saint Leo, however, did not accept this canon because the order of precedence in the Church is regulated by other laws than those determining political precedence, and also to avoid anything that might be detrimental to the rights of the established, ancient Sees of the East. Nevertheless, in the course of time, Rome recognized the Patriarch of Constantinople as the Ecumenical Patriarch and highest authority in the Eastern Church. Within the Orthodox Church itself, the Patriarch of Constantinople is considered as having jurisdiction over Eastern Christians who live in regions where their Church has no established hierarchy. It was because of this canon that a part of the Russian Orthodox emigration submitted to the jurisdiction of Constantinople.

Concerning the rights of the Patriarch of Constantinople, and his relations with Rome and with other Eastern Churches, we strongly recommend to historians and theologians of ecumenism an outstanding book published by the *Institut Français d'études byzantines* (The Assumptionist Fathers), under the title *Les Regestes des actes du patriarcat de Constantinople*, series 1. (The Acts of the Patriarchs.) Three volumes, by Venance Grumel, have now been published. Another, by Vitalien Laurent, is in preparation.

8 This title belongs properly to the Pope. In the *Annuario Pontificio,* his titles appear as follows: Bishop of Rome, Vicar of Jesus Christ, Successor of the Prince of the Apostles, Sovereign Pontiff of the Universal Church, Patriarch of the West, Primate of Italy, Archbishop and Metropolitan of the Roman province, and Sovereign of the State of Vatican City.

9 The Encyclical *Aeterna Dei Sapientia,* November 11, 1961. The second part of this Encyclical relates the fifteenth centenary of Saint Leo to the Second Vatican Council. This part pertains to the bishop of Rome as the center of visible unity, and mentions the prerogatives of the Magisterium of Saint Peter and his successors. The Encyclical especially quotes the following text of Saint Leo the Great: "The Lord takes special care of Peter and prays particularly for his faith, so as to show that the perseverance of the others would be best assured if the courage of the leader were not overcome. In Peter, it is the strength of all of them that is protected, and the order of divine grace is as follows: fortitude, which is given to Peter by Christ, is then

communicated to the apostles through Peter" (*Documentation Catholique,* no. 1367, January 7, 1962, col. 15).

[10] Cf. *The Council of Florence,* by Fr. Joseph Gill, S.J. (Cambridge, 1959), pp. 270–305.

[11] Press release, November 30.

IX

The Church

THE COUNCIL UNDERTOOK EXAMINATION OF THE SCHEMA ON the Church on Friday, November 30. Cardinal Ottaviani suggested that the proposed dogmatic constitution on the Virgin Mary be included in the discussion, but this was not approved by the presiding Cardinals. There is no reason to regret their decision, because the short Marian schema could not possibly have raised fewer questions than the large schema on the Church.[1] However, if we keep in mind that such an important text on a fundamental matter should properly be the subject of prolonged debates and stimulate the expression of different points of view, the faithful would have been less inclined to say that the Fathers of the Council were divided in matters pertaining to Marian theology. Furthermore, the ecumenical spirit, which has been so strongly affirmed during the Council, might have suffered from a too hasty or superficial examination of a question that lies at the heart of the ecumenical dialogue. In Mariology, according to the recommendation of Pius XII, we must avoid two opposite excesses: according too much to Mary or not according her enough.[2]

A Composite Summa on the Church

Materially, the schema De Ecclesia is a considerable document. It is printed in a booklet of 122 pages which constitutes the second series of projects distributed to the Fathers. The fascicle includes a kind of *imprimatur* specifying that Pope John XXIII had decided that these texts of constitutions and schemas would be transmitted to the Fathers for discussion at the Second Vatican Council.

The schema has eleven chapters: 1. The Nature of the Church Militant; 2. On members of the Church Militant and the necessity of the latter for salvation; 3. On the episcopate as the highest degree of the sacrament of Holy Orders and on the priesthood; 4. Residential bishops; 5. The States of Evangelical Perfection; 6. On laymen; 7. The Magisterium of the Church; 8. Authority and obedience in the Church; 9. The relations between Church and State; 10. The need for the Church to proclaim the Gospel to all peoples throughout the world; 11. On Ecumenism.

Finally, the schema on the Blessed Virgin Mary, Mother of God and Mother of men, can be considered as chapter 12.

A theologian, who had participated in the elaboration of the schema and had explained it to an episcopal conference, warned the bishops that they would be disappointed by everything that concerned the episcopate in this treatise. Bishops are sensitive on this matter, not because their personal authority is at stake, but because the common mind of the Church, just prior to the opening of the Second Vatican Council, clearly seemed to expect doctrinal clarifications on the question of the episcopate.[3] The First Vatican Council defined the powers of the Pope. The decisions concerning his infallibility and universal jurisdiction are irreformable. However, the Council of 1870, in view of the tribulations of those days, was unable to define the powers of a bishop in the government of his diocese, the rights and powers of the episcopate in any given region, or the collective responsibility of the episcopate, exercised either in an ordinary way or an extraordinary manner, as in the Council.

The whole question of the episcopate is found at the heart of the orientations which the Council has taken. These orientations are pastoral, missionary and ecumenical. The last of these is particularly important. Often, from the Protestant side, as well as the Orthodox, we hear it said that Roman primacy is the principal obstacle to unity. What a tremendous misunderstanding, what incomprehension, and what prejudices have built up during the centuries, if separated Christians consider as the principal obstacle that which the Catholic faith regards as the visible center and the foundation of unity!

To dispel equivocations, the Council must throw light upon various aspects of the Magisterium: the Sovereign Pontiff, the bishops; the different ways in which it is exercised; its relationship with Holy Scripture and the faith of the Church.

The discussion of the schema on the Church could not in such brief time culminate in a vote on the text, but it did suffice to single out the precise orientations for a new document. It is increasingly apparent that a dogmatic constitution, *De Ecclesia,* will likely be the very heart of this Council and the monument that it will leave to future centuries. Vatican II will doubtless go down in history as the Council which promulgated the dogmatic constitution *De Ecclesia.* In this respect, the initial contact of the Fathers with this project will have been of great usefulness.

Three aspects, in fact, which are not all of equal importance, became clearly apparent when the debating was over:

1. The definition of the Church as the Mystical Body of Christ must take into account the progress of ecumenism.

2. The rights of the Church must be formulated in terms of the mission entrusted to the Church by Jesus Christ, and not as something to which the Church lays claim. It is less a matter of claiming rights for her than the accomplishment of a service and fulfillment of a mission for the greater welfare of mankind.

3. The relations of Church and State must be conceived in terms of the present rather than the past, and not with reference to any particular country but in view of situations that are varied to the extreme.

4. The schema on the Church cannot disregard a problem that is decisive for the future of ecumenism: the matter of religious freedom. Modern man, whether believer or unbeliever, wants to know what the Church now teaches about this question, and in a more general manner what she thinks about the values of this present world and everything that contributes to the ordinary happiness or misfortune of men from day to day.

5. The Fathers must reach agreement on whether they now intend to propose a complete treatise on the Church or merely discuss particular points, controversial at present, that require a clear response from the Church.

The discussion seemed to prepare us for a complete treatise in which certain elements would be simply reviewed or repeated because they have already received very definite outlines, for instance, the primacy and infallibility of the Pope. Others are urgently in need of clarification and definition, such as the place and role of laymen in the universal responsibility of the Church with regard to the human race, and especially the role of bishops considered as the college of the apostles. The Lord's command, "Go, and teach all nations, . . ." is still addressed to them and imposes responsibilities that the Council must clearly illumine, in order to enable the bishops to assume those responsibilities more effectively.

The Members of the Church

Cardinal Ottaviani introduced the schema.[4] He praised its theology and warned the bishops against any tendentious questionings or criticisms. This schema, he said, was carefully prepared, and then seriously examined by the central Commission, reviewed by the Commission for amendments and by the Sovereign Pontiff who made the decision to transmit it to the conciliar Assembly. Whatever may be said by critics who condemned it without even knowing what it contained, it was written in a biblical and pastoral sense and in language that can be understood by everyone.

Cardinal Liénart was first to intervene in the discussion. *"Gaudeo,"* he said, thus almost astonishing the Assembly, "I rejoice to see the schema's emphasis upon the mystical aspect of the Church. However, the schema goes too far in accentuating the equation between the Roman Church and the Mystical Body of Christ. Such a formula ejects the mystery. For baptized Christians, separated from the Roman Church, we must regret that they are deprived of certain graces, but can we say they do not adhere to the Mystical Body?"

Cardinal Ruffini was satisfied with the theology of the schema, but he found the division of chapters inadequate. He suggested a more logical, and therefore more coherent arrangement, which would compromise the following chapters: the nature and end of the Church, the members of the Church, the power of Orders, the power of jurisdiction, the Magisterium, obedience in the Church, and the Church and civil society. The Cardinal also laid stress upon the unity and unicity of the Church founded upon Peter.

Cardinal Koenig, Archbishop of Vienna, would have preferred a shorter schema, and a more precise specification of the relations of the Church and the State. On this point, it would be inappropriate to refer to particular nations or be concerned only about the rights of the Church.

It is also important to mention her duties, her mission, which is to bring salvation to mankind. Another important point is the matter of freedom of conscience. Finally, the Cardinal remarked, the schema insists upon the necessity of belonging to the Church to ensure one's individual salvation, but we must not let ourselves forget the collective salvation of mankind and, consequently, the necessity of the Church for the human race.

Cardinal Alfrink, Archbishop of Utrecht, emphasized the Church's role as the Mystical Body, and expressed surprise that the schema, in chapter 4, referred only to residential bishops, whereas a third of the bishops taking part in the Council are titular bishops. Moreover, he felt that the college of bishops was mentioned too negatively. With regard to the rights of the Church, the Cardinal believes that, instead of the proclamation of these rights, the world is more interested in hearing what the Council will say about freedom of conscience.

The intervention of Bishop de Smedt of Bruges must also be mentioned. His statement concerning an ecumenical mode of expression had won the support of nearly all the voting Fathers. But this was not the case with regard to his intervention on the Church and a certain ecclesiastical manner and phraseology, in which three defects are apparent: triumphalism, clericalism, and legalism.[5] No doubt the Bishop of Bruges was right in what he said about each of these points, but he was mistaken in considering only one aspect. The style of glory is not appropriate for the Church which Christ called *"Pusillus grex,"* of course. But it was to this little flock that it pleased the Father to give the Kingdom and its glory. The flaw of clericalism may indeed be found in the schema, but one cannot avoid the fact that the Church is a hierarchical society with degrees including the Pope, the bishops, clerics and laymen. The Church must certainly be maternal, but this set of mind cannot suppress her laws or juridical rules.

During the same session, Msgr. Elchinger, Coadjutor Bishop of Strasbourg, made special mention of the perspectives of a theology of the Church, inspired by a pastoral concern. Heretofore, the Church was considered primarily as an institution; today, we are more aware of the Church as a communion. Formerly, we saw only the Pope, but now we are in the presence of a bishop united to the Pope. Yesterday, we thought in terms of the bishop alone; but now we confront the whole college of bishops. In the past, theology affirmed the value of the hierarchy; in our day it is discovering the people of God. Previously, it emphasized whatever divides and separates, but at present the stress is upon whatever unites. Until now, the theology of the Church considered especially its internal life; today, however, it contemplates the Church turned also toward the exterior.

These new aspects, Msgr. Elchinger concluded, should not make us forget the ancient truths. It is in their light that it is fitting to constantly respond to new needs. Only then will the Church be the leaven of the masses, the salt of the earth and the light of the world.

The Place of Laymen and Priests

The same arguments were developed in the course of the following days. But two points were given special emphasis. As the Council seemed to be increasingly tending toward a complete treatise on the Church, the absence of a chapter devoted to priests and another to laymen was particularly regretted.

It has been said that priests are the forgotten men of the Council. This remark, expressing disappointment, can be explained by the omission of any schema specially considering the priests and their role in the life of the Church. Actually, however, they are less forgotten than they suppose. Many texts pertain to the pastoral ministry and the parish, new forms of apostolic action and the formation of clerics. Not to mention the schema on the liturgy which concerns them above all others. Nevertheless, if the Council intends to produce a treatise on the Church, it must certainly give consideration to the place of the priest in the Church's life and his relations with the bishop and the faithful.

His Excellency, Bishop Renard of Versailles, laid stress upon this with authority and conviction. The schema, he said, has a great deal to say about bishops, religious, the states of perfection and laymen. And that is all good and right. But nothing, or almost nothing, is said about priests. This omission painfully affects a large number of priests, and the hearts of bishops should be sensitive to it. Priests, in fact, are a vital force of the Church. They are the sons of the bishop in the priesthood. Consequently, the schema should affirm the bond that exists between the bishop and his priests in a more positive way. Priests participate in the bishop's priesthood, the *sacerdotium secundi ordinis,* as the *Pontificale* calls it. They are not merely ordained for the Mass and the sacraments, but also for preaching. The priests together form the presbyterium, which the apostolic writings associate with the bishop for pastoral action in general. It is also well to distinguish the obedience which priests owe to the bishop from that which is required of the faithful. The priest's obedience is derived from the sacrament of Holy Orders and entails acceptance of all the apostolic labors.[6]

With regard to laymen, it was Cardinal Spellman who made himself their determined advocate. He greatly regretted that the chapter devoted to them is not more explicit concerning the fundamental role of Catholic Action in the Church.

After all that the Holy See has said about Catholic Action, the organized apostolate of laymen must not be considered only with reference to schemas directly devoted to their apostolic mission. It is indispensable that Catholic Action be included in the constitution of the Church. Several interventions also requested that the specific role of Catholic Action in the Church should now be fully recognized. The laity, organized and commissioned by the hierarchy, must hereafter have its full place in any treatise on the Church.

Several Fathers finally criticized the schema for considering the Church and its members only insofar as their mutual relationship and interaction are concerned. Bishop Huyghe of Arras urged the Fathers to consider the Church in relation to the world also, for the modern world is awaiting the Church. Depending upon the way in which the Church approaches the world, it will be welcomed or disregarded by men of our day. When the Council is finally over, men will ask the Church, "But what have you to say about yourself?" And Bishop Huyghe went on to express his regret that the schema does not sufficiently express a more open and Catholic spirit, a missionary spirit and the spirit of service and humility.[7]

It was during this same session that one Father thought it well to remind the bishops of the need for sound doctrine. Quoting the beginning of the fourth chapter of the second epistle to Timothy, in which Saint Paul recommends to his disciple to be firm in the teaching of doctrine, the Bishop of Aquino, the homeland of Saint Thomas, Msgr. Musto, intimated that in his opinion certain Fathers could benefit from this remark. . . . This provoked various reactions in the aula, more amused than indignant.

The Infallible Church

On December 3, Cardinal Doepfner told the Assembly that it would be ridiculous to attribute to the Fathers any desire to limit the primacy of the Pope. The Archbishop of Munich was doubtless alluding to a news item in the *Frankfurter Allgemeine,* and repeated in the Italian newspapers, which reported that Cardinals Liénart and Frings had expressed the opinion to the Council that the Pope could not be infallible without the Church.[8] Neither the one nor the other had spoken about this matter.

In fact, two bishops seem to have merely touched on this question. In their concern for ecumenism, they hoped that the First Vatican Council's definition of papal infallibility could be explained more satisfactorily to the Orthodox. When the Catholic Church says that the Pope is infallible by himself and apart from the consent of the Church, this does not mean that the Pope is infallible outside of the Church. The Pope cannot be separated from the Church, nor the Church from the Pope. The function of governing and teaching is a relationship wholly orientated toward the Church. Whenever therefore the Pope proclaims the faith of the Church in an infallible way, he is fulfilling a function that is eminently ecclesiastical. It is in this sense that one of the Fathers could tell the Council that infallibility *ex sese* did not exclude the Church and did not mean "without the Church."

The history of the only dogmatic definition that has been made since the First Vatican Council proves this in its own way. It was not until theologians had made careful studies and the whole Catholic episcopate had been consulted, that Pius XII defined the doctrine of the bodily Assumption of the Blessed Virgin Mary.

In the course of the conciliar debates, other points received useful clarifications. The schema, which was formulated in a juridical manner, tended to reserve the guardianship of the revealed deposit of faith exclusively to the teaching Church. But preserving the faith is the function and duty of the whole Church; for the faithful also, as Cardinal Ritter, Archbishop of Saint Louis, commented, must preserve the faith of the

Church, not by special favor or grace, but by virtue of their character as baptized Christians.

This intervention brings to mind an old quarrel between the Catholic Church and the Orthodox Church. I mention it because it is continually recurring in conversations between Catholics and Orthodox. When Pope Pius IX, in 1848, addressed an appeal to unity to the Churches of the East, the four Orthodox patriarchates (Constantinople, Alexandria, Antioch and Jerusalem) answered harshly:

> Among ourselves, neither patriarchs nor Councils have ever been able to introduce innovations, because the defender of religion is the very body of the Church, that is to say, the people, who desire to preserve their faith forever unchanged and according to the faith of their fathers. Many Popes, and the patriarchs who were friends of the Latins after the schism, have learned this by costly experience, for they never achieved any results.

This declaration had an unusual destiny. Instead of *defender of the faith,* the Russian translation said *guardian of the faith.* The famous Russian theologian, Alexis Khomiakov, considered this a confirmation of his theory affirming that the Church alone, as a body of believers, is infallible. The definitions of Councils are not infallible unless they receive the consent of the faithful in general.

Theologians call this thesis the theory of *Sobornost* or the conciliarity of the Church, infallible in its totality. It has received wide acceptance in the Orthodox Churches if only because of the brilliant theologians who have championed it.[9] However, in nearly all the Orthodox Churches there has been a reaction among the hierarchy who, conceivably, are not very favorable to a thesis that tends to deprive them of their principal prerogative.

Khomiakov's theory is not traditional, nor is it Catholic. But it has the merit of at least raising the question of the laity in the Church, including their role and their functions. Once again we see that the same profound currents are arousing the Church both in the East and in the West.

Authority and Obedience in the Church

Laymen say that their role in the Church is simply tantamount to simple obedience. There has been considerable talk in the Council about the crisis of obedience in the Church. The Superior General of the Marist Fathers made a philosophical intervention on this subject that was new for many. It is not sufficient to say there is a crisis of obedience today; we must also be able to see the reasons. Nor is it sufficient to say that we must obey the Church and the State because all power comes from God. Obedience, in our time, is considered as a relative perfection, whereas freedom is an absolute perfection. God is free. He does not obey. Christ was obedient, but according to His human nature. A doctrine of obedience must begin with freedom. The Church's authority comes from Christ, but we must carefully distinguish between the various authorities within the Church. There is a considerable difference between a definition of the Pope and an order given by a Father Superior. A great deal is often said about the necessary connection between the superior's will and the will of God. It is God's will that we obey, but prudence is necessary to the superior in order to command. The State's authority is based upon the fact that man is a social being. It is false to assert that political leaders will only account for their deeds before the tribunal of history. The principle of authority must always be tempered by the principle of the autonomy of intermediary bodies, as Pope John XXIII pointed out in his encyclical, *Mater et Magistra.*

On the same subject, Archbishop de Bazelaire of Chambéry objected from a psychological point of view. In these times, when there is a real crisis of obedience, it is good to bring to mind the authority of the Magisterium. However, authority is one thing, and the exercise of authority is something else again. We must speak of authority in terms that will make it acceptable. The schema, unfortunately, uses harsh language in referring to it, as though it entailed the right of coercion. The Church is *magistra* with regard to teaching and education. But the Church is a mother also who knows the faults and failings of her children. Men do not reject the word of the Gospel if it is presented with love.

It was about love, also, that Cardinal Lefebvre spoke in expressing regret that the texts on the Church and the Magisterium of the Pope and the bishops make very little mention of charity. For the mystery of the Church is a mystery of love. Charity is essential in every member and in the structure of the Church, so that "those who live will live no longer for themselves."

117

Primacy of the Pope and Collegiality of the Bishops

There were many interventions on the collegiality of the bishops and its relationship with the Roman primacy. This point, quite obviously, needed doctrinal clarification. As Archbishop Guerry said in a pastoral letter devoted to the Council,[10] *"Jesus Christ founded His Church on the apostolic college of the Twelve with Peter as the visible Head."* The First Vatican Council defined the powers of the Pope. But the defining of the powers of the college of bishops remained to be done. Certain forms have already been experienced precisely in the course of the present Council. One of the revealing moments of the Council was the intervention of Cardinal Liénart concerning an external matter, namely, the election of Commission members. When the Cardinal requested that the national episcopal conferences should be permitted to meet together for consultation about this, his intervention received almost unanimous approval. This incident established the factual existence of various forms of episcopal collegiality in the Church.

Until recently, the appointed and consecrated bishop considered himself especially and sometimes exclusively as the bishop of a diocese. However, by his episcopal character, the bishop is primarily a member of the whole body of bishops. This incorporation, Archbishop Guerry again remarked, entails for each bishop, in a distinct manner, and over and above his role as the pastor of his own diocese, a participation in *"the universal responsibility of the apostolic mission of the Church, in the solidarity of the body of bishops under the direction of the Pope as Head."*[11]

The collegiality of the bishops signifies, in fact, the corporate responsibility shared by the whole episcopate, under the authority of the Pope, for the evangelization of the world, and the establishing of the Church everywhere on earth. The modalities of this government and the exercise of this power are still to be determined. This task was scheduled for the second Session of the Council. The forms would have to be largely and broadly determined by the new social and political structures of various national or linguistic groups that are constantly in process of change; however, primarily, the bond with Rome and communion with that Holy See, as the foundation and symbol of visible unity, and secondarily, a respect for the rights of the bishop in his own diocese must always be preserved. These episcopal rights, however, will undergo certain limitations. There are some powers and initiatives that will hereafter appertain to various competent, episcopal assemblies, organized territorially and legitimately constituted, as mentioned in chapter I of the Constitution *de Sacra Liturgia,* such as the provincial council, the regional episcopal conference or the national conference, as circumstances determine.

During discussions of the schemas on unity and on the Church, many bishops pleaded in favor of a collegiality that would be continuously effective and not merely an extraordinary manifestation like that of the Council. Others, believing that the papal primacy was in peril, ardently defended the rights and privileges of Peter. There were some, however, who tried, in the interests of unity, to show that the two truths were complementary and correlative.

Bishop Ancel expressed his conviction that the antinomies of authority and freedom, primacy and collegiality, law and spirit, would be resolved by a return to the Gospel. It is inadequate to say that the contrast or opposition is simply apparent, or that the realities are complementary. The charter of the Church is set forth in the Gospel. Christ founded a kingdom that does not rest upon force or money or the secular power; it does not exist for the wise alone, but also for the poor. And what Christ has said and done must be observed forever. Consequently, we cannot put a legal society in opposition to a community of love, but we should instead strip the legal element from whatever, in the eyes of believers and unbelievers, threatens to disfigure the true face of the Church.

Msgr. Hakim, Melkite Bishop of Okka, Israel, also thought that the Gospel would enable us to surmount the antinomy of the primacy and collegiality. It would be contrary to the Gospel if the truth and authority of the apostolic college were diminished, and he reminded the Fathers that the Eastern Churches had preserved the tradition of collegiality (while occasionally warping or falsifying its real purpose and function whenever the primacy was denied or excluded). A return to the practice of the Eastern Church in this matter, according to Bishop Hakim's concluding remarks, would not be fanaticism, but rather an act of fidelity to the apostles and to our origins. It would in no way diminish our love for Peter or our obedience to him. "This is

119

eminently true of us who live on the shores of Lake Tiberias where Our Lord's words still echo clearly: 'Thou art Peter, and upon this rock I shall build my Church.'

These words worthily ended the historic session of the 6th of December, distinguished by the intervention of Cardinal Lercaro on the subject of poverty, and by the reading of the pontifical norms for the rest of the proceedings. It remains for us now to tell of these matters, and the projects and orientations which emerged in the course of the final sessions.

NOTES

[1] The schema on Mary comprises six large pages, followed by extremely copious notes that fill twenty-four pages. This schema considers the close bond between Christ and Mary, the place of Mary in the economy of salvation, Marian mediation through divine grace and benevolence, the privileges of Mary, the veneration of Mary and unity.

[2] Encyclical *Ad caeli reginam* of His Holiness, Pope Pius XII, "On the Queenship of Mary and the institution of her feast" (October 11, 1954). "Let (theologians and preachers) guard themselves against opinions that are without any foundation, whose exaggerated expressions go beyond the limits of truth, and also from excessive narrowness of mind when it is a question of that singular dignity, wholly sublime and almost divine, of the Mother of God, which the Angelic Doctor teaches us to attribute to her, 'because of the infinite goodness of God' " (*Documentation Catholique*, No. 1186 [November 14, 1954], col. 1418).

[3] With regard to the sacramental character of the episcopate as the supreme degree of the sacrament of Holy Orders, there was unanimity among the Fathers. Some of them, however, had hoped that this article, which constituted the third chapter of the schema, would be the object of a debate and definition. The text is due, in large part, to a French theologian, Father Lécuyer.

[4] The Cardinal limited himself to a formal presentation and a juridical defense of the schema. His tone was cordial, but his words were severe in referring to those who intended to criticize the schema: "It is in vain that they would come to tell us that this schema is scholastic rather than pastoral or ecumenical, etc."

[5] This intervention provoked many rejoinders on the following days. The bishops who disagreed with Bishop de Smedt attempted to find in Scripture or Tradition any texts in which the Church was mentioned in terms of glory. This was not hard to do, but in the process they themselves fell into the same mistake for which they were reproaching the Bishop of Bruges. In this respect, as in so many others, it is easier to separate than to unite. What is necessary, of course, is to discover the affirmation that unites, by comprising within one organic truth the two contradictory aspects between which the human mind tends to choose the one or the other.

[6] *La Semaine religieuse* (December 14, 1962) published a rather extensive account of Bishop Renard's intervention. (Cf. *Documentation Catholique* [January 6, 1963], No. 1391, col. 54–55.) It concludes as follows: "For the renewal of the Church, it is high time that the bond between priests and their bishop be made more clearly apparent. The Council must not forget this vital matter. The necessary legal norms must be orientated to the spiritual life. Moreover, it is important that our priests, in order to live their priesthood in a holier manner, be helped by the Council: 'You are the salt of the earth; but if the salt loses its strength, what shall it be salted with?' (Matt.

5:13). Archbishop Guerry intervened to lay emphasis upon the paternal role of the bishop: *Episcopus, imago patris.* The Holy Father, who listened to this intervention from his office in the Vatican, as was his custom, sent a letter that same evening to Archbishop Guerry, together with three volumes of his writings, with the exact indication of a long quotation from his book on the bishop" (Msgr. Jenny, *La Quinzaine diocésaine de Cambrai* [December 23, 1962]).

[7] *Les Informations religieuses* (weekly bulletin of the diocese of Arras), on December 14th, published a detailed account of the intervention of Bishop Huyghe. The three points were explained and developed:

1. *A truly Catholic and open mind.* We are no longer living in Christendom. Bishops feel themselves responsible for both unbelievers and believers. And all of them, as the college of bishops, feel responsible for the whole world.

2. *A missionary spirit.* Concern for those who are "far off" is our primary pre-occupation. And it is inadequate to consider the missionary spirit in some single chapter, for it is on every page of the schema that this concern ought to be expressed. The Church is not merely a society that protects its members from error; it is a community open to new sons, a body in process of spiritual growth.

3. *A spirit of humble devotion and service.* The Church is described throughout the schema as a "power" that seeks to subject all nations to its service. This legalistic and dominating spirit was not the spirit of Christ. In the Church which He founded, does authority mean anything other than service to others?

[8] According to the *KIPA* Agency (December 4, 1962), the origin of this news item was the Italian newspaper, *Il Tempo.*

[9] Cf. Serge Bulgakov, *Orthodoxy,* on the question of *Sobornost.*

[10] Published in the *La Quinzaine diocésaine de Cambrai* (January 6, 1963). A long summary of this letter, under the signature of F. V. (Fausto Vallainc), appeared in *Osservatore Romano* on January 25th. It was reprinted in *Documentation Catholique* (February 3, 1963), No. 1393, col. 175–190.

[11] *Ibid.,* col. 176.

X

Principal Orientations

THE FATHERS HOPED TO BRING THE FIRST SESSION OF THE
Council to a splendid conclusion. It seemed, toward the end, that they
were hoping to make up for lost time. The discussion of the schema on
the Church, as we noted, produced impressive interventions and profound theological statements. However, the Fathers did not want to let
the field lie fallow after their laborious tilling and partial seeding.

Concentration of the Schematas

The Council had finally found its true course. In the Assembly,
divergent opinions continued to be heard. But everyone felt that the
Council was inspired by only one heart and one soul in its concern for
truth and its desire to make the Church's presence meaningful to the
world of today. Seeing the first session's end approaching, and fearing
that the flame might go out, the Fathers spoke with greater ardor.
Propositions came forth abundantly and were given persuasive expression by the voices of bishops and cardinals who, until then, had kept
silence.

On Monday, December 3rd, Cardinal Léger, Archbishop of Montreal, took up the matter of work to be done between sessions, and
traced the prospective outlines that made a profound impression upon
the Assembly:

The first session now drawing to a close, already appears as a precious
gift—*donum magnum*—which God has granted to His Church. Doubtless
this session did not enable us to advance very far in the enormous program
of conciliar tasks and proceedings.[1] But during this first session we have attained to a better understanding of the amplitude of effort required for the

renewal of the Church. This experience was necessary, *etsi aliquando dolorosa,* even if it proved to be occasionally painful. Now the way is open, that chosen way in which the Council has manifested its determination to engage itself.

However, if the spirit of renewal is to fulfill its task, the Archbishop of Montreal suggested that an organism be constituted to maintain the orientations already established and stimulate the conciliar Commissions, so that in the next session they could present schemas that would be more likely to win the approval of the Assembly without delay.

The following day, Tuesday, December 4th, during the thirty-third general Congregation, Cardinal Suenens, Archbishop of Malines-Brussels, in his turn entered into the question of the organization and spirit of the future proceedings. More especially, he touched on the problem of a comprehensive plan. It is important, he said, to constantly return to the Council's goal and purpose. This condition is essential if there is to be a better ordering of the proceedings and if the work of the Commissions is to be clearly understood as a particular task for integration within the total effort of the Council. The Cardinal went on to say that the First Vatican Council was known for its definition of the primacy of the Pope. The Second Vatican Council must now show forth the Church as the light of the nations: *Ecclesia lumen gentium.* That is why the schema on the Church truly appears as the very node of the Council.

The Cardinal then suggested a procedural program that would successfully consider the Church *ad intra* and the Church *ad extra,* that is to say, orientated first toward herself and then facing the world around her. Cardinal Suenens compared this plan to the Gospel that tells of Our Lord sending forth the apostles. This same Gospel, as we recall, was read at the opening session of the Council. *"Go"* which was the command, sending the Church forth; *"and teach"* which entrusted the teaching mission to the Church; *"all nations"* clearly manifesting the universality of the mission; *"baptizing them"* which constitutes the sanctifying work of the Church.

The Church must go forth to meet the expectant world, and then make known her response to the problems that confront all men today, concerned as they are about respect for the human person, the invioliability of all life, procreation, social justice, the third force in international affairs, the evangelization of the poor, peace and war, so that the Church's doctrine may shine brightly as the light that lightens the nations. For the Church is not only responsible for her own members; she must also give thought to the separated Christians and undertake a dialogue with the world, in accordance with the orientations given by the Sovereign Pontiff in his message of September 11th and repeated in his opening address to the Council on the 11th of October.

On December 5th, it was Cardinal Montini's turn to bring his stone for the building of the edifice. His intervention was impatiently awaited. Until then, he had not spoken except for his comments concerning the schema on the Liturgy. The Cardinal, however, had been writing a "Letter from the Council" from time to time, which appeared in *l'Italia* of Milan. In the edition of Sunday, December 2nd, he had commented critically with regard to the preparatory work:

The material is immense, and excellent also, but heterogenous and of unequal quality. It should have been abridged and boldly classified if an authority, not merely extrinsic and disciplinary, had governed the logical and organic preparation of these magnificent volumes, and if a central, architectural idea had "finalized" and polarized this considerable task. In conformity with the principle of freedom and spontaneity which prevailed at the origins of the Council, the program of Vatican II lacked a central point. However, the latter was outlined solemnly and wisely in the words of the Holy Father during the years that preceded the Council, and especially in the two addresses of September 11th and October 11th.

The Cardinal informed his readers that there was talk about reducing the material and combining it in a few schemas that would be of general interest, corresponding to pastoral necessities. After this task of clarification and simplification was completed, the Council would finally undertake consideration of the principal theme concerning the Church.

In his intervention, Cardinal Montini first expressed his total adherence to the "comprehensive plan" proposed on the previous day by Cardinal Suenens (who, like Cardinal Montini, belonged to the Secretariat for Extraordinary Affairs). Then he brought up the question of the schema on the Church, acknowledging that it contained many useful elements, but he could not keep silent about the inadequacy of the text itself. It was necessary, in his opinion, to make a deeper study of the doctrine set forth and then prepare a schema that corresponds more satisfactorily to the end and purpose of the Council, one that constitutes the central theme.

The Search for an Organ of Orientation

These successive blows tended to shatter the whole edifice of the preparatory work. The Cardinals could not have acted in such a critical manner if they had not at the same time prepared a positive plan. The very concordance of the last interventions seemed to proceed from concerted action. Several projects had also been taking shape in the minds of the Council Fathers for some time, including, for instance, a conciliar Secretariat for human problems. On Thursday, November 22nd, bishops of several nationalities had taken steps to make this desire known to those who were close to the Holy Father. They did not want to return to their dioceses empty-handed, and they hoped to reach out toward all men, even non-Christians, by a conciliar proclamation relative to the vital problems of our day, touching on peace, war, underdevelopment and other concerns of humanity everywhere. On Sunday, November 25th, Helder Pessoa Camara, Auxiliary Bishop of Rio de Janeiro, confirmed to journalists that bishops of all countries had requested the Pope to create a Commission or Secretariat that would specially undertake a study of these great problems in an effort to bring the response of Christian doctrine to bear upon them.[2]

Other bishops were more concerned about the rest of the proceedings. The first session had made it possible to discover the Council's principal orientation, prefigured in the message of September 11th, and stated in the address of October 11th. However, this orientation was more implicit than explicit. The long period between sessions tended to diminish remembrance of it, not to mention the possibility that negative influences would be exercised. It was important to avoid repeating the errors of the preparatory phase in the future.

The preparatory proceedings had not sufficiently kept in mind the real nature of a Council. And simply because Vatican II had not been convoked against any particular heresy, it was supposed that the Fathers

125

should give consideration to all dogma and morality and to all the Church's institutions. Obviously, however, it was apparent that no Council could digest such a quantity of material. Beyond question, the number of subjects would have to be reduced. But this reduction could not be left to the initiative of the Commissions involved, because they are naturally inclined to extend their competency and prolong their work. Special Commissions sometimes become self-enclosed and lose sight of the concrete function of the Council in its relations with the world.

This revealed the need for a superior organ that would determine the subjects and specify the methods. This Commission, moreover, would exercise a role of coordination. Not merely was there no material coordination during the preparatory phase, but the proceedings and documents were also lacking in unity of viewpoint and in inspiration. The organ of control and coordination under consideration would provide all of this, safeguarding the spirit, maintaining proportions and assuring fidelity to the Council's end and purpose as the Pope had defined them, in which the Council had recognized its own aspirations.

Several projects were proposed, of which one had certainly inspired the norms promulgated by the Pope on December 6th. This project suggested that the Commission under consideration possess a regulatory arrangement that would, among other things, formulate the *Council's charter,* determine the general subjects, and give practical instructions to the various Commissions. This charter could comprise: 1. evangelization of the poor and the poverty of the Church; 2. the unity of the Christian family; 3. the relations between Christianity and the different cultures and civilizations of mankind, and the vocation of each nation.

The address of October 11th could once again provide the point of departure for these declarations in its passages on poverty, Christian unity and the respect of human values.

There still remained the matter of appointing or electing the members of this organism. It was unlikely that the Council would be asked to elect a deputation. This procedure, which had once seemed appropriate in the opinion of some of the Fathers, appeared on second thought less favorable to the sessional recurrence that would be quite frequent from January to September. It is not by holding meetings at long intervals that a relatively numerous deputation could give the necessary impetus and provide remedies or corrections for the drawbacks or omissions that were noted during the first session.

Consequently, in the first days of December, it was expected that the Holy Father would designate, either among the presiding Cardinals, or among members of the Secretariat for Extraordinary Affairs, a small committee of Cardinals who would be assisted in their task by the secretaries of the Council.[3]

On Wednesday, December 5th, a fascicular program was distributed to the Fathers in which the seventy-odd preparatory schemas had been regrouped under twenty principal subjects. A rather prophetic preliminary note explained that the fascicle "contains the summary of the schemas of the preparatory Commissions which will be submitted to the Commissions of the Council for reduction, if necessary, to general principles and for combination or unification whenever the resemblance of topics or mixed subject-matter may require it." The list of schemas included the following subjects:

1. Divine Revelation (text prepared by the Ottaviani-Bea mixed Commission);
2. The Church (this discussion already broached);
3. Mary, the mother of God and mother of men (printed);
4. The preservation of the faith (printed);
5. The moral order;
6. Chastity, virginity, marriage, family (printed);
7. The social order and the community of nations; moral principles;
8. The Eastern Churches;
9. The clergy;
10. Bishops and the government of the dioceses;
11. Religious;
12. Laymen;
13. The sacrament of marriage;
14. The Liturgy (already discussed, but not definitely adopted);
15. The care of souls or the pastoral ministry;
16. Vocational recruitment and training;
17. Catholic universities and schools;
18. The Missions;
19. The media of social communication (discussed);
20. The reunion of Christians (partially discussed).[4]

Cardinal Lercaro: Poverty, the Major Theme of the Council

On December 6th, Cardinal Lercaro, Archbishop of Bologna, put the crowning touch on the Council's task, clearly defining its essential spirit. First of all, he expressed his agreement with the opinions of Cardinals Suenens and Montini with regard to the elaboration of doctrine. Now we understand more perfectly what the Council must accomplish in proclaiming the mystery of Christ, the Word of God, living and working within the Church. Now the mystery of Christ in His Church was always, and more than ever before is today, the mystery of Christ in the poor. The Church, as Pope John XXIII declared, is the Church of all men, but especially the Church of the poor. (It is likely that the Cardinal, in making this intervention, was aware of the papal directions concerning the rest of the proceedings, which were to be read a few moments later, with references to the passage on poverty quoted from the opening address.)

Poverty is the sign of the Incarnation, proclaimed and foretold by the prophets, apparent in the Mother of God who was its servant in Bethlehem. We see it all during the public life of the Savior, and in the preaching of the Kingdom. We find it among the apostles. Poverty is the seal of evangelical expansion. We would neither be fulfilling our task nor measuring up to mankind's expectation if we did not bring forth a document concerning the evangelization of the poor. In our time, the poor seem to be forsaken and left outside the Church. This is an affront to the poverty of two-thirds of the human race. The evangelization of the poor is the great problem before us. Unity can only be a consequence. This is the central theme of the Council, imposed upon us by the era in which we live; it is not merely one of the themes we are considering. The schema on the Church should therefore include: 1) a theology of the eminent dignity of the poor in whom God conceals His glory; 2) a doctrine of poverty in the Church.

We must keep in mind the connection between Christ's presence in the poor and His presence in the Eucharist and the hierarchy. These are three mysterious forms of His presence, all of them different, but not foreign to one another. Finally, our methods in regard to the apostolate will only be fruitful if the apostles are poor.

Consequently, with wisdom and moderation, but without hesitation or compromise, we must set limits to the use of material things in the Church; reduce the pomp and display that surround our bishops, in order to avoid giving scandal; many bishops are really poor, and should appear to be so. Priests should practice sacerdotal poverty. Religious communities ought to extend poverty not only to their individual members, but also to institutions.

If we are faithful to poverty, the Archbishop concluded, we will find in it both the light and method for an integral presentation of the Gospel. We will then be the imitators of Him who, although He was rich, made Himself poor to bring us His wealth.[5] Enthusiastic applause greeted this intervention.

Creation of a Commission of Coordination

Immediately after the Cardinal's conclusion, Archbishop Felici read a regulation issued by the Sovereign Pontiff to ensure the continuity of the proceedings in faithfulness to the spirit of the address of October 11th. Two excerpts from the opening address were cited: the first pertaining to the method of doctrinal instruction, and the second on pastoral care and love of the poor. The literary style and spirit of the conciliar definitions were specified, and a Commission was instituted for the co-ordination and control of the proceedings. Precise regulations defined the relations of this Commission with the bishops individually, or with the episcopal conferences "if the latter prove to be more practical."[6]

The reading of this regulation greatly impressed the Fathers. All of them listened with reverent respect. When they realized that the Pope's decisions were in conformity with their own hopes and desires, and even went beyond them, an immense joy filled their hearts and there was hearty applause in the Council hall.

Following this memorable assemblage, we had the impression that the first session of the Council was already terminated. Rome was throbbing with the excitement that resembles the joy that follows child-bearing. The regulations issued by the Pope echoed beneath the vaults of St. Peter's like a solemn reminder that the end of the session did not mean the end of the Council. The Pope had taken all the necessary dispositions to ensure the continuity of the proceedings in the spirit defined by the opening address, which had rallied the vast majority of the Fathers.

The Pope brought this spirit to mind again. It is not a question of reformulating ancient doctrine, which has already been done very well, but the Gospel must be presented to men of today in language that they understand, making the message attractive and the Church which bears this message appealingly maternal. It is also a question of manifesting the Church as the society of men redeemed by Christ, but especially as the Church of the poor. For they are the men who, sometimes in fact, and nearly always according to appearances, are rejected from the Church.

The intervention of Cardinal Lercaro had been brought to bear upon this particular point, which inspired lively comments. It is obvious that the Church, in her concern for the poor, can never lose interest in the rich, for all men are called to enter the Kingdom of God. Nor should we let anyone suppose that the Church preaches poverty for her own sake. The love of predilection which she bears for the poor is a compensatory wealth. The Church does not put up with poverty in a passive, resigned manner, but inspired by the spirit of poverty in her ministers and institutions, she struggles, on the contrary, for greater justice and well-being, for the sake of the poor.[7]

The interventions of Cardinals Léger, Suenens, Montini and Lercaro had been like battering-rams. A breach was opened, and the norms promulgated by the Sovereign Pontiff gave the Fathers the assurance that the Council could and would follow through accordingly. Certain interventions, following the proclamation of the rules issued by the Pope concerning the agenda and spirit of the future proceedings, now seemed anachronistic and already irrelevant.

The great usefulness of the first session becomes evident when we see that it enabled the Fathers, in their examination of a few schemata, to pass judgment on the entire conciliar preparation. Although there were no spectacular results, the first session did not labor in vain. Those who, from the first days to the last, were witnesses of its gropings, quests, and confrontations can only marvel at what the Holy Spirit, by means of human discussions, had achieved. As on the first day, we now said on this last day, *Confirma hoc Deus:* "Confirm, O God, what you have done in us, in your holy Temple of Jerusalem, in that Jerusalem which, in all truth, has been the conciliar Assembly of Vatican II, gathered here in the Cathedral of Saint Peter."

Closing of the First Session

On Saturday, December 8th, the feast of the Immaculate Conception, the Pope closed the first session of the Council which had been inaugurated two months before, on October 11th, the feast of the divine Maternity of Mary. In his closing address, he made allusion to this Marian sign. The maternal protection of Mary had blessed the work of the Council.[8]

The Pope rapidly summed up the achievements of the session, but then pointed especially to the future. The Council would continue, and the bishops must keep themselves in readiness for this task. In spirit, he gave the kiss of peace to the bishops "in expectation of their early return." This was the voice of one who had risen from his sickbed, following serious illness that had suddenly taken hold and had thus darkened the final days of the conciliar session. On Wednesday, November 28th, alarming rumors had begun to circulate in Rome. It was whispered that the Pope would have to undergo a serious operation. Thursday, at noon, *Osservatore Romano* published, not a press release, but an unofficial news report stating that it had been reliably informed that the Holy Father had found it necessary to interrupt the audiences with the bishops on the previous Tuesday "because symptoms of gastritis had become worse. This illness, for quite some time, had made it necessary for the Pope to follow medical and dietetic regimens which had resulted in serious enemia (*piuttosto intensa*)." Late Tuesday night and early Wednesday morning, the Pope began to hemorrhage. Some of the Fathers were fearing the worst would happen. They even spoke about a conclave, although in dread of its possibility.

The Pope showed courage and will-power that led him, perhaps, to fall short of his personal ideal: *Obedience and Peace*. The physicians and those close to him wished, in fact, that he would take greater precautions. But John XXIII felt that the Council was a higher imperative which required the Pope to give fully of himself to the very end and hold fast to the helm of the Church. He spoke to a large crowd from

131

the window of his apartment in the Vatican on Sunday, December 2nd. And on Wednesday, the 5th, he addressed the bishops who had completed their tasks a little early in order to gather in St. Peter's Square to hear the Pope's remarks and recite the *Angelus* with him.[9]

Finally, on Friday the 7th, the Fathers learned with joy, mixed with surprise, that the Pope planned to be present among them in the conciliar aula to close the first session with a short allocution and the prayer of the *Angelus*. Those who saw him appear on that day, exhausted and pale, walking and speaking by sheer will-power alone, felt greater anxiety than joy. It was with heavy hearts that the bishops left Rome.

The Pope, however, showed that he was determined to defy his illness. On December 9th, he proclaimed the canonization of three new saints of the Church: Julian Aymard, Anthony Pucci and Francis Camporosso. At the same time, he instituted the Coordinating Commission. The names of the members were not formally announced until December 17th, but as early as Monday, the 10th, we published a list of the appointed Cardinals in the newspaper *La Croix*. Besides Cardinal Cicognani, the Vatican Secretary of State, the Commission comprised Cardinals Achille Liénart, Bishop of Lille; Francis Spellman, Archbishop of New York; Giovanni Urbani, Patriarch of Venice; Carlo Confalonieri, Secretary of the Sacred Congregation of the Consistory; Julius Doepfner, Archbishop of Munich; and Leon Joseph Suenens, Archbishop of Malines-Brussels.[10] The Secretariat of the Commission included the Secretary General and five subsecretaries of the Council.

Instructions to the Bishops for the Rest of the Proceedings

On January 6th, the Pope addressed the letter *Mirabilis ille*[11] to the bishops. Reminding them that they were still assembled in Council, he emphasized the importance and the role of the new Coordinating Commission and precisely defined the relations between the Pope and the bishops taking part in the Council. He wrote:

The Council as is normal receives its general orientation from the Pope who convoked it. At the same time, however, it appertains to the bishops to ensure its free development. It will be necessary for the Pope to confirm decrees in an official and definitive manner, and such decrees will then receive the value and force of law from his apostolic authority. But it devolves upon the Fathers of the Council to propose, discuss, and prepare in the desired form the different determinations and finally to place their signatures upon them along with the Roman Pontiff.[12]

There were various reactions to this statement.[13] Some believed that the Pope was attempting to reaffirm his own authority with regard to the bishops. For our part, however, we would say that he was exalting the episcopate and its collegial function in the Church. As a matter of fact, on several occasions, the Pope made a sharp distinction betweeen those members of the Council who possess episcopal character and others who, like the superiors general of religious communities, had been called to the Council by courtesy or favor, although they are not members of the teaching Church. He asked

that the venerable college of all the bishops who, in union with the Sovereign Pontiff, constitute the mind and fundamental motivation of conciliar action, remain the object of unimpaired respect. This must be ascertainable especially in Rome, on the Vatican hill, in the vast premises of the universal government, readily accessible and always obliging; and in the institutes of the sacred sciences, the places of prayer and devotion, and finally in the personal presence of the Vicar of Jesus Christ.[14]

Osservatore Romano reacted against tendentious interpretations by stressing the fact that the Pope had simply recalled canon law:

There are some who preferred to see in the passages devoted to bishops a more accentuated authoritarianism of the Pope in the Council, or else a more conspicuous episcopalism. But nothing could be less objective. In the typical, efficacious, and direct language of John XXIII, the document confirms the common doctrine of the Church and the very principles of canon law concerning the Council. When the Pope says that it is necessary for the Sovereign Pontiff to approve in an official and definitive manner the decrees which, by his authority, will acquire force of law, but that it is incumbent on the bishops to prepare them and subscribe to them with the supreme pastor, he is reflecting, in a complete way, both theology and law, without accentuation or particular application.[15]

In the last part of the letter, the Pope recalled the objectives of the

133

Ecumenical Council that concern the whole body of Christians and the entire human family.

For if we devote our attention only to ourselves and to Catholics, would not this procedure, as we have always thought, seem to be insufficiently corresponding to the word of the Divine Redeemer?

To have remained, and still remain faithful to the purity of Catholic doctrine, according to the teaching of the Gospel, Tradition, the Fathers of the Church and the Roman Pontiffs, is certainly a great grace, a claim to merit and honor. But this is not sufficient for the fulfillment of the Lord's precept, when He tells us, "Go and teach all nations" (Mt. 28:19), or again in this passage of the Old Testament, "each of them he gives precepts about his fellow men" (Eccl. 17:12).[16]

We have, consequently, entered into a new phase of the Council, which we could never have imagined in the past and which the techniques of social communication make possible today. The present period is a time of theological maturing, made of study and consultation.

At the base, the bishops meet together according to regions or nations, or according to their competences and sometimes their particular affinities. And since the fruits of the Council are anticipated in three domains—the renewal of the Catholic Church, the reunion of all Christians, and the well-being of all humanity—the bishops are inspired by a triple concern that is pastoral, ecumenical and also temporal to the extent that the problems of peace and justice are the fundamental aspiration of men of our time. For in a world of greater justice and peace, the maternal call of the Church to salvation will resound with greater efficacy.

At the summit, the Coordinating Commission met in Rome at the end of the month of January. Jointly responsible for the work in general, the Cardinals nevertheless divided the various schemata between them.

—Cardinal Cicognani: the Eastern Churches and ecumenism;
—Cardinal Liénart: Revelation and the deposit of faith;
—Cardinal Spellman: chastity, marriage, the family;
—Cardinal Urbani: the apostolate of the laity, the clergy, the sacraments;
—Cardinal Confalonieri: seminaries, schools, studies, missions;
—Cardinal Doepfner: the bishops (pastoral aspect), the pastoral care of souls, members of religious orders;

—Cardinal Suenens: the Church (and the world), the Virgin Mary, the social order.[17]

At the end of the month of March, the Coordinating Commission met again. The members examined the schemata on bishops and the government of dioceses, the Religious, the seminaries, universities, and the clergy. It is not impossible, when they meet later on, that they may change the order and subject matter of the schemata. The schema *De Ecclesia*, especially, has been found to be complex. It comprises the mystery of the Church, the hierarchical institution, the episcopate, the laity, and the states of perfection. These last two subjects are also studied by the Theological Commission in collaboration with the Commission of the Apostolate of the Laity and the Commission concerned with Religious.

There were some who wanted the schema on the Virgin Mary to be incorporated and considered as the conclusion of the schema on the Church. But it was decided to keep these schemata separate. According to Cardinal Suenens, in a press conference held in Paris, March 21, 1963, the text ought to show forth the riches of the spiritual maternity of Mary as the Eastern Churches have done, while also finding formulas that would enable Protestants to understand the Catholic doctrine exactly.

On the other hand, the original projects pertaining to the preservation of the deposit of faith, the moral order, etc., were combined in a single schema, numbered the seventeenth and titled: *De Ecclesiae principiis et actione ad bonum societatis promovendum:* "On the principles and action of the Church for fostering the welfare of society." It comprises six chapters concerning man's admirable vocation; the human person in society; marriage, the family and the demographic problem; human culture; the economic order and social justice; the community of peoples; and peace.

The schema on ecumenism is studied in a mixed sub-Commission composed of members of the Theological Commission, the Secretariat for the Promotion of Christian Unity which prepared the basic text, and the Commission for the Eastern Churches.

A shadow hung over the outcome of the Council. The bishops and faithful knew that the Pope's health was precarious. From the human point of view, the success of the Council and the pontificate of John

XXIII were closely linked. Theoretically, of course, a new Pope could dismiss the Council. The Code of Canon Law, Article 229, states that if the Pope dies while the Council is still in session, the Council is then legally suspended until the new Pope orders it to reconvene and continue. However, the hope which the Council inspired in the world was too great to allow any frustration of its fulfillment.

The Holy Spirit who, in the course of the first session, let it be seen where He intended to lead the Church, assists that Church in all circumstances and under any pontificate. The ecumenical, pastoral, and apostolic orientation which was affirmed in the first session could no longer be thwarted. In double fidelity to the past and the future, the Church, through the Council, is taking the measure of this present time in order to give men a message transcending all time. As the messenger of the Gospel, and the light of Christ, the Church establishes her role in the world as the light of the peoples: *Ecclesia Christi lumen gentium*. This is the Council's first and final word.

NOTES

[1] On his return from Rome, Cardinal Léger addressed a gathering of thirteen hundred militant Catholics in Montreal, on December 17th, speaking on the Council. "Everything must be done over again," he said, replying to someone who had asked about future proceedings. This expression greatly surprised the audience, and the Cardinal felt it necessary to explain what he meant. He was certainly not saying that whatever had been done at the Council so far was bad. The schema on the liturgy, for instance, was excellent, in everyone's opinion. And the debates of the first session provided splendid contributions to the conciliar task. (Cf. *La Croix,* January 4, 1963.)

[2] The text of his allocution to the press was published in *Documentation Catholique:* "It has been asked that a special Commission be set up to study in a concrete way the problems now confronting the world, and more especially the relations between industrialized countries and the underdeveloped regions, and also the problem of world peace." (December 16, 1962, No. 1390, col. 1611–1613.)

Furthermore, Bishop Pioger, of Sées, in a letter dated from Rome on November 15th, published in *la Semaine religieuse* on November 23rd, already made mention of this Commission: "While we have been applying ourselves in the general congregations to the study of a pastoral and living liturgy, we have been becoming increasingly aware that the Council must also mark a great moment in human history, as the source of real hope for the world.

The Church must take all the concerns of men to heart. And that is why, in addition to the conciliar Commissions and along with the Commission for the unity of Christians, another extra-conciliar Commission is being formed, which will serve as a Commission of charity concerned with "peace" and the "poor." Indeed, the Church must not be merely intent upon bringing to her own children the treasures of enlightening faith and sanctifying grace which flow from Our Lord's words as their source. Nothing is alien to the Church."

Here we discover, as though at its source, the origin of a project of which certain elements received a kind of effective realization with the forming of the Coordinating Commission. Other elements, however, would become effective later.

As things turned out, no particular or special Commission was actually instituted, but the tasks which, in the minds of the Fathers, should have devolved upon it, were assumed by the Theological Commission and the Commission of the Apostolate of the Laity which established an organic collaboration between themselves with regard to these problems. The principal questions are set forth in schema XVII of which we give a summary analysis toward the end of this chapter.

3 That is what Jean Pélissier reported in *La Croix*, in the issue of December 5th. (His text had been sent from Rome on the 3rd, in the evening.) It should be noted that this information exactly defined the composition of the Commission of co-ordination in an even more precise way than was suggested in the text published on December 6th, in which mention was made of a few Cardinals and *a few bishops*. This implied that the bishops would be members of the Commission. But these bishops, who are conciliar secretaries, are assisting the Cardinals in their task, as Pélissier had said in reporting the news.

4 Complete distribution of these schemata among the various Cardinals of the Commission of co-ordination will be listed later in this chapter.

5 Cardinal Lercaro repeated the essentials of this intervention in a declaration made on the Italian television network, December 22nd, 1962: "The Church and the Council, men and problems." Cf. *Civiltà Cattolica*, February 2, 1963, p. 285, and *Documentation Catholique*, March 3, 1963, col. 317–321. The same issue published the pastoral letter of Msgr. Huyghe, Bishop of Arras: *Eglise et pauvreté*, which gives a nearly literal text of Cardinal Lercaro's intervention.

6 The text of the regulation is published in *Documentation Catholique*, No. 1391, January 6, 1963, col. 21–24.

7 B. Matteucci, in an article of *Osservatore Romano*, January 17th. "Motifs d'actualité" also speaks of poverty and lays stress on the biblical notion of poverty as a disposition of abandonment to God (the poor of Yahweh).

8 The address was published in *La Croix*, December 11th, and in *Documentation Catholique*, January 6, 1963, col. 7–12.

9 Nothing could be more impressive than this image of the universal Church. At the summit, the Pope, united with the bishops all gathered around himself, and in all directions the throng of priests and faithful hastening to see the spectacle beneath a sun that was finally shining again, eager to hear the voice of the Father for whom everyone felt the greatest anxiety.

10 *La Croix*, December 11, 1962.

11 This letter was sent to the bishops, January 6th, by the nunciatures. After the bishops had received the text, translations were prepared by the Secretariat of State and transmitted to the nunciatures. *Osservatore Romano* published the Latin text and the Italian version, on February 8, 1963. The same day, *La Croix* (dated February 9th—provincial edition), published the French version. By this delay, the Pope marked the respect for the episcopate which his letter had asked the faithful to show forth.

12 *Documentation Catholique*, March 3, 1963, col. 291.

13 The newspapers had commented about the text in terms of authoritarianism. I do not know on what dispatches they based their stand. *Agence France-Press* had given a judicious and correct interpretation of the text, as usual. R. Millet, in *Figaro*, wrote about the text as follows: "It has been pointed out, in well-informed circles in Rome, that the vigorous terms used by the Pope obviously pertain to points on which, until now, there has been conciliar discussion (essentially liturgical questions). The purpose was to show that the supreme authority does not intend to let itself be placed in the presence of the *fait accompli* on the part of those who act as if the preliminary acts, recorded thus far, already possessed a definitive value."

Fr. Rouquette, whose chronicles of the Council in *Etudes* were remarkable for accuracy of information and critical spirit, wrote on this subject: "(Mr. Millet) reports, he says, the interpretation that 'Roman circles' had given to the Pope's letter. It is difficult not to see in this naively reported information one of those very disagreeable *manoeuvres* that we have been constantly observing during the first session on the part of certain ecclesiastical circles in Rome, opposed to the very idea of the Council, opposed to freedom of speech for the bishops, hostile to any reorganization of their bureaucracy, and even opposed to the Pope's attitude in leaving full freedom to the Council, only intervening as the supreme arbiter." (*Etudes,* March, 1963, p. 399.)

14 *Documentation Catholique,* March 3, 1963, col. 290.

15 *Osservatore Romano,* February 10, 1963.

16 *Documentation Catholique, ibid.,* col. 296.

17 It will be noted that the schemata on the liturgy and on the media of social communication were not attributed or assigned because they were fully and definitively discussed by the Council.

pARt II
The Council and Unity

1

The Invitation to Christian
Churches and Denominations

"IT'S A MIRACLE, A REAL MIRACLE!" Cardinal Bea addressed these words to the observers representing non-Catholic Christian Churches, who had been received in audience by the Pope on Saturday, October 13th. But the Cardinal was not only referring to that audience, but rather to the whole succession of events and developments that occurred since the establishment of the Secretariat for the Promotion of Christian Unity and culminated in the presence of over forty observers at the Council. These observers represented the major federations of Christian communions of Reformation origin and a considerable number of Eastern Churches as well.[1]

The presence of these observers greatly impressed public opinion because of the spectacular aspect. But even Christians themselves sometimes failed to understand the interior aspect and ecclesiastical significance of the fact,[2] because this presence marks a milestone in the relations between the Catholic Church and the separated Christian Churches. Weary of going their own way in division and disunity towards greater dissimilarity and mutual ignorance, the Churches decided to change their courses in order to draw nearer together and enter into a dialogue regarding the faith, in a spirit of love and mutual respect.

How the Invitation Originated

In this instance, as in so many others, the first indications came from the Pope. During an audience at Castelgandolfo, on Sunday, August 30, 1959, the Pope declared that if representatives of our separated brethren wanted to attend the Council, "it would be only reasonable to welcome them because the Church is still their home from which they wandered away in the course of the vicissitudes of history."[3]

The idea was broached. The press—to its honor—laid hold of it and was first to bring it to the attention of public opinion everywhere. During the first press conference on the Council, October 30, 1959, a journalist asked Cardinal Tardini whether members of the hierarchy of the separated Churches would be present at the Ecumenical Council. The Cardinal replied:

> The matter is under consideration. The Council is concerned about the internal life of the Catholic Church, but it is probable that those who wish to attend as observers will be allowed to do so. They will be very welcome, and if they are to follow the proceedings intelligibly, it seems evident that they should receive the more important preparatory documents.[4]

Neither the question nor the answer can be found in the recorded *Acts* of the Ante-Preparatory Commission which, however, contains an appendix in which the text of Cardinal Tardini's statement to the press is printed.[5]

On the other hand, for the first time the possibility of the presence of observers was publicly mentioned in the televised interview which Cardinal Tardini granted to the French television network on the occasion of the Church Unity Octave, January 25, 1960. With considerable circumspection, I said to him,[6] "Pope John XXIII said that, in his opinion, this Council of the Catholic Church would also be an invitation to think seriously about reunion, which so many souls desire. In this perspective, can we suppose that representatives or heads of the Churches separated from Rome will be able to attend the Council?"

The Cardinal said,

> You know better than I do that the Ecumenical Council is an internal event of the Church. Canon law regulates and determines who has the right and duty of attendance at the Council. Consequently, it may be inferred that members of other religious denominations cannot participate in the Council. However, I believe that if some of them want to be present, they may certainly come to the Council, obviously not as members, but as observers, because we have nothing to hide. The Council will be a splendid manifestation of truth, unity and charity. This is an absolute certainty. And then, this

wonderful spectacle which the Catholic Church will enact, and the renewal of life that will result from it, as we hope, will facilitate the unity and reunion which so many souls desire, as you expressed it so well yourself, a unity that was asked for by Our Lord in His prayer to the Father.[7]

Apparently Cardinal Tardini envisaged this presence of non-Catholic observers in a perspective that was more apologetical than ecumenical. But the idea itself then seemed to be quite audacious in Roman circles. The Holy Office, notably, was not very favorable to it. The Pope spoke about it only in veiled terms. In his address of November 16, 1960, to members of the Preparatory Commission, he alluded somewhat enigmatically to a possible participation of the separated Churches in the Council.[8]

The Central Commission studied the question during its second meeting at the beginning of November, 1961. It was divided on this matter, as on many others. In view of the seriousness of the whole question and the consequences that might result in later relations with non-Catholics if news about the subject was not accurate, *Osservatore Romano* published an official communiqué:

All the members of the Central Commission freely expressed their opinions about the matter and voted on it following the discussion, after Cardinal Bea and Cardinal Cicognani, respectively president of the Secretariat for the Promotion of Christian Unity and the Commission for the Eastern Churches, had made their reports. Needless to say, this was simply a consultative vote, since the final decision on a matter of such importance must be made by the Holy Father. Any conjecture in one sense or another would consequently be premature. And any news concerning decisions not yet made with regard to procedures to be followed in addressing a possible invitation to non-Catholics would be even more premature.[9]

A few weeks later, however, on December 25, 1961, the Pope settled the question in the conciliar Bull of Indiction *Humane Salutis.* Or rather, he made it known that it was settled in a positive sense. After mentioning the interest expressed in the Council by separated Christians, the Pope went on to say, "They are now happy to be able to send to the Council, in the name of their ecclesiastical communions, their own representatives who will make it possible for them to follow the proceedings more closely. This is a great hope and consolation to Us," the Pope added.[10]

The Secretariat for the Promotion of Christian Unity dedicated the year 1962 to a sustained effort of contact with all Christian Churches and denominations, to inform them of Rome's intention and officially invite those that manifested a desire to be represented at the Council to arrange for the appointment of observers.

Msgr. Jean Willebrands, Secretary of this body, was a tireless pilgrim in the cause of unity. With different results, he traveled to Constantinople and to Athens, to Alexandria and the Near East, to Geneva and London, and finally to Moscow.

A Warmer Welcome from the Protestants

It may seem surprising that conversations regarding representation at the Council were easier with the Churches of Reformation origin than with the Eastern Orthodox Churches, which, however, are nearer the Catholic Church in their faith and their ecclesiastical structures. This is because Protestants, through the ecumenical movement, already possess a long ecumenical apprenticeship. They always desired contacts with Catholics and regretted the reticence and hesitation of the Roman hierarchy with regard to these openings. And now that an opportunity for contact was at hand, they did not want to let it pass.

A historical survey of contacts between the Catholic Church and the various Protestant Federations would be too long here. In most cases, the reports and documents remain in the archives of the Secretariat for the Promotion of Christian Unity and in the keeping of the other Churches concerned. However, we shall say a few words about the way in which the decision of the World Council of Churches was made. During a meeting of the central committee in Paris, in August, 1962, the question of sending observers to the Council was under discussion. The committee members finally reached a favorable decision in three procedural stages:

1. The report of the Secretary General defining the attitude of the World Council of Churches with regard to Vatican II in general and the sending of observers in particular;

2. Discussion of the matter by the central committee;

3. The final resolution unanimously approved.

Mr. Visser't Hooft was personally in favor of it. The spirit of his report, the definition he gave of the dialogue, and the manner in which he answered all questions showed that he hoped to see the World Council share his opinion. The debate, moreover, did not reveal any serious opposition. Some members of the committee merely wanted explanations or enlightenment on the status of the observers.

The Lutheran Bishop of Hanover, Hanns Lilje, asked three questions:

1. Under what conditions are observers invited and what will be their status at the Vatican Council?

2. How can they have recourse to the dialogue during the Council?

3. We are not only interested in the juridical nature of the Council, but also in its content and theological significance. The Council will raise the question of the true Church. Where among ourselves (in the World Council of Churches) is this question discussed?

Mr. Visser't Hooft answered these three questions both precisely and pertinently:

Concerning the status of the delegated observers, he made known to the assembly that the letter of invitation, signed by Cardinal Bea and Msgr. Willebrands, in the name of Pope John XXIII, set forth the nature and role of delegated observers in four points:

a. The observers will provide the separated Churches with reliable news concerning the Council;

b. They will be able to attend the solemn public sessions and the closed general assemblies in which the conciliar decrees will be discussed;

c. They will not possess the right to speak or vote;

d. The Secretariat for the Promotion of Christian Unity will serve as intermediary between the organisms of the Council and the observers in order to provide the latter with necessary information that will enable them to follow the proceedings of the Council more easily and more efficaciously, and the Secretariat will arrange interviews for them with qualified persons, including Fathers of the Council, regarding the topics discussed at the Council.[11]

With regard to the methods and limits of the dialogue undertaken

145

with the Catholic Church while the Council is in session, the Secretary General explained his personal opinion:

The Council's agenda is still unknown. But some questions, if they are to be given consideration, pertain by their very nature to the inter-denominational dialogue. For example, such questions as religious freedom and mixed marriages, and the unity of the Church. What we already know about the schemata shows that the Council is fully aware of the ecumenical dimension and aspect of these problems. Without becoming indifferent in matters of faith and order,[12] the dialogue presupposes that each side will listen to the other and that each is conscious of the other's position.

Moreover, the dialogue, in the fullest meaning of the term, can be carried on in the meetings arranged by the Secretariat for the Promotion of Christian Unity, and Mr. Visser't Hooft emphasized that such an opportunity was but rarely encountered heretofore.

As for the place of discussion on the nature of the Church, with reference to the World Council of Churches, Pastor Visser't Hooft mentioned that this question is the permanent object and purpose of the Faith and Order Commission. Providentially, moreover, the fourth World Conference on Faith and Order would be held in Montreal in 1963, at a time when the Vatican Council would still be in session.[13]

Mr. Alivisatos, of Athens, raised a question which is of special importance to the Eastern Orthodox Christians: What will be the position of the observers representing the World Council of Churches? Within the latter organization, for instance, each delegate is still a member of his own Church, and he is primarily representing the faith of that particular Church.

The Secretary General admitted that it was a difficult question. It would be necessary, in fact, to make a distinction between the observers representing the World Council of Churches and those representing international organizations of various Churches and denominations (the World Alliance of Reformed Churches, the Lutherans, Anglicans, Methodists, etc.).

Observers representing the World Council of Churches will not comment upon denominational matters or questions, but they will be free to express the point of view of the organization when there is question regarding the World Council itself, or the ecumenical movement and its ecclesiological implications. In no case, however, will the delegates officially engage or commit the World Council of Churches.

The voting took place on Monday, August 13th. The central Committee had to consider and decide upon the following text:

> The Committee accepts the invitation received from the Vatican Secretariat for the Promotion of Christian Unity to send one or two observers to the Second Vatican Council.
>
> It is agreed that:
>
> The purpose of sending observers is to obtain direct information concerning the proceedings of the Vatican Council which will examine a certain number of questions that pertain to relations between the Churches and to Christian unity in general.
>
> The observers will have no authority to speak officially in the name of the World Council of Churches or its member Churches, nor can they undertake negotiations of any kind on their behalf.
>
> They can give unofficial explanations concerning the position of the World Council of Churches, according as this is expressed in the decisions of the Assembly or the Central Committee. During the course of the Council, observers will make their reports through the bureau of the World Council of Churches. It has also been decided to grant authority to the executive Committee to name and appoint the observers.

This resolution was unanimously adopted. The President, Mr. Franklin Clark-Fry, pointed out that this unanimity was even more spontaneous than in previous voting, for he seemed to see that hands were raised higher than ever to express approval.

Orthodox Difficulties and Reservations

The question of observers was more difficult for the Eastern Orthodox Churches. First of all, it should be remembered that an Eastern Christian feels uneasy when the term *Ecumenical* Council is used in reference to a gathering that comprises only *Latin Rite* bishops. Of course, according to the Catholic faith, a Council is ecumenical whenever it assembles the whole body of bishops in union with the See of Rome, even if these bishops are, in fact, overwhelmingly of the Latin Rite.

On this point, however, the Eastern Orthodox Church holds a dif-

147

ferent opinion, at least in practice. This Church also claims to be the one true Church of Christ, and consequently believes that it has the right to convoke an Ecumenical Council. Would Catholic bishops be invited to such a Council? Theologians discussed this matter at the first Orthodox Theology Congress at Athens in 1936.[14] Since the Catholic Church possesses a valid apostolic succession, Orthodox theologians held the opinion that there could be no Ecumenical Council without the participation of bishops of the Latin Rite. Another aspect of this question was whether these bishops would come to a Council to be judges in matters of faith or to be judged concerning their faith.

Consequently, we should not be surprised to find the Eastern Orthodox Christians rather perplexed and amazed. For them, the announcement on an Ecumenical Council without convoking Orthodox bishops who possess a valid apostolic succession is simply to vitiate the ecumenicity of the Council at the very start. Such a Council, in their eyes, could only be a synod of the Latin Church, legislating for Christians of the Latin Rite.

The difficulty, however, is not insurmountable, since the Catholic Church itself has often stated that the Council is an internal matter, and therefore the sending of observers in no way implied recognition of the Roman primacy on the part of the Orthodox Churches.

A difficulty of another kind, but quite as serious, pertains to the political situation. The Eastern Orthodox Churches are found on both sides of what is called the Iron Curtain. This physical division made a common decision more difficult, although such a decision would have been preferable both for the Orthodox and for Rome as well. The emulation between Constantinople and Moscow added to the difficulty, with the latter envious of the former's primacy and fearful that an honorary primacy could become a real one. Constantinople, for its part, is afraid that the Patriarchate of Moscow, with its powerful status and political support, will identify itself with all of Eastern Orthodoxy.

At the Pan-Orthodox Conference held at Rhodes, September 24 to October 2, 1961, the Eastern Orthodox Churches decided to adopt a common attitude with regard to problems that concern Eastern Orthodoxy in general. But there was no explicit reference to the matter of sending observers to the Council. Rome considered this unity as an established reality and did not want to send separate invitations to the various Orthodox Churches. This same procedure was followed with regard to other Churches and denominations. Only the world federations of the various Christian communions were invited to send delegates. Consequently, the invitation to the Eastern Orthodox Churches was transmitted to Patriarch Athenagoras of Constantinople, the Ecumenical Patriarch and first-ranking prelate of Eastern Orthodoxy.[15]

This Roman initiative was the original cause of the misunderstandings between Moscow and Rome, and later between Constantinople and Moscow, and finally between Constantinople and Rome. Nevertheless it is not apparent what other means or methods should have been used instead.

NOTES

[1] A list of observers, as published by the Secretariat for Promoting Christian Unity, will be found in Appendix III, pp. 192–195.

[2] Jean Guitton, in his inimitable manner, expressed the real significance of the event in a commentary published in *Figaro,* October 17th:

"Last Saturday, Pope John XXIII received the thirty-eight observers. . . . It was a solemn date, perhaps unique in the history of the Church, if we keep in mind that priests, being part of *ecclesia docta,* have no part in the Council. The thirty-eight observers are quite dissimilar, among themselves, and for the sake of unity their obligation to be together and see one another is already an initial blessing. . . . The Pope revealed that the secret maxim of his life was abandonment to God, from moment to moment, and from day to day, being always available to serve God and never seeking to know what the future might hold. It was in accordance with this principle that he had been appointed to Paris and had later been made Pope, and convoked the Council. And this had meaning now: 'With regard to the reunion of Christians, let us not seek to know the hour or the manner. This does not concern any of us.' As for myself, I can only recall Newman's hymn which the Anglican Church has kept among its beautiful hymns: *"Lead Kindly Light . . . One step enough for* me *. . ."*

[3] *La Croix,* September 1, 1959. We must point out that *Osservatore Romano* not only had never published any such text, but even denies having any knowledge of the audience in question (*Unitas,* December, 1959–January, 1960, p. 25).

[4] The death of Cardinal Tardini had repercussions upon the Council. His strong personality certainly left its mark upon the conciliar proceedings. From conversations which I had with the Cardinal, I always felt that from the very beginning he had a very precise and clear idea of the organization of the Council. We have evidence of this in his reply, because at that very moment he had in mind the possibility of communicating certain preparatory material concerning the Council to the separated Churches.

[5] *Acta et documenta Concilio oecumenico Vaticano II apparando. Series I (ante-praeparatoria). Volumen I: Acto summi pontificis Ioannis XXIII,* a magnificent volume published by the *Polyglotte Vaticane,* in collaboration with the Secretariat of the Central Commission, pages 153–158.

[6] The Cardinal was very ill on that day. Even in Rome there were rumors of his resignation, and Cardinal Marella was being mentioned as his possible successor. However, Cardinal Tardini received Msgr. Glorieux and myself in his private office to prepare the questions and answers. When I expressed the wish to interrogate him con-

cerning the representation of the separated Churches, he corrected me, good-naturedly, with reference to the word *Church:* "You know," he said, "in Catholic theology and Roman practice and usage, the word Church is reserved for the Catholic Church alone." This explains the manner in which the question was asked during the televised interview. The Cardinal improvised his replies, which is apparent in his rather spontaneous and sometimes impulsive style of speaking.

[7] *Acta et Documenta,* page 160.

[8] "It is Our hope," he said, "that those who, although not sharing the whole Catholic faith, sincerely desire news and information concerning the proceedings of the Council, will not think it inappropriate or discourteous if we ask them to wait until the Fathers have completed their work and everything is ready and better disposed for more elevated contacts of the mind, the heart and supernatural vision, in which the spirit of the Lord may preside for the glory and love of Christ Jesus, the founder of His holy and glorious Church." (*Documentation Catholique,* December 4, 1960, col. 1483).

[9] *Osservatore Romano,* November 11th, and the communiqué of the press service of the Central Commission, No. 4, dated November 9, 1961.

[10] *Documentation Catholique,* January 21, 1962, col. 104, which gives a somewhat different translation: "Many among them (Christians of the separated Churches) have promised to pray for the success of the Council and have great hope that their communions will be allowed to send representatives to closely follow the proceedings of the Council."

[11] A fact worthy of notice must be emphasized here. The status of observers figures in the conciliar regulations, as published in *Documentation Catholique,* October 7, 1962. This was done *de facto,* although the regulation in question still remains, *de jure,* a text reserved to bishops and experts. *Osservatore Romano* never published it.

However, since the discussions of the World Council of Churches are generally public and the press is admitted, we learned about the status of observers on August 12, 1962.

The way in which we then reported the matter in *La Croix,* which was wholly unofficial, differs but little from the official text which follows here:

1. The delegates of Christians separated from the Apostolic See who are authorized by the Holy See to attend the Council as observers, may attend the public sessions and general congregations, except in particular cases that will be determined by the presiding Cardinals. They will not attend the meetings of the Commissions, unless this is authorized by competent authority. They do not have the right to speak or vote during the discussions of the Council.

2. Observers may inform their ecclesiastical communities regarding events and happenings of the Council, but they are required to observe secrecy towards others, as required of the Fathers also, by virtue of article 26.

3. The Secretariat for the Promotion of Christian Unity is responsible for relations between the Council and observers, in order that they may follow the conciliar proceedings.

[12] The Secretary General of the World Council of Churches is obviously alluding, in this instance, to the communiqué of the press service of the Central Commission which reviewed and surveyed the efforts made by the separated Churches to achieve reunion among themselves. This report implied that the World Council of Churches was seeking unity without concern for doctrinal differences, in a kind of federation of all Christian Churches which would then enjoy equal status. Mr. Visser't Hooft protested energetically against such an interpretation in a public conference given at Berlin, July 2, 1962. "This text," he said, "gives a completely false image of the attitude of the World Council of Churches . . . and in no way serves the cause of unity."

[13] This important conference was scheduled for July 12–26, 1963. The foresight

of the Secretary General was correct. As the second session of the ecumenical Council was to open on September 8th, the discussions held at Montreal would be, from the ecumenical point of view, nearly as important for the Catholic Church as for the World Council of Churches, inasmuch as the subjects and topics would be partly the same.

[14] The Acts of this Congress were published in a magnificent volume through the efforts of Professor Alivisatos. This collection is of utmost importance for study of the trends and problems of Eastern Orthodox theology. Unfortunately, I have noted that the latter is very little known, whether among Catholics or among Protestants. (Cf. *Procès-verbaux du premier Congrès de théologie orthodoxe à Athènes,* November 29– December 6, 1936. Editions Pyros, Athens, Greece, 1939.)

[15] It is not impossible that certain Roman circles thus hoped to avoid the real difficulty of sending invitations to Orthodox Churches in countries behind the Iron Curtain. In Rome, it might have been embarrassing to have a large number of observers coming from countries in which the Catholic bishops were not allowed to attend the Council.

151

Appendix I
Delegate Observers at the Council

RUSSIAN ORTHODOX CHURCH (Patriarchate of Moscow)

Archpriest Vitalyi Borovoi, professor at the theological faculty of Leningrad

Archimandrite Vladimir Kotliarov, vice-rector of the Russian Orthodox Mission in Jerusalem

RUSSIAN ORTHODOX CHURCH (Outside Russia)

Most Rev. Antony, Bishop of Geneva

Archpriest Igor Troyanoff, rector of the Russian Orthodox Churches of Lausanne and Vevey (Switzerland)

COPTIC CHURCH OF EGYPT

Rev. Youhanna Girgis, former inspector in the Ministry of Public Instruction

Dr. Mikhail Tadros, former magistrate of the Court of Appeal, Alexandria (Egypt)

SYRIAN ORTHODOX CHURCH

Rev. Ramban Zakha B. Iwas and Rev. Paul Varghese

ETHIOPIAN ORTHODOX CHURCH

Abbas Petros Gabre Sellassie
Dr. Haile Mariam Teshome

ARMENIAN CHURCH (Catholicate of Cilicia)

152

Archimandrite Karekin Sarkissian, rector of the Armenian Seminary of Antelias (Lebanon)

OLD CATHOLIC CHURCH (Union of Utrecht)

Canon Pierre-Jean Maan, New Testament professor at the Seminary of Amersfoort and canon of the Old Catholic Cathedral of Utrecht (Holland)

ANGLICAN COMMUNION

Rt. Rev. Dr. John Moorman, of the Church of England, Bishop of Ripon

Rev. Dr. Frederick Grant, of the American Episcopal Church, professor emeritus of biblical theology, Union Theological Seminary, New York City

Ven. Rev. Dr. Harold de Soysa, of the Church of India, Pakistan, Burma and Ceylon, Archdeacon of Colombo, and rector of the Divinity School of Colombo, Ceylon

LUTHERAN WORLD FEDERATION

Dr. Kristen E. Skydsgaard, professor of systematic theology at the University of Copenhagen (Denmark)

Dr. George Lindbeck, professor of historical theology at the Yale University Divinity School, New Haven, Conn.

WORLD PRESBYTERIAN ALLIANCE

Rev. Hébert Roux, pastor of the Reformed Church of France, in charge of interdenominational relations, Paris

Rev. Dr. Douglas W. D. Schaw, Church of Scotland, assistant pastor in Edinburgh

Rev. Dr. James H. Nichols, of the United Presbyterian Church, professor of modern Church History at Princeton Theological Seminary

EVANGELICAL CHURCH OF GERMANY

Dr. Edm. Schlink, professor of dogmatics at the University of Heidelberg

WORLD CONVENTION OF THE CHURCHES OF CHRIST (Disciples)

Rev. Jesse M. Bader, Secretary General of the Convention (New York)

WORLD SOCIETY OF FRIENDS (Quakers)

Dr. Richard Ullmann, professor at Woodbrooke College, Birmingham, England

INTERNATIONAL CONGREGATIONAL COUNCIL

Rev. Dr. Douglas Horton, former Moderator of the Council

Rev. Dr. George B. Caird, Mansfield College, Oxford, and

Dr. G. H. Williams (substituting for Dr. Caird), professor of historical ecclesiology at Harvard University, Cambridge, Mass.

WORLD METHODIST COUNCIL

Bishop Fred P. Corson, president of the Methodist World Council, Philadelphia, Pa.

Dr. Harold Roberts, head of the Theological College of Richmond (England)

Dr. Albert C. Outler, profesor of theology at Southern Methodist University, Dallas, Texas, replaced by

Dr. F. Hildebrandt, professor of Christian theology at Drew University, Madison

WORLD COUNCIL OF CHURCHES

Rev. Dr. Lukas Vischer, secretary of the Department of Faith and Order (Geneva, Switzerland)

INTERNATIONAL ASSOCIATION FOR LIBERAL CHRISTIANITY

Dr. L. J. Van Holk, professor at Leiden University, Holland

Dr. Dana McLean Greeley, president of the Universalist Unitarian Association, Boston, Mass., replaced by Professor J. L. Adams, of Harvard Divinity School, Cambridge, Mass.

INVITED BY THE SECRETARIAT:

Pastor Roger Schutz, prior of the Protestant monastic community of Taizé (France)

Pastor Max Thurian, of the same monastic community

Dr. Oscar Cullman, professor at the Universities of Basle and Paris

Dr. G. C. Berkouwer, professor at the Protestant University of Amsterdam

Most Rev. Cassian Bezobrazov, titular Archbishop of Catana, Rector of Orthodox Theological Institute, Paris

Rev. Dr. Stanley I. Stuber, Jefferson City, Missouri

Rev. Dr. Joseph Jackson, President of the National Baptist Convention, Chicago, Illinois

Canon Bernard C. Pawley, of the Church of England, canon of Ely Cathedral

Archpriest A. Schmemann, vice-dean of St. Vladimir's Orthodox Seminary, New York

ALTERNATES OF THE DELEGATE OBSERVERS:

Dr. Vilmos Vajta, World Lutheran Federation

Rev. Robert E. Cushman, Dean, Duke Divinity School, Durham, N.C.

Rev. Reginald Kissack

Rev. Victor Subilia, dean of the faculty of theology of the Waldensian Church in Rome

Dr. Serge Grotoff

Dr. José Miguez Bonino

11

Relations Between Rome and Moscow

THE RUSSIAN CHURCH INITIALLY REMAINED SILENT AROUT THE Council. Only when *Il Tempo* published a story about exchanges between the Nuncio at Vienna, Msgr. Dellepiane, and representatives of the Synod of Moscow, did an official declaration from the Patriarch Alexis appear in *Izvestia* on June 21, 1959: "The Patriarchate of Moscow," said the communique, "considers the Catholic Council as an internal matter of the Roman Church. The Patriarchate has no reason, and certainly no intention, of becoming involved in this affair."[1]

An Initially Cautious Attitude

The Russian Orthodox Church was thus adopting a cautious attitude as much towards Rome as toward the Kremlin. Soviet authorities in fact expected no good of the Council, and could possibly have been tempted to use the Russian Orthodox Church against it. The first reactions of the new bishop at the head of the department of external relations of the Orthodox Church, Archbishop Nicodemus,[2] of Yaroslav and Rostov, gave evidence of these reservations concerning the Council. At the Pan-Christian Peace Conference of Prague, in June, 1961, Archbishop Nicodemus, among others, declared:

The absence of Catholics from this Congress is to be regretted. It betrays a lack of love of peace on the part of the leaders of the Catholic Church. The dogma of the primacy of the Pope has isolated the Catholic Church from the other Churches. Today she is trying to emerge from this isolation through the Council. Conversations are taking place with representatives of the other

156

Churches. But it is not difficult to understand that the aim of the Council is not directed towards the unification of Christians, but rather towards their division according to political criteria which have not been changed, and which remain unchanged by the Vatican.[3]

The remainder of the text makes it clear that the line of demarcation for the Vatican passes between Socialism and Capitalism.

We would have preferred not to have to recall these harsh words, but they contain for us a double lesson. They teach us not to attach too great an importance to certain excesses of language, and never to lose sight of the mobility of situations when these do not depend entirely on individual persons. Situations can very quickly change either for good or evil.

At the first Pan-Orthodox Conference of Rhodes, in September-October of 1961, Archbishop Nicodemus was again very reserved about the Catholic Church. He declared that the Russian Church was in favor of unity, but could not tolerate that certain elements in the West—and he designated the Vatican by name—should lay hold of this aspiration and make it the ideological basis for a struggle against peoples committed to the democratic way of life.[4]

Previously, the *Journal of the Patriarchate of Moscow* in May, 1961, had published an unsigned article about the Council.[5] Its tone is revealed by its title, *"Non Possumus."* The article explains first of all the reasons for the communique of June 21, 1959. The Patriarchate had expressed these sentiments regarding the future Council by virtue of its conviction that the See of Rome, proclaiming itself the center of Catholic truth and ecclesiastical unity, had not yet manifested any desire to renounce the demands which, in 1869, had compelled the Eastern Patriarchs to reject their convocation by Pope Pius IX to the First Vatican Council. Quite evidently, their participation in the Council at that time would have constituted an unconditional recognition of the primacy of the Pope. For the same reason they felt that nothing could now be expected from the present conversations of Catholic personalities on the subject of Christian unity except an effort to extend the power of Rome over the Orthodox Church.

The pretext for these unkind insinuations, and the refusal of association with the Council, was the reply that Cardinal Bea was said to have given to a journalist of the *Giornale del Popolo*. He had been asked whether a representative of Moscow would be acceptable to the Council. *"If the Patriarch of Moscow wishes to send an observer to the Council,"* the Cardinal answered, *"we shall welcome him gladly."* This reply had been very displeasing to a Church which had decided from the outset to deal with Rome only on a basis of equality.

"The declarations of Cardinal Bea," the article goes on, *"bear witness to the claim of the See of Rome to absolute power in the Christian world. It is in virtue of this claim that new dogmas were forged which have separated the Church of Rome from the universal Church."*

There was worse to come. The suspicion of political motives which the author attributed to the Council would have much graver consequences in regard to public opinion. The author concluded:

It is impossible not to take account of the fact that the future Council, called together in the difficult situation created by the political division of the world and the arms race, will not be prepared to raise itself above the contradictions of our time and speak to humanity the necessary words of peace. On the contrary, there are many reasons—historical, political and psychological— for predicting an orientation of the Council's activities that will turn it into an arm for political ends incompatible with the spirit of Christianity.

This being the case, we must counter the well-known *Non Possumus* of the Roman Church with the *Non Possumus* of the Orthodox Church.[6] Our Orthodox *Non Possumus* does not, however, imply hostility towards Catholics or efforts to subject them to ourselves, or indifference to the idea of Christian unity. However, we cannot agree to the Roman conditions for this unity, conceived as a world union of Christians under the authority of the Pope. And we cannot agree for the reason that our Lord Jesus Christ, before the beginning of His public ministry, refused the diabolical temptation of power (Mat. 4:5–11), and by His act of redemption appeared before the world as Divine Love. In His Church, He does not tyrannize over the souls of the faithful, but unites them by a bond of love in His Body which is the Church.

That is why, for us, the basis of Christian unity is compatible neither with the principle of the monarchic centralization of ecclesiastical power, nor with hostility towards other believers. It is not power but love which must unite Christians. It is by virtue of this conviction, which excludes any participation whatsoever by us in the work of the new Vatican Council, that the Patriarchate of Moscow replies to Cardinal Bea, *Non Possumus.*[7]

We criticized this article somewhat severely in *La Croix* of August

158

29, 1961. To refute the allegations of Moscow, we quoted an address of the Pope to the General Chapter of the Fathers of the Holy Sacrament, in which John XXIII defined once more the aim of the Council and the relative importance of each of its goals: the internal reform of the Catholic Church, the reunion of all Christians, and greater efficiency in missionary efforts among men everywhere. The Pope added:

> The Ecumenical Council seeks the attainment of the whole heritage of Our Lord Jesus Christ. God grant that to the work concerning the condition of the Church and its adaptation to new circumstances, after twenty centuries of life (and this is the principal task) there may be added—as a result of the edification that we may be able to give, but especially because of the almighty power of God—another outcome: a movement towards reunion of the whole of the mystical flock of Our Lord.
>
> We must reject facile illusions; for if this ideal were completely realized, the blessed hour would truly have come for us to shut our doors, close up our houses and set out on our journey to Paradise, singing choruses of praise. It will need a great deal of time for all the nations of the world to come to a perfect realization of the Gospel message; and it will need, besides, immense efforts to change the mentality, tendencies, and prejudices of all those who have a past behind them. Moreover, it will be necessary to examine in some sense what time, traditions and usages have tended to establish, all the while obscuring reality and truth. Nevertheless, the desire to respond to the aspiration towards unity expressed by the Divine Master remains complete and ardent. The same may be said about all the efforts we are making in order that, some day, all peoples shall be closely united by the gentle bonds of the sole *Credo* of Christ's Holy Church.
>
> Years, months and days have a relative value: we must each of us be constantly ready to respond to Our Lord's call. But we must also, with all the vital forces of our souls, work tirelessly to carry out the Lord's will in the spreading of His Gospel which, bringing grace and charity everywhere, fills the whole earth with serenity and joy.[8]

How could this statement be reconciled with the will to dominate, or a yielding to the temptation of power? To quote the text of Matthew 4:5–11 these days in reference to the Papacy is at best reminiscent of the Grand Inquisitor. But literature, even if it be a work of genius and marked with the seal of Dostoevski, has nothing to do with the image that the Papacy manifests to the world in our time. And so we remained hopeful that this was not the last word of the Russian Orthodox Church, and we expressed the wish that our Eastern brothers might find other images and other symbols to describe the See of Peter.

Fear of an Anti-Communist Attitude

Meanwhile the Russian Orthodox Church had asked to be admitted to the World Council of Churches. Because of the prevailing ecumenical climate inspiring its work, the Council of Churches contributed considerably to the evolution of the Church of Russia in its feelings towards Rome.[9] After New Delhi, Archbishop Nicodemus had a much more favorable opinion of the Catholic Church.[10] We were able to assure ourselves of this when we interviewed Archbishop Nicodemus on the subject of relations between the Church of Russia and the Catholic Church.

"It is still being stated in the press," said Archbishop Nicodemus,

that the Russian Orthodox Church has inimical feelings towards the Church of Rome. I must state that these affirmations do not conform to reality. Russian Orthodox Christians harbor most fraternal feelings for the whole of the Roman Catholic Church, including both the hierarchy and the faithful. But the Russian Church does not approve of the activity deployed by the Vatican in the political domain. In this respect, the Vatican often shows itself inimical to our country. We, the faithful of the Russian Orthodox Church, are also loyal citizens of our country and have a deep love of our land. And that is why anything directed against our country is not going to better our mutual relations. We disapprove of and condemn this political activity of the Roman Catholic Church, but we are not against the Catholic Church as such.[11]

What did Archbishop Nicodemus mean by the political activity of the Vatican? From the Archbishop's writings and from certain private conversations, it appears that the acts for which the Vatican was reproached were as follows: anti-Castro activities by the clergy of Cuba; some public manifestations at the World Eucharistic Congress at Munich, in August, 1960, in favor of the Church of Silence; anti-Communist declarations and activities of Cardinal Spellman as Chaplain General to United States Armed Forces; the intervention of Cardinal De Barros Camara, Archbishop of Rio de Janeiro, against the establishment of diplomatic relations between Brazil and the Soviet Union; and the speeches of Cardinal Ottaviani on the Church of Silence, notably that of January, 1961, along with his foundation of the Pius V Institute, which was destined in Russian eyes to promote an ideological crusade against Communism.

The acts and words of the Pope were never called in question. John XXIII, to avoid giving any grounds for the accusation of being politically biased, borrowed his language from the Gospels and spoke of peace and justice without any political coloration. His speech of September 10, 1961, after the building of the Berlin wall (August 13, 1961), in which the Pope asked for negotiations and the respect of rights and liberties, had even received the support of Mr. Khrushchev. This approbation made possible a more favorable position of the Russian bishops toward Rome. Archbishop Nicodemus told us that he loved the discipline of the Roman Church and its law of celibacy. He said that he was an admirer of the vigorous theology of St. Leo the Great.

More particularly as touching the Council, we asked Archbishop Nicodemus if he still held to his refusal of participation either as an observer or as an invited member, as expressed in the article *Non Possumus.* He replied evasively that there was no invitation for the moment, that the doors were not closed, but that prudence was necessary.

The Attitude of Patriarch Alexis

In July, 1962, the Patriarch Alexis himself had occasion to express his feelings about the Council. Jean Boulier, formerly lecturer at the Catholic Institute of Paris, had come to Moscow as a member of the French delegation to the "World Congress for General Disarmament and Peace," and had asked Patriarch Alexis for an audience. The Patriarch, who was ill at the time, designated Archbishop Nicodemus to receive Mr. Jean Boulier in his name, but was anxious to reply himself to the latter's questions. We reproduce this conversation which has documentary value.[12]

Question. The convocation of the Ecumenical Council at Rome in October, 1962, has aroused lively interest in the East. Has Your Holiness been invited to the Council, and if so, will the invitation be accepted? The Western press has brought this question before the public.

Answer. The Russian Orthodox Church has not yet received an invitation to the Council of the Roman Catholic Church, and this makes it difficult for me to reply to the second part of the question.

Question. Does it not seem to you that the Russian Orthodox Church occupies a position somewhat apart among the other Orthodox Churches, since there has never been any official rupture between the Russian and the Roman Churches, although an unfortunate situation has gradually been created as a result of historical factors, and particularly following the wars with Poland?

Answer. The Russian Church occupies a position in relation to the Roman Catholic Church that is determined by certain circumstances common to all the Orthodox Churches. This position does not admit of any substantial difference with respect to existing relations between the Roman Catholic Church and the other autonomous Orthodox Churches.[13] At the time of the great separation, the Russian Church was a part of the Eastern Orthodox Church; for that reason the rupture between Christians of the East and the West embraced also the Russian Orthodox Church. The problem of mutual relations between Russia and Poland constitutes in the present context a special problem.

Question. Can we affirm that there is nothing of great importance in matters of faith and discipline separating the two Patriarchates of Moscow and the West,[14] except the Roman dogma of papal infallibility and of universal jurisdiction—a dogma rejected by the Russian Orthodox Church?

Answer. We can affirm that the Orthodox and the Roman Catholic Churches are close in matters of faith and liturgy, and we believe that the differences which separate them can be eliminated with time, thanks be to Christ, if the two parties offer proof of good will.

In matters of dogma, we are essentially separated by the doctrine of the infallibility and supremacy of the Pope, and also by certain problems of Mariology, the *"Filioque,"* etc.

Question. Does Your Holiness agree that if the Patriarch of the West claims the title of successor to Peter and asks for himself the same rights that Peter had among the twelve Apostles, an agreement might be possible; but that in the Latin Church, bureaucratic centralization and the abasement of the episcopate have reached a stage which does not allow consent to this state of affairs in the universal Church?

Answer. The Orthodox Church believes that the Apostle Peter was one of the twelve Apostles without any privilege, even though he was named, as also was Paul, leader of the Apostles of God.

The unification of the Orthodox and the Roman Catholic Churches can certainly be achieved on condition that they profess the same rules of faith and the same canonical norms.

Question. The reformation of the Curia and the re-establishment of the rights of the bishops is one of the tasks of the Council; nevertheless, political factors in today's divided world hinder the reunification of Christians. What does Your Holiness think about this?

Answer. We are convinced that the drawing together of Christians on the road of unification will greatly contribute to the union of their efforts in the normalization of the international situation and the intensification of their activity in the work of establishing a just and enduring peace.

Question. Western politicians are coldly discussing the matter of using devastating atomic weapons. They menace the Soviet people with these weapons. Priests and bishops have even gone so far in their hatred of the Soviet Union as to declare the use of these terrible weapons permissible, and to threaten recourse to them.[15] Do you not consider that this attitude represents an extremely grave attack on Christianity?

Answer. We consider that any action of the Christian leaders, as of all Christians, which tends to stir up hatred between people is incompatible with their belonging to the religion of love and peace.

The denunciation of these false brothers, and the protection of the flock against the destructive influence of such sowers of hate and preachers of evil, is the duty of the religious conscience of all true Christians.

Question. If the Pope or even the Council should approve, in a form that they would find admissible, the resolutions of the Congress of Moscow which were approved by the Christians present at the Congress, would not this evident manifestation of aspiration towards peace on the part of the Latin Church constitute an important step towards the unification of the two Churches of Rome and of Moscow?

Answer. Approval by the supreme power of the Roman Church of the Congress's appeal for general disarmament and peace would be welcomed, we are sure, with enthusiasm, not only by believers, but by public opinion of the whole world.

We are convinced that any concrete actions of the supreme power of the Roman Church tending towards the consolidation of a just and lasting peace would provide a solid basis for the healing of the international situation, and the establishment of reciprocal understanding between our Churches. Such positive actions would contribute to the co-operation of our Churches in a practical domain, and this would greatly help the unification which we desire.

This interview is revealing, with regard to both the thought of Mr. Boulier and of the positions of Moscow. Mr. Boulier, for example, takes the view that in relation to the Catholic Church, the Church of Russia occupies a privileged place, since there was no formal schism between

Rome and Moscow, the latter Church not being in existence when the separation occurred.

This optimistic thesis, upheld by some Catholic ecumenists and by Pius XII in his letter to the Russian peoples,[16] does not fully correspond to reality. When the Russians were completely converted to Christianity, the schism between Rome and Constantinople had already been consummated (1054). The Christianity that Russia received from Byzantium carried the brand of anti-Latin polemics. Bulgakov was able to say in this sense that the schism was the "original sin" of the Russian Church, a sin which she had not committed herself, but of which she had to suffer the sad consequences.[17]

Patriarch Alexis said that with regard to the Catholic Church, the Russian Church finds itself in the same condition as Orthodoxy in general: a great closeness in matters of faith and liturgy, with some fundamental divergences, nevertheless: the primacy of Rome and papal infallibility, and the *Filioque,* more a divergence of expression than a fundamental difference, and Mariology. The Orthodox Church does in fact believe in the mystery of the Assumption of Mary, but formulates reservations about the Immaculate Conception, because its theology of original sin is different from that of the Latins.

Mr. Boulier endeavored to present a formula for the Roman primacy which might be acceptable to the Orthodox: the Pope enjoys in the college of bishops the same rights that Peter possessed in the college of the Apostles. Patriarch Alexis saw the cleverness of this repetition of former statement and replied: "Peter was one of the twelve Apostles and had no special privilege." This is a very recent opinion which the Orthodox borrowed from the Reformers, but not at all in conformity with ancient Eastern tradition.[18]

The conditions expressed by the Patriarch as likely to bring about reunion are those constantly affirmed by the Orthodox in attempts to reach a closer understanding with the Anglican Church and the old Catholics: to profess the same faith and be ruled by the same canonical norms.

In conclusion, Mr. Boulier speaks in a concrete manner about the action of Christians in favor of peace as helping to promote unity. We are fully in agreement on this point; never to preach hate against any people is the duty of all Christians. But this charity does not in any way imply spiritual disarmament, nor require that we shut our eyes to the struggle carried on against the Church and the faith by Communism.

The Council, according to Mr. Boulier, could give its approbation to the appeal of the Moscow Congress in some form which it would find admissible. This support, said the Patriarch, would be received with enthusiasm, as would any concrete action in favor of peace.[19]

These declarations of the Patriarch Alexis came to our knowledge when John XXIII had just addressed to the world his radio broadcast of the 11th of September, in which the Pope particularly emphasized the contribution that the Council could make to world peace. Here, in advance of the Council, was a reassuring answer to the questions that were being asked in Moscow. In his message the Pope said:

> It is natural that the Council, in its work of doctrinal construction, and in the pastoral action that it must promote, should give expression to the aspirations of peoples who wish to advance along the paths marked out for each by Providence and to unite, in the triumph of peace, so that existence on earth may become nobler, more just, more rich, and more rewarding for all men.[20]

First Interview between Archbishop Nicodemus and Monsignor Willebrands at Paris

During August, Archbishop Nicodemus returned to Paris, on the occasion of the meeting of the Central Committee of the World Council of Churches. We renewed with him the conversation that had taken place at New Delhi. "Is your Church," I asked, "thinking of replying affirmatively to the invitation of the Roman Church?"

"What invitation?" replied the Archbishop. "We have only received the report of the Patriarch of Constantinople on the visit of Monsignor Willebrands."

The Russian Church was of course hardly disposed to reply favorably to an invitation that came by way of Constantinople, fearing that its acceptance might imply a recognition of the latter's effective primacy. The primacy of Constantinople, as Archbishop Nicodemus was to say when he was passing through Paris in December, 1962, is nothing more than appearing at the top of the list of the autonomous Orthodox Churches.

In view of these new developments, some Catholic ecumenists decided that it would be useful to bring the matter before the Secretariat for the Promotion of Christian Unity. Monsignor Willebrands was able to meet the Archbishop on the occasion of the meeting of the Central Committee of the World Council of Churches at Paris in August, 1962. The first interview took place during the reception held by a group of Catholic organizations (*La Croix* among them) for the members of the World Council of Churches. It was no doubt at Paris that a visit of Msgr. Willebrands to Moscow was decided in principle, so that he might inform the Holy Synod on the subject of the Vatican Council, and transmit an invitation in the event that the Holy Synod found it possible to accept one.[21]

The role played by Mr. Visser't Hooft in these negotiations deserves special notice. The Secretary General of the World Council of Churches, who had been instrumental in the favorable decision reached by the Central Committee, was anxious that the World Council not be the sole representative at the Vatican Council.

Archbishop Nicodemus had other contacts during his stay in France. The Metz newspaper, *Le Lorrain,* published on February 9th a report on a press conference held by Bishop Schmitt. The Bishop of Metz had some interesting details to add to the subject.

It was at Metz that Cardinal Tisserant met Archbishop Nicodemus, the Archbishop in charge of Foreign Affairs of the Russian Church, and it was here that the message was prepared that Msgr. Willebrands took to Moscow. Archbishop Nicodemus, who had come to Paris during the first weeks of August, had expressed a desire to meet Cardinal Tisserant. The meeting took place at the house of M. l'abbe Lagarde, Chaplain of the Little Sisters of the Poor at Bordes. Legarde had been always interested in international problems. Following this interview, Archbishop Nicodemus agreed that someone should go to Moscow to bring an invitation, on condition that guarantees would be given concerning the non-political attitude of the Council.[22]

From then on, the journalist lost track of the negotiations. The Secretariat for Unity was shrouded in silence. Passing through Rome at the end of September, I learned without further details that a new approach had been tried. On my return to Paris on the 29th of September, Father Trubnikov informed me that the Synod of the Orthodox Russian Church outside the Soviet Union had decided to reply favorably to Cardinal

Bea's invitation. This Church, representing the great majority of Russian emigrants, was formerly called the Church of the Synod of Karlovsty; now established in the United States, it had on the 13th of September designated as observer-delegates Bishop Antony of Geneva and Father Igor Troianox, theologian at Lausanne, and also an assistant, Mr. Serge Grotoff, professor of Russian at Rome.

Fearing that the presence of observer-delegates from a Church which in several circumstances had shown its hostility to the Patriarchal Church of Moscow might make it impossible for observers to come from the latter, I made it clear in *La Croix* that the Russian Church outside the Soviet Union was a member of the World Council of Churches, of which the Russian Orthodox Church had equally been a member since the Assembly of New Delhi, in November 1961.[23] I wrote:

> The Orthodox Russian Church outside the Soviet Union has been invited by Cardinal Bea as an autonomous jurisdiction, and has thought proper to use its freedom in accepting the invitation. This decision does not break the unity of faith of Orthodoxy, or the unanimity which is its rule, since it is not concerned with an active participation in the Council, nor even with the opportunity for discussion, but simply with being present, which is in truth a sign of interest and a mark of esteem. In questions of this order, it would seem natural that the autonomous Orthodox Churches, which are so concerned about their independence, should decide upon their attitude in complete freedom.[24]

When I wrote this I hardly thought that the Church of Moscow would advance precisely the same argument to justify its own decision.

Monsignor Willebrands goes to Moscow

Msgr. Willebrands went to Moscow on September 27 and came back on October 2, all in the greatest secrecy. Not until Sunday, October 7th was any rumor of his journey heard in Moscow. The *France-Presse* Agency published on Monday a statement by Mr. Alexis Bouievsky, spokesman for the Holy Synod. He made it clear that Msgr. Willebrands had not met Patriarch Alexis, who was absent from Moscow at the time.[25] He explained that Msgr. Willebrands' visit was for the purpose of information, and that he had not brought an invitation for the Russian Orthodox Church with a view to its participation in the Council. But if such an invitation were addressed by the Vatican to Moscow after this visit, it would receive consideration.

Later, the *Journal of the Patriarchate of Moscow,* in its issue of October, 1962, published an informative official text which gave more details on Msgr. Willebrands' stay.

The Secretary to the Secretariat for the Promotion of Christian Unity, Msgr. Willebrands, was in Moscow from September 27 to October 2. The object of Msgr. Willebrands' journey was to inform the Patriarchate of Moscow of final stages of the preparations for the Second Vatican Council, and also of the tasks of the Council, the questions of agenda and conciliar procedure. Msgr. Willebrands was received by the Archbishop Nicodemus of Yaroslav and Rostov, a member of the Holy Synod and President of the Department of External Affairs of the Moscow Patriarchate, with whom he had several interviews.

Msgr. Willebrands also made a statement about the Second Vatican Council in the course of a meeting with the members of the Holy Synod, the members of the Synodal Commission for Inter-Christian Exchanges, the Rectors of the Ecclesiastical Academies of Moscow and Leningrad, and the responsible collaborators of the Patriarchate of Moscow. The participants in this meeting asked Msgr. Willebrands numerous questions, in reply to which he explained the official point of view of the Roman Catholic Church.

While he was at Moscow, Msgr. Willebrands visited the Cathedral Church of the Theophany and a number of parish churches. On Sunday, September 30, he was present at the Liturgy celebrated by Archbishop Nicodemus at the Church of St. Peter and St. Paul of Lefortovo. Msgr. Willebrands also visited the Monastery of the Trinity and the Ecclesiastical Academy of Moscow. Every day, Msgr. Willebrands celebrated Mass at the Catholic Church of Saint-Louis at Moscow (that is, the Church of Saint-Louis-des-Francais). Msgr. Willebrands visited the Kremlin and other monuments of the capital.

The meetings and the conversations between the representatives of the Russian Orthodox Church and Msgr. Willebrands took place in a friendly atmosphere and in a spirit of Christian brotherhood.[26]

It is not hard to guess that reports of Msgr. Willebrands' journey to Moscow found their echo at Rome. On the eve of the Council, this and the eventual coming of Russian observers were subjects of lively discussions. Msgr. Willebrands confirmed that he had gone to Moscow on his own initiative to inform the Episcopate of the Russian Orthodox Church concerning the development of preparations for the Council. He added that these contacts were the sequel to those established verbally and in writing, both with the representative of the Orthodox Church at the World Council of Churches at Geneva and with Archbishop Nicodemus. Now, he said, it belonged to the Synod of the Orthodox Church to decide whether it would eventually be represented by observer-delegates.

Since contradictory rumors persisted, the Secretariat for the Promotion of Christian Unity published, on October 10, a communique confirming the journey, but allowing doubt to remain about the coming of observers. It was the first news given to journalists. The communique said:

> Following the contacts which have been taking place for several months between the Secretariat for the Promotion of Christian Unity and certain personalities of the Patriarchate of Moscow, Msgr. Willebrands, Secretary of the Secretariat, undertook a journey to Moscow between September 27 and October 2, so as to give in person to the patriarchal authorities information concerning the Second Ecumenical Council of the Vatican. As far as the possible sending of observer-delegates is concerned, it must be pointed out that the final decision belongs to the Holy Synod of the Church of Russia.

The Russian Orthodox Church Accepts the Invitation

The *Journal of the Patriarchate of Moscow* for the month of November brought further details which allow us to reconstruct the order of events. Returning to Rome on October 2 or 3, Monsignor Willebrands made a report of his conversations to Cardinal Bea. The Cardinal addressed a telegram to Archbishop Nicodemus on October 4, advising him of the sending of an official invitation: "I thank Your Excellency for the welcome extended to our Secretary. We are forwarding today the official invitation to His Holiness the Patriarch to send two or three observer-delegates to the Council. With my religious respects. Cardinal Bea."[27]

It was not until October 10 that the Holy Synod held a full meeting with Patriarch Alexis presiding. He examined the invitation from Rome and the report of Archbishop Nicodemus on the preparations of the

Second Vatican Council of the Roman Catholic Church, and on the discussions which had taken place with Msgr. Jean Willebrands. Following this report, the Holy Synod took the historic decision which deserves to be given in full. It was decided:

1. To accept the invitation to send observers from the Patriarchate of Moscow to the Second Vatican Council of the Roman Catholic Church;

2. To designate as observers from the Patriarchate of Moscow to the Second Vatican Council the Archpriest Vitalyi Borovoi, provisional representative of the Orthodox Church to the World Council of Churches and professor at the Ecclesiastical Academy of Leningrad, and the Archimandrite Vladimir Kotliarov, auxiliary head of the Russian Mission at Jerusalem;

3. To promulgate the following ruling on the subject of the observers from the Patriarchate of Moscow to the Second Vatican Council:

(a) The observers will inform the Patriarchate of all details concerning the work of the Second Vatican Council, and of the results of this work insofar as ecclesiastical circles and public opinion are concerned. They will regularly send, at least once a week, reports on the proceedings of the Council to Archbishop Nicodemus of Yaroslav and Rostov and head of the Department of External Relations of the Patriarchate of Moscow, accompanying these reports with written material about the Council along with related periodicals and publications.

(b) The observers, within the limits of the Council's statute concerning observers, will disclose, if need be, to the competent authorities of the Roman Catholic Church, the exact position of the Patriarchate of Moscow.

4. To give a mandate to Archbishop Nicodemus, head of the Department of External Relations of the Patriarchate of Moscow, regularly to inform the Holy Synod of the work of the Second Vatican Council.[28]

On the evening of October 10, it was learned in Rome that Moscow had decided to send observers. But in the absence of an official declaration concerning such a serious matter, doubts persisted among the journalists.[29] Early the next morning, while a depressing, endless rain drenched Rome, the journalists who had since half past six been crowded under the Arch of the Bells, were still talking of nothing but the Russians. I was in suspense during the whole of the ceremony. Seeing opposite me, in front of the tribune of Saint Longinus and the very *parterre* of the Confession, the ranks of observers, I wrote in my notebook: "About the Russians, if they are here, we must say *Confirma hoc Deus quod operatus es in nobis.* It is the beginning of miracles. So many efforts finally crowned by the presence of observers. May they remain at the Council to the end. And may the Council see in their presence the desire for unity and question itself about the causes of division."

The news of the arrival of the Russian observers was confirmed only on the 12th of October by a communique from the Secretariat for the Promotion of Christian Unity: "On the subject of the news recently given out by the information agencies, the Secretariat for the Promotion of Christian Unity officially confirms that the Patriarchal Church of Russia has announced in a telegram, dated October 11, that two observer-delegates have been appointed to attend the Council: the Archpriest Vitalyi Borovoi and the Archimandrite Vladimir Kotliarov."

The two observers arrived in Rome on the afternoon of the 12th of October.[30] They were welcomed at Fiumicino airport by Msgr. Willebrands and Msgr. Arrighi. On the way to the Rome of the Prince of the Apostles, they passed in front of St. Paul's Outside-the-Walls. They expressed the desire to stop and venerate this place where the glorious Apostle had finished his earthly course. At Rome, they immediately wanted to make a pilgrimage to St. Peter's. They were not attracted by the immensity of the Basilica, nor by the imposing hall of the conciliar sessions, but went straight to pray before the Confession of St. Peter. On the following morning, October 13, they were present at the Council for Mass, and were witnesses of the first surprising incident, the postponement of the elections. That evening, during an audience with the Pope, they were the most observed of all the observers! What Pope John XXIII might have thought about this fraternal meeting, and the feelings that inspired the two observers in prostrating themselves before the successor of Peter, may easily be imagined.

An Acceptance without Conditions but not without Consequences

The *France-Presse* Agency published the conditions that were said to have been laid down by the Holy Synod for the sending of observers: the receipt of an official invitation; the obtaining of assurances that such participation did not imply recognition of the primacy of the Pope by the Holy Synod, and finally an assurance that the Council would not become an anti-Communist forum.

Le Monde even reported that the Russian observers did not leave Moscow until after the broadcast of the Pope's opening address. "As much as to say," Mr. Fesquet remarked, "that if the Pope had spoken one word considered unacceptable by the Russians, they would not today be represented at Rome. This again would explain why Moscow waited until the end of the morning of October 11 before sending a telegram to Cardinal Bea announcing the arrival of the observers." (*Le Monde,* October 17, 1962.)

Others have hinted that the text of the address may have been transmitted to the Russians in advance, but that would have been showing them too much deference. Msgr. Willebrands had certainly given assurances that the observers would never be placed in a delicate situation. But this could only have pertained to matters openly discussed. "In no case and in no manner," I wrote at the time, "can the presence of observers hamper the sovereign liberty and independence of the Fathers of the Council. Always and on all subjects, and notably on peace, on religious freedom, and on practical and ideological atheism, the Fathers will say what is in conformity with the faith and what will be given to them to say by the Holy Spirit."

One magazine went so far as to write that the two observers were functionaries of the Soviet State and belonged to the Communist Party.[31] I would like to report here some facts that testify, on the contrary, to their intense faith and courage. I met Archpriest Vitalyi Borovoi for the first time on the *Marilena,* the ship that was transporting the members of the first conference of the Orthodox Churches from Athens to the isle of Rhodes in September-October, 1961. He talked to me then about my articles on the Russian Orthodox Church, of which the last, a reply to the *Non Possumus,* had been severe.

At New Delhi, I noticed his interventions, emphatic, but moderate and strictly orthodox, on the subjects of Tradition, the Trinitarian formula of baptism and the apostolic succession.

In Paris, at the meeting of the Central Committee (August, 1962), he intervened in opposition to a resolution of the Committee, protesting the measures taken by President Nkrumah against the Christian Churches. On another occasion Borovoi spoke with great assurance. The

Committee was discussing the place and role of Christ in the world of today. Borovoi said:

> There is nothing in the report of what Christ means to and within a society hostile to God. Do not expect me to make a statement about it here, but I could at least tell you what should be avoided. One has to be extremely prudent in speaking of the Bible. If we say that the origin of the world as it is related in the Scriptures is simply a literary description of events, then in our country the atheists of *Science and Religion* will repeat your words and add that the creation of the world by God is a myth. I have a son who is passionately fond of exegesis. To save his faith, I am obliged to forbid him this kind of reading. . . .

At Rome, on all public occasions, the journalists and photographers, and even the Fathers of the Council, had eyes only for the Russians.[32] This attitude was no doubt natural because the fact of their presence was so extraordinary, but it was very difficult for them. They extricated themselves creditably from this delicate situation by the surest means: they remained silent. A story that was told about them was an amusing example of mutism. To a journalist who came to question them about their impressions, their answers were invariable: nothing, to no one, never![33]

The Ukrainian Bishops Bring Up the Case of Metropolitan Slipyi

One critical situation, however, did arise for them. On Friday, November 23, a rumor was circulating in Rome that the Russian delegates had packed their bags. Archpriest Viatlyi Borovoi had in fact left for Geneva, where his duties in the World Council of Churches no doubt made his presence necessary. But in Rome itself there had been great alarm. It was provoked by a proposed declaration of the Ukrainian Catholic bishops in exile, residing in Europe and America.

Because of the tragic division of the world, there were many occasions for these bishops when the Council added to the burden of their suffering. They could not but feel deeply the absence of the Catholic bishops of Russia, particularly of Metropolitan Slipyi, who had for seventeen years been exiled somewhere in Siberia, while the Russian

173

Orthodox Church was represented at the Council. This Church had, in 1946, at a time of grave difficulty and under circumstances not yet historically clear, but very painful for the Catholic Church, "reintegrated" into Orthodoxy the flourishing Uniate Church of the Ukraine.

Already the fifteen Ukrainian bishops had expressed a wish that the existence of the Church of Silence should be more clearly expressed in the message to the world from the Fathers of the Council. As they had told us themselves, exercising their freedom of speech, they felt unable to approve the form of the message. With the sufferings of their Church always in their hearts, they wanted to show the world their continuing spiritual concern for what had been done to it. At one point they thought about making a declaration. They had agreed upon the wording of a draft for this purpose, but not upon the right moment for publishing it. The draft was, however, made public by the *Associated Press* and printed in a number of papers. *La Croix* gave a summary of it on November 22, 1962: The fifteen bishops of the Byzantine-Ukrainian rite regretted that observers from the Russian Orthodox Church should have been invited to the Council, while a Catholic prelate, the Metropolitan Josyf Slipyi, Archbishop of Lvov (Ukraine) was still held prisoner in Siberia.

Sounding the first discordant note with regard to the presence of the Russian observers, who had been welcomed until then with satisfaction, the draft affirmed that their presence had given rise to feelings of uneasiness, discontent, and discouragement among Catholic Ukrainian clergy and faithful.[34]

The Russian observers were of course upset about this statement and felt very unhappy. Msgr. Willebrands took the occasion of the press conference given by Professor Cullmann on Friday, November 23, to make an official declaration:

The Secretariat for the Promotion of Christian Unity wishes it to be known that all observer-delegates have been invited by the Secretariat, which was most happy to welcome them. All, without exception, have manifested a sincerely religious and ecumenical spirit. The Secretariat in consequence deplores the appearance of a statement contrary to the spirit which inspired the loyal contacts made with the observer-delegates, and must dissociate itself from it.

Msgr. Willebrands' declaration dispelled the uneasiness of the observers. As for the Ukrainian bishops, the lasting impression from contacts with them was that they felt deeply the sufferings of their people, and those of their leader, Metropolitan Slipyi, and that they were offering up this anguish and their prayers for the unity of all Christians and the peace of the world. Their chief anxiety was that the faithful would not undertsand what was happening in Rome. Those whose faith was not very great were on the verge of thinking that Rome had abandoned the weak in favor of the strong.

When Archbishop Nicodemus, who was responsible for external relations of the Patriarchate of Moscow, came to France in December, a number of people had the opportunity of talking to him about the fate of the Ukrainian Metropolitan. Questions were even publicly put to him by students at a meeting in the University City. He replied that the matter was not within the province of the Orthodox Church.

There was a feeling that the case of Metropolitan Slipyi had now been brought out into the open, and might come up on any occasion. There was the danger that if a satisfactory solution were not found, it might compromise the happy results of the Council's discussion with the Eastern Christians and affect the improved relations between East and West. The solution was both sudden and unexpected.

On the morning of Sunday, February 10, 1963, the Pope gave the world news that left many Catholics speechless with emotion: Archbishop Slipyi had been liberated and was returned to the Pope as to his own father. "A touching consolation came to Us yesterday evening from the east of Europe," the Pope said, at the end of an audience for a group from Milan, "for which We humbly thank the Lord, as for something which, in the divine secrets, can prepare for Holy Church and for all righteous souls a new impetus of sincere faith and peaceful and beneficent apostleship."

Archbishop Slipyi had arrived in Rome on Saturday evening. He was immediately received by the Holy Father. When Cardinals Cicognani, Secretary of State, and Testa, Secretary of the Congregation for the Eastern Church, introduced him, the Pope welcomed him with emotion and quoted the words of the *Imitation* that he had just been reading: *"Felix hora quando Jesus vocat de lacrimis ad gaudium Spiritus:*

175

Happy the hour, when Jesus calls us from tears to the joy of the Spirit!"

On Tuesday, February 12, the *France-Presse* Agency published some details about the liberation of the Ukrainian Metropolitan that gave the background of this outstanding event in the contemporary history of the Church.

Msgr. Willebrands, Secretary of the Secretariat for the Promotion of Christian Unity, had gone to Moscow to meet the Archbishop after his eighteen years in captivity. The two observers, Archpriest Vitalyi Borovoi and Archimandrite Vladimir Kotliarov seemed to have delegated themselves as interpreters to the Soviet authorities of the grief caused to the Pope and to the Catholic hierarchy by the prolonged detention of Archbishop Slipyi.

It appears from certain indications that Cardinal Testa, a personal friend of the Pope and Secretary of the Eastern Congregation, together with Cardinal Bea, President of the Secretariat for the Promotion of Christian Unity, had spoken to the two observers on the question while they were in Rome. They emphasized the fraternal spirit in which they had been received there, and also the fact that responsible authorities had publicy disassociated themselves from the newspaper articles that contrasted the captivity of Archbishop Slipyi and the presence in Rome of observers from Moscow, apparently to cast doubts on their integrity, their intentions, and their religious spirit.

In January, the two observers let it be known that they had presented a report on the question to the competent Soviet authorities. Next, a telegram to Rome announced that Archbishop Slipyi had left his place of detention and arrived in Moscow. It was then that Msgr. Willebrands went by plane to the Soviet capital, leaving there by train on February 5 with Archbishop Slipyi. At Vienna, the Metropolitan was received with joy by the exiled Ukrainian priests in Austria, and on the evening of February 9, the two prelates arrived in Rome.

NOTES

[1] The communique, so often mentioned, was in fact a denial from the Patriarchate of Moscow, published in *Izvestia* on June 21, 1959 and reproduced in the *Journal of the Patriarchate of Moscow* in July, 1959. Here is the integral text: "In number 20 of the Italian review *Tempo* of May 19, under the title *'Will the Russians Take Part in the Ecumenical Council?'* it was stated that '. . . during the last two months the

Apostolic Nuncio at Vienna, Msgr. Dellepiane, had several meetings with three Orthodox bishops, sent especially by the Synod of Moscow to meet him, and perhaps even for conversations on the participation of the Russians in the Catholic Council.' From this fact the author draws the conclusion that the Patriarch of Moscow would be prepared to participate in the Council.

"The Patriarchate of Moscow considers it to be its duty to declare that all this, from beginning to end, is a pure invention of the author. The Holy Synod of the Russian Orthodox Church has not, either during recent months or at any former time, sent bishops or other representatives to meet the Papal Nuncio in Vienna or elsewhere, and there have been no negotiations with him.

"The Patriarchate of Moscow considers the future Catholic Council as a purely Roman Catholic matter, and for its part, it has no reason to become, and still less any intention of becoming, involved in this affair."

[2] Born in 1929, in the village of Frolovo, province of Riazan, Boris Georgeievitch Rotov belongs to the new Soviet generation. He completed all his studies at a Soviet school, and his secondary studies at the pedagogic institute of Riazan. In 1947 he became a monk and took the name of Nicodemus. Ordained deacon, and then priest in 1949 at the age of twenty, he was given a parish in the province of Yaroslav. In January, 1952, he was named pastor of the Cathedral of Yaroslav and Secretary to the Archbishop. In 1950 he enrolled in a correspondence course of the Seminary of Leningrad. After matriculating at the Ecclesiastical Academy, he was made Doctor of Theology for his thesis entitled *History of the Russian Mission at Jerusalem*. He became attached to this mission in February, 1956, and was made its head during the following year, with the title of Archimandrite. In March, 1959, he was recalled to Moscow to serve as Chancellor of the Patriarchate. On July 4, 1959, he was appointed as Vice-President, and on July 21, 1960, as President, of the important Department of External Relations. Because of this appointment he was named Bishop of Podolsk when he was only thirty-one years old and soon after he became Archbishop (on the eve of the Peace Congress of Prague) of Yaroslav and Rostov. He succeeded the famous Metropolitan Nicolas de Krutitsy (✝ 1962) who had retired apparently because of poor health. The Patriarchate and the Communist Party, obviously for different reasons, disliked his overbearing personality. (Cf. *La Croix*, February 9–10, 1961.)

[3] This was actually a collective report of the Russian delegation at Prague. It was published in the *Journal of the Patriarchate of Moscow*, n. 6 (1961), pp. 41–59. The passages concerning the Catholic Church are on pp. 54–56.

[4] Cf. *Journal of the Patriarchate of Moscow*, n. 11 (1961), p. 16.

[5] Archbishop Nicodemus gave an explanation about this article to a journalist of *Informations Catholiques Internationales*, n. 175 (September, 1962): "The article 'Non Possumus,' published by the *Journal of the Patriarchate of Moscow*, carried no signature. Accordingly, although it was published in the official organ of the Patriarchate, the article in no way engaged the latter. It must therefore be considered as expressing the opinion of its author, A. V. Vedernikov, editorial secretary of the *Journal of the Patriarchate of Moscow*. The Patriarchate had in consequence no need to deny it." The article, however, appeared in the official review and spoke in the name of the Patriarchate. The very absence of a signature gave greater authority to the recurrent expression: *the Patriarchate of Moscow believes, thinks, etc.*

[6] We notice here the tendency of Russian Orthodoxy to substitute itself for Orthodoxy as a whole.

[7] *Journal of the Patriarchate of Moscow*, n. 5 (1961), pp. 73–75.

[8] *La Croix*, August 29, 1961.

[9] We know that the leaders of the World Council of Churches informed the heads of the Russian Church that they must not expect to find in the World Council an echo of any activity directed against Rome, whatever might be the private thoughts of in-

dividual members on the subject, because such activity would be contrary to the aims of the Movement.

[10] The third assembly of the World Council of Churches took place at New Delhi, from November 18, 1961, to December 5, 1961.

[11] Cf. *La Croix*, December 13, 1961.

[12] The text of this interview was sent to *La Croix* by the *Novosti* Agency very late—at the beginning of September. The offices of the Agency in Paris were not able to give us the reasons for the delay. The text, they told us, still remained valid. (Cf. *La Croix*, September 18, 1962.) It was published in the *Journal of the Patriarchate of Moscow*, n. 9 (1962), pp. 14–16, under the title *"The Defense of Peace."* The interview did include some questions on peace that have been omitted here but were published in *La Croix*.

[13] The translation of the *Novosti* Agency, which we published in *La Croix* in default of the original text that did not reach us until November, made the Patriarch say exactly the contrary: "The position of the Russian Orthodox Church does not admit of the serious differences which exist between the Roman Catholic Church and the autonomous Orthodox Churches."

[14] Put in this way, the question asked by ex-Abbe Boulier seems to make the Roman Church co-terminous with the Patriarchate of the West.

[15] Since *La Croix* had strongly criticized this way of putting the question, Mr. Boulier replied to me: "You say it is lacking in charity to attribute to leaders of other nations a hatred of the Soviet Union when there is no proof of this. But surely it is respect for truth to recall that the United States is cold-bloodedly preparing for Moscow the same fate as Hiroshima, and threatening the Russians with it? If that is not hate, what name are we to give to these designs of Cain?

"You certainly know, for you alluded to it I think, that Father Gundlach, a Jesuit in *Stimmen der Zeit,* and five theologians, with the approbation of the bishops, also in the German religious press, have said that the use of atomic weapons is permissible. They even dared to attribute this opinion to Pope Pius XII. Thus they have acquitted themselves of 'their duty to study the problems that modern forms of war bring before the conscience of Christians.' When I think that the Second Lateran Council excommunicated *crossbow-men* and *ballestarii* because of the cruelty of those 'modern forms of war'! There was a Christian conscience at that time; but today? Is it wanting in charity to denounce such ignoble laxity? What we need is Pascal's fiery pen to flay these casuists and their complacent attitude toward these attempts on human life!"

[16] Apostolic Letter, *Sacro vergente anno,* to the peoples of Russia (July 29, 1952): "It should be most carefully noted that Isidore, Metropolitan of Kiev, at the Ecumenical Council of Florence signed the decree by which the union of the Eastern and Western Churches under the authority of the Roman Pontiff was solemnly affirmed, and this was binding upon the whole of his own ecclesiastical province, that is to say, for the whole kingdom of Russia. For his part, he remained faithful to this restored unity until the end of his earthly life.

"And if in the course of time, and because of a number of adverse circumstances, relations on both sides became more difficult, and, in consequence, the union of minds also became more difficult—although until 1448 there was no public document which declared your Church separated from the Apostolic See—this must nevertheless not be imputed in a general way to the Slavic peoples, and certainly not to Our predecessors, who always surrounded those peoples with paternal love, and whenever it was possible, took care to support them and help them in every way." (*Documentation Catholique,* n. 1128, August 24, 1952, col. 1027–1028.)

[17] Mr. Boulier, in a letter dated October 1, explained the meaning of the question

178

that he had put to the Patriarch, and added some clarifications to the remarks which we had published in *La Croix*.

"In opposing my 'optimistic' summary of the Russian schism, you adopt the version that is current in Moscow. This is rather taking liberties with the history of the Church of Kiev, which was supplanted by Moscow at a relatively recent date. The conversion of Russia is generally dated from 988, and as you remember, the schism of Cerularius dates from 1054. It seems to me that, when Bulgakov speaks of 'original sin,' he is thinking rather of the birth of the Patriarchate of Moscow in 1589. This was at the time, as I suggested, a political act in the struggle against Polish Latinism.

"Optimistic or pessimistic, my opinion rests on incontestable facts, which Muscovite tradition, to prevent divergence from the other Orthodox Churches, prefers to gloss over. But I do not understand why Roman Catholics should want these well-established facts to be forgotten, when they bring us closer to our Slav brothers.

"1. The Church of Kiev, which was then unquestionably the Church of Russia, *Ecclesia Ruthena*, remained in communion with the Church of Rome for more than a century after the schism of Cerularius.

"2. The Metropolitan of Kiev, accompanied by all his suffragan bishops, took part for several months in the Council of Constance (1415), and solemnly celebrated the Orthodox liturgy there. He supported the complaints about atrocities (already!) brought before the Council by the King of Poland and the Grand Duke of Lithuania, against the 'lords of Prussia,' those Teutonic knights of sinister memory.

"3. Isidore, Metropolitan of Kiev, along with Bessarion, Metropolitan of Nicea, was an active promoter of union at the Council of Florence.

"At this period, the Grand Duke of Lithuania, at whose court Russian was spoken, had gathered under him all the Russian territories with the exception of Moscow, which was still tributary to the Mongols.

"After 1453, the Greek emigrants, who were violently anti-Latin, escaping from Byzantium following its capture by the Turks, declared Moscow to be *the third Rome*. The Czar Basil raised the Metropolitan of Moscow above Kiev; after having been 'Russian,' the Lithuanian territories became more and more 'Polish,' and finally, a century later (1589), came the creation of the Patriarchate, born as Bulgakov said, in the 'original sin' of schism.

"Consequently, the history of the Russian Church shows her to have been in more ancient and more enduring communion with Rome than Byzantium and the Greeks. I hoped, in asking my question, that the Patriarch, who knows this history, would have taken the opportunity to mention it."

[18] Among others may be quoted the witness of Hesychius of Jerusalem (beginning of the 5th century): "Peter is brilliant in himself. He shines above those who shine, as leader of the chariot of the Apostles, as the eye of the accepted teaching, as the monument of zeal and representative of the faith, as the trumpet of the mystery, as the mouth that itself teaches many other mouths, as the irreproachable shepherd, the ever-watchful pilot, the infallible leader." *Unpublished homily for the feast of St. Peter and St. Paul,* Vat. gr. 1667 and 1165.

[19] Mr. Boulier went to Rome and handed to several Fathers a text on the law of war and peace. The text is based upon the following principles:

1. Declarations of pure moral theology should be avoided and reference should be made only to the existing body of international law.

2. To be accepted by all governments, definite political positions should be avoided.

3. In practical ways a sure and firm course for the action of Christians and of all men of good will should be opened so as to rally world opinion in favor of peace.

4. For this reason, our aims in this domain should be limited to the realizable minimum rather than the desirable maximum.

The summary of the schema is as follows:
1. Sins without number result from war.
2. Pacts against war are precarious.
3. The Church must show that there is a *practical way* to prevent war. This way is suggested in the following propositions:
    (a) Peace is the tranquillity of the order of human brotherhood.
    (b) War can never be legally justified.
    (c) But in wars, law and equity must be respected.
    (d) Conscience is bound by law and equity.

Mr. Boulier thinks that in the present state of human relations, and because of the immense forces of destruction that are brought into play, war can only engender evils infinitely worse than those which it is supposed to eliminate. Therefore, no war can any longer be regarded as just, whatever may be the motive or pretext for it.

He affirms that atomic weapons are "in themselves criminal arms. Their use, and the threat of their use, must be forbidden forever, and therefore their manufacture also. Even the desire to prepare and experiment with such means of human massacre is criminal. Nothing can excuse the governments which engage in it."

[20] *Documentation Catholique,* October 7, 1962, col. 1220.

[21] In an interview given to *Informations Catholiques Internationales,* Archbishop Nicodemus denied the statements attributed to Patriarch Alexis at Belgrade (May, 1962): "The Synod of the Russian Orthodox Church has not yet taken any decision, positive or negative, on the subject of the Second Vatican Council. The Patriarchate of Moscow declared as far back as 1959 that it considers Vatican II as an internal matter of the Catholic Church—which this Church itself recognizes—and that declaration still remains in force. No other has since been made by the leaders of the Russian Orthodox Church either denying or modifying it, not even that which the press attributed to Patriarch Alexis during his stay at Belgrade. I am able to confirm that the correspondent of the Italian newspaper who was the source of this information did not even speak to Patriarch Alexis. It was only with myself that he spoke, and I made no declaration of this kind to him."

And since the journalist of *Informations Catholiques* was bent on knowing what the Russian Church would do if an invitation were received, the Archbishop replied: "We must not put the cart before the horse. . . . The Russian Orthodox Church has as yet received no invitation. It would, therefore, be difficult for me to give a positive or negative reply to a question which in reality is just a simple hypothesis. What I can say is that if in the near future we received sufficient information on the subject of the Council, and if the Vatican were to send us an invitation in view of an eventual participation of our observers at Vatican II, this would furnish the Holy Synod with a basis for study of the question, and then it would be possible to take up an official position on the subject, and to give a reply which would engage the responsibility of the Russian Orthodox Church. But in any case we must not try to push things, or instruct the Vatican what it ought to do in the matter. The Vatican knows very well how it should act on the point." (*Informations Catholiques Internationales,* September 1, 1962).

[22] *La Croix,* February 15, 1963.

[23] The Russian Church outside the Soviet Union had expressed reservations about the admission of the Patriarchal Church of Moscow to the World Council of Churches. Bishop John of San Francisco said, first in English, and then in Russian: "I consider it our duty, from deep religious considerations, to abstain, by reason of certain circumstances, from voting in favor of the admission of the Russian Orthodox Church. But we hope that our apprehensions, which are the reason for our abstention, will be dispelled in the near future, thanks to the providence of God."

[24] *La Croix,* October 7–8, 1962.

180

[25] Patriarch Alexis was then resting at Odessa. He could not come back to Moscow to meet a lesser Roman prelate.

[26] *Journal of the Patriarchate of Moscow*, n. 10 (1962), p. 43.

[27] *Journal of the Patriarchate of Moscow*, n. 11 (1962), pp. 9–10.

[28] *Ibid.*, p. 10.

[29] They seemed to be the only ones who were excited about the matter. The bishops were too busy with the problem occasioned by their registration, the ceremony of October 11, and the imminence of the Council's work.

[30] They were very soon joined by Nicolas Anfinogenov, Secretary of the delegation of the Patriarchate of Moscow at the World Council of Churches at Geneva, who arrived in Rome on October 16, to serve as official interpreter to the two observers of the Russian Orthodox Church.

[31] *Itinéraires* (January, 1963), p. 59: "The two representatives of the Orthodox Patriarchate of Moscow are functionaries of the Soviet State: they are subservient to the Communist Party. The Patriarchate of Moscow is an instrument in the hands of the Soviet government and the Communist Party in their totalitarian dominion over the Russian people and their colonialist dominion over the non-Russian peoples of Europe and Asia."

[32] There was one journalist who said that they had not knelt at the moment of the consecration, when they were present for the first time at the Mass, on Saturday, October 13. Apparently they were not aware that the moment had come to do so. Although according to Orthodox theology, the Real Presence occurs after the invocation of the Holy Spirit (*epiklesis*), the moment of the consecration is more solemn in the Byzantine than in the Latin rite. The words *This is my Body; this is the chalice, etc.,* are sung by the priest, and the people reply "Amen."

[33] They did, however, depart from this rule of silence, since interviews were often published which they had granted to newspapers and magazines, but these were a witnessing for the Russian Orthodox Church rather than an expression of opinion concerning the Council.

[34] The draft of the declaration added: "For certain sections of public opinion, it seems that the coming to Rome of the Orthodox observers has been loudly hailed, while the absence of Metropolitan Slipyi and his detention are passed over in silence. Archbishop Slipyi was 'illegally deported and has been imprisoned in Siberia for seventeen years.' He is the sole survivor of eleven Ukrainian Catholic bishops who were sent to Siberia. The Patriarchate 'assumed ecclesiastical jurisdiction over four and a half million Ukrainian Catholics contrary to all divine, ecclesiastical, or human law in open collaboration with the atheistic civil power, because this was the only way in which the Ukrainian Catholic Church could be suppressed and liquidated.' "

It will be seen how fortunate it was that this text, which was both severe and out of place during the Council, remained no more than a project and was never published. But it was no doubt good that the case of Metropolitan Slipyi was brought before public opinion. The Moscow government was consequently obliged to make a gesture which it would not itself have initiated.

III

Constantinople-Moscow

THE DAYS THAT PRECEDED OCTOBER 11 WERE DRAMATIC IN Constantinople. Patriarch Athenagoras wanted with all his heart to send observers in the name of the Orthodox Church. He did everything he could to remain in touch with Rome and the other Orthodox Churches. On October 6, he sent a telegram to Rome to find out if anything new had been heard from Moscow. He sent a telegram to Moscow, also on the 6th. On the 7th, the Patriarch of Moscow answered that there was nothing new to communicate. With heavy heart, the Patriarch notified Cardinal Bea that, to maintain the unity of Orthodoxy, he could not send any observers to the Council:

1. The Orthodox Church of Constantinople and the other national Orthodox Churches answered the invitation of His Eminence Cardinal Bea, saying they could not send any observers to the Second Vatican Council.

2. However, the Orthodox Church would continue to observe with interest all the acts of the Vatican Council at Rome and to pray for its success.

3. The Orthodox Church is certain that the Council in Rome will open a new opportunity for a dialogue with the Orthodox and for reunion of the three Churches,[1] a union which is desired on all sides.

Equivocations and Misunderstandings

The Patriarch made this decision known to all the Orthodox Churches. But, on the evening of the 10th, the radio broadcast to the world that Moscow would send two observers to the Council. They arrived in Rome on the 12th with credentials in good and due form, the like of which no other Church had furnished to its delegates. On Thursday morning, October 11, while the Council was opening its proceed-

182

ings, Constantinople was in a quandary. On that day, the Patriarch felt the weight of suffering which is always the other side of the joyous events of the Church. He published a message to emphasize his astonishment at not having been informed of the trend of developments in Moscow:

Before renouncing the idea of being represented at the Council, we consulted the autonomous Churches, as we are accustomed to do. We had addressed a letter and two telegrams to the Patriarch of Moscow asking him to let us know his point of view concerning the sending of observers to the Ecumenical Council. The Patriarch of Moscow acknowledged the receipt of this letter and of the first telegram without expressing his point of view. Then we sent him another telegram in which we clearly asked him to express his opinion. The Patriarch answered us on last October 7, letting us know in this new telegram: "We have nothing new to communicate to you." Consequently, the announced decision of the Patriarchate of Moscow to send observers to the Second Vatican Council astonished us.

As we see, Patriarch Athenagoras does not mention Rome. However, some time after, Archbishop Iakovos, Orthodox Bishop of the Americas, under the jurisdiction of Constantinople, one of the six presidents of the World Council of Churches (who was recalled to the United States because of the Cuban crisis), made a severe declaration against Rome. He accused the Vatican of having wanted to break the unity of Orthodoxy in sending separate invitations to the Orthodox Churches. Only the Church of Russia responded to the wish of the Vatican. The reasons which caused that Church to change its position were purely political. However, Patriarch Athenagoras was not angry with Russia. "On the contrary, we are praying that the Russian participation adds to the usefulness of the Council and to the good of the Christian Church."[2]

The proof that the Russian Church had acted only for political motives seemed apparent to Archbishop Iakovos because of a declaration of Msgr. Willebrands, written before his trip to Moscow. "If the Russians do not send any observers," the prelate said, "this would mean that there are reasons which prevent them from doing so."

The argument is not conclusive. The fact that the absence of Russian observers might have been motivated by political reasons does not prove that her presence must be attributed to these same reasons. On the other hand, in the grievances presented to the Secretariat for the Promotion of Christian Unity, we must be logical and not reproach Rome, as some do, for having wanted to divide Orthodoxy by sending separate invitations or, as others do, for not having invited each Church separately, thus recognizing a *de facto* primacy in Constantinople.

The Undecided Church of Greece

Athens was even more annoyed, but with less justification, because it had always shown reluctance to send observers. In February, 1962, Msgr. Willebrands had passed through Athens on his way back from Constantinople. In June, Patriarch Athenagoras was questioning the Greek Church concerning the possible sending of observers. Then came a direct invitation from the Holy See, sent by the Secretariat for the Promotion of Christian Unity.

For some months, however, because of certain efforts and more particularly those of the Metropolitan of Kitros, Archbishop Varnavas, the Holy Synod of Athens had constituted a committee charged with international ecclesiastical affairs. This committee included the Archbishop of Athens, His Beatitude Chrysostom; the following Metropolitans: Procopios of Corinth; Varnavas of Kitros; Dionysios of Kozani; Antonios of Xanthi and professors of the Faculty of Theology of Athens, Messrs. P. Bratsiotis, B. Ioannidis, J. Karmiris, and A. Alivisatos. The invitation was first considered by this committee.

From the beginning then the Orthodox Church of Greece seemed to hesitate in giving a favorable response to Rome's invitation, either because of the rapid development and progress of the idea of reunion in these past few years, or the habitual slowness and excessive prudence of the Orthodox Church with regard to adaptation, or an age-old attitude of suspicion of Rome, or especially the lack of more immediate preparation by frequent and cordial contacts between Orthodox and Catholics.

The Holy Synod met Wednesday, August 8. The results were rather disappointing for the partisans of reconciliation of the Churches. First of all, five of the twelve members of the Synod were missing at this meeting which proves, at least, their reluctance to declare themselves. Finally the Holy Synod shirked this responsibility by sending the question back for decision by the whole hierarchy, which could not normally meet before October 1. Thus the Church of Greece was not able to be present at the Vatican Council, at least not at the beginning.

To critical observers, it did not appear that opposition to Rome could alone explain this hesitation. Many of the Orthodox, both clergy and laity, were frankly favorable to the idea of reconciliation and would gladly welcome the idea of having Orthodox observers at the Council. Even among members of the Holy Synod there were metropolitans favorable to sending observers. But, as in everything else, there are indeterminate factors that are always preponderant.

"We should not be surprised," our correspondent in Athens remarked, "if in the end, the attitude of the Russian Orthodox Church finally influenced the decision of the Eastern Orthodox Churches." It should be noted that as soon as it was announced that a Council would be held, all of Orthodoxy, in spite of internal difficulties, felt the need to manifest a united front in a common attitude regarding the Catholic Church. All over the world, even behind the Iron Curtain, the watchword was unity and a common attitude. As a matter of fact, it would not do for a divided and discordant Orthodoxy to be present in Rome. However, in Rhodes, at the Pan-Orthodox Conference in September, 1961, against all expectation, the question had not been broached. But the Russian Church, the most powerful and influential of all the Orthodox Churches, seemed resolutely determined to refuse. At least, it was in this sense that its attitude was interpreted by the other Orthodox Churches. Furthermore, in Rome, at the Secretariat for the Promotion of Christian Unity, they had been convinced for a long time that the Russians would not come.

The sudden decision of the Russian Orthodox Church to send observers irritated the Church of Greece. Its head, the Archbishop Chrysostom of Athens, declared to a reporter that the decision of the Patriarchate of Moscow, inspired by political motives, was a severe blow to the unity of Orthodoxy. Consequently, the Church of Greece could only refuse to go to Rome.

The most perspicacious minds deplored the absence of Greek Orthodoxy at the Council. Professor Alivisatos wrote in a letter published by the Athenian daily *To Vima* that the refusal of the Orthodox Churches, especially the Church of Greece, to send observers to the Vatican

Council constitutes *"an inexcusable historical mistake."* This has become *"the irony of the entire Christian world."* The mistake was all the more grave as it occurred "at a time when a unique occasion offered itself to the Orthodox Church to make the Christian world aware of its prestigious and unquestionable majesty." In place of this, Orthodoxy merely revealed its *"hesitation and irresolution."* The situation was doubly serious and tragic because the Russian Orthodox Church *"had modified its tactics and its policy. We should have foreseen it and, as I asked from the beginning, the Ecumenical Patriarch and the Church of Greece should have sent observers in time. It is too late now."* Professor Alivisatos concluded: "Therefore we remain alone rejoicing in our Orthodoxy and in our ecumenicity; we learn what is happening in the newspapers, whereas other Churches hold the place which belongs unquestionably to us, and go resolutely forward, leaving behind those who trail along lackadaisically."

Rome: "A Momentary Failure"

How did all this occur? It is not our duty to pass judgment or to designate responsibilities. The Secretariat for the Promotion of Christian Unity will say that unfortunate occurrences created misunderstandings. Any interpretation which could place blame on particular persons or Churches was carefully avoided. When, on November 8, 1962, Cardinal Bea received the press to speak to us about the Secretariat for Unity, he warned us in advance that he would not answer any questions that we might want to ask him. An unfortunate word might have disastrous effects for the cause of unity. In saying this, he surely was thinking of the relations between Rome, Constantinople, and Moscow. In the course of this press conference, he stressed that the absence of Greek observers was regrettable for all concerned:

Our joy and when I say "our joy," I mean also that of observers and the denominations they represent—is diminished by the absence of a good number of the venerable Eastern Churches. We must always realize that great efforts have been made to overcome existing obstacles. And although we did not quite succeed, we have carefully tried to prevent deterioration of our mutual relations in Christ as a result of this temporary set-back.[3]

Moscow: The Legitimate Autonomy of Churches

The Russians took pains to affirm their good faith during the contacts prior to October 11. The most detailed account is undoubtedly a conversation between Archpriest Borovoi and a German reporter, Eva-Marie Jung, published in *Echo der Zeit,* December 16, 1962.[4] The substance of the interview is as follows:

We knew that Msgr. Willebrands had visited Patriarch Athenagoras and that he had given him an invitation. We also knew that he had returned to Eastern Europe in May and that he had met the heads of all the Churches there, except the Russian Orthodox. We knew that the Greek Patriarch was quite willing to send observers to the Council. We, too, were following the preparation of the Council with much interest. And Patriarch Athenagoras did send us, as we confirmed, an account of his encounter with Msgr. Willebrands, but with no mention at all of an invitation. Msgr. Willebrands came to Geneva, where he had talks with the representatives of the international Protestant federations. I was there myself, but he did not speak to me because we Orthodox are a Church, and not a denominational federation. I waited in vain. We met again in Paris in August, during a session of the central committee of the World Council of Churches. This time, I had to act as the interpreter for Msgr. Willebrands and Archbishop Nicodemus, head of the Department of Foreign Affairs of the Patriarchate of Moscow. We told Msgr. Willebrands that if Rome desired our presence, we would have to receive a personal invitation. Even though we respect the Patriarch of Constantinople, we are still an autonomous church. Msgr. Willebrands asked us if a visit by him to Moscow would be well received. We answered that if he wanted to come, he would be cordially welcomed. We waited again. August and almost all of September passed without hearing a word from him. Suddenly, on September 26, a telegram informed us that he would arrive in Moscow on the next day. We gave him a cordial reception. I myself had been called from Leningrad."

Question: But why wasn't the Patriarch there?

Answer: The Patriarch was at that time far from Moscow, at his summer home in Odessa. Why should he have come to Moscow? Msgr. Willebrands is a mere prelate, like my colleague and myself, without important rank.

Question: I understand. The Cardinal himself would have to come for the Patriarch to be present.

Answer: I do not believe that a Cardinal would have been enough. A

187

Cardinal is only a bishop, while a Patriarch is much higher in rank.[5] Msgr. Willebrands stayed six days in our country. He had some talks with certain members of the Holy Synod. But he did not bring an invitation with him. He said that he wanted first to know if we were willing to accept his invitation. We answered that we could not make any decision if we did not have the invitation in hand. So Msgr. Willebrands left without having obtained any results, and he promised to give us an answer when he arrived in Rome.

Question: Let me interrupt you. Were there any conditions set down, either on your part or on the Vatican's, regarding the sending or accepting of observers?

Answer: Conditions? I do not understand. What do you mean? How can one Church set down conditions for another?

Question: All right, another question: Was Constantinople informed about these negotiations?

Answer: Constantinople has been kept abreast of the proceedings since August. On October 6 we received a telegram from Patriarch Athenagoras asking us what we intended to do. The only answer we could give was: "We have nothing new to communicate to you." We still had not heard from Rome.[6] The official invitation did not reach us until the day before the opening of the Council. The Holy Synod met immediately and decided to send two observers. They made this decision known to us the evening of the same day. We were convinced upon our arrival in Rome that we would find the observers of the Greek Patriarchate already there. You can imagine our disappointment at finding ourselves alone.

Question: Do you think they still may come?

Answer: We do not know, but we hope so.

Question: Also, why have we not seen the other Orthodox Churches which are dependent on Moscow, for example, the Rumanian and Bulgarian Churches?

Answer: If they were dependent on Moscow, they would have come, but they are autonomous like ourselves. It appears that the Roman Church still does not understand this.

Question: But Patriarch Athenagoras stated: "Before renouncing the idea of being represented at the Council, we consulted the autonomous Churches." How do you account for that?

Answer: He did not consult us. He told us of his decision on October 10 by telegram.[7] When it arrived, we had already let it be known that we would send two observers and we could no longer go back on our word. We were so stupefied by Patriarch Athenagoras' decision—because he was the one who had previously expressed such a strong approval of the Council—that the man who opened the telegram couldn't believe his eyes and asked someone who knew Greek better than he to translate it. You see, if there were a commission of Orthodox Churches in which all the autonomous Churches of Orthodoxy would be represented, as was decided at Rhodes, these misunderstandings would not have arisen. All information and opinions would be exchanged and discussed right away. We are forever insisting on the need for this commission, but Patriarch Athenagoras still has not done anything along these lines.

Eva-Maria Jung next questioned Archpriest Borovoi on the manifesto attributed to the Ukrainian bishops regarding the Metropolitan Archbishop Slipyi who, at that time, was still deprived of his liberty. She reports his answer in the following manner:

The Archpriest stated that he was not at all offended by it. The Ukrainian bishops' declaration was no reflection on the person or the good faith of the Russian observers. "I myself would also like Metropolitan Slipyi to be here. But what can we do if the State has condemned him and is keeping him in confinement?"[8]

The last question was this: "Do you believe that unity of all Christians is possible?"

Answer: Why not? All the Orthodox Churches are united among themselves in matters of faith and doctrine and it could be the same for all Christian Churches. An organic unity is not necessary. We would recognize in the Pope, because of his historic importance, a primacy of honor, but *inter pares.*[9]

Athens: Was Orthodox Unity Compromised?

In Greece, neither Moscow nor Rome had yet been pardoned for the separate contacts. The complaints against the Churches are suggested rather than expressed in a series of questions asked of Patriarch Alexis in the Greek paper *Ethnos* (*The Nation*) published in Athens. Questions and answers were preceded by a lead editorial. This was a new item to add to the record.

According to *Ethnos,* the sending of observers by the Russian Church to the Vatican Council last October has shaken the unity of Orthodoxy affirmed at the Pan-Orthodox Conference of Rhodes in September, 1961. No other Church, not even the Ecumenical Patriarchate, accepted the Pope's invitation. The Russian Patriarchate's action was considered the consequence of political intervention resulting from relations between the Soviet Government and the Vatican.[10]

Ethnos, through its collaborator in charge of ecclesiastical affairs, Mr. Spyros Alexiou, asked Patriarch Alexis of Moscow to give information to the Orthodox regarding the sending of observers and his own views concerning the reunion of the Churches.

Patriarch Alexis did the newspaper the honor of speaking of this delicate question for the first time since the sending of the observers. Through Archbishop Nicodemus of Yaroslav and Rostov, who is responsible for foreign relations of the Patriarchate of Moscow, Patriarch Alexis agreed to give the appropriate explanations which were most useful for the progress of Orthodox unity.

Question: From the moment that you knew that the Catholic Church had invited the Orthodox to send observers to the "ecumenical" Vatican Council, you stated, "The Council of Rome constitutes an internal matter of the Western Church, and Orthodoxy has no place in it." So that is what was communicated and written. Is this true?

Answer: When Pope John XXIII announced his plan to convoke the Second Vatican Council (and even now) the Russian Orthodox Church considered this Council as an internal matter of the Roman Catholic Church.

Question: Would this declaration on your part mean that you had no intention of sending observers?

Answer: This position of the Russian Church did not signify its intention *not* to recognize a wholly natural fact—the fact that an event of such great importance for the life of the Roman Catholic Church would certainly arouse the interest of the rest of the Christian world and in particular the Orthodox Church.[11] In this way, such a declaration did not carry the sense of a refusal by the Russian Church to send observers to the Council.

Question: Why, after the visit of Rome's envoy, Msgr. Willebrands, only a few days before the inauguration of the Council's work, did you agree to send observers?

Answer: It was natural that the Holy Synod of the Russian Church would consider the question of sending observers to the Second Vatican Council only after the invitation was received; it arrived just before the opening of the Council.

The visit made by the secretary of the Secretariat for the Promotion of Christian Unity, Msgr. Jean Willebrands, to the Patriarchate of Moscow enabled us to gain direct information and an accurate conception of the character of the Council. Consequently, this visit contributed to the decision taken by the Holy Synod of the Russian Orthodox Church regarding the sending of observers to this Council.

Question: The Archbishop Iakovos of North and South America in his recent statements said: "The Vatican, after having said at the outset that it would invite the Orthodox with the Ecumenical Patriarchate acting as intermediary, so that the Churches could reach a common decision, later invited the Churches separately by its envoys, thus creating a division among the Orthodox Churches."[12] Is it possible that the sending of Russian observers was meant to bring about a division?

Answer: In sending invitations to the local Orthodox Churches asking them to send observers to the Council, we, for our part, see nothing which could (as you have written) provide a division among them. We do not consider the presence of Orthodox observers at the Council as a problem requiring Pan-Orthodox agreement. We see this in the light of contemporary ecumenical activity at the level of the local Orthodox Churches.

In fact, it is not within the competence of the observers, for example, to deal with the problem of re-establishing liturgical and canonical relations between the Russian Orthodox Church and the Roman Catholic Church, nor with problems whose solutions depend upon the consent of the entire Orthodox Church and not any particular Church, whatever it may be.

The affirmative answer to the question of sending observers was determined, on our part, in conformity with certain rules universally accepted among us (taking into account the principles of mutual esteem which, of course, remain complete and entire) and also in a way that does not touch upon interests of the Roman Catholic Church and the Russian Orthodox Church.[13]

For that reason, the different opinions of the various Orthodox Churches regarding the sending of observers to the Vatican Council cannot, as we see it, be exploited as the cause or consequence of any division that there may be between us. To the extent that each Orthodox Church is an autonomous Church, it is independent of the other Churches.

Question: Does the particular decision of the Russian Church advance the cause of the unity of the Churches and of the reunion of the Christian world in the future?

Answer: As we have already said, the Russian Orthodox Church welcomed the invitation to send observers to the Council in an ecumenical spirit. The Russian Orthodox Church prays for Christian unity and makes serious efforts to attain it. Its entrance into the World Council of Churches constitutes a step toward the realization of this goal.

Question: Don't you think that the isolated act of your sending Orthodox observers will lead to difficulties for the preparatory work of the Pan-Orthodox pre-synod which will eventually be meeting?[14]

Answer: In the undertaking of our Church that you mention, we see nothing, on our side, which could complicate the unanimous effort of the various Orthodox Churches to resolve the general problems of Orthodoxy, as for instance the very important matter of convoking a Pan-Orthodox Council.

Constantinople: Silence and Reserve

At Constantinople, Patriarch Athenagoras seems to have adopted a policy of silence. This silence is eloquent in its own way. It hides the great grief of the Patriarch, but also his unimpaired hope for Christian unity. As the mother Church of the various European Orthodox Churches, Constantinople believes that its role is to suffer and be silent regarding the possible divergences of her children. As for Rome, the separation has been too long, and the historic rivalry too great, for this negative past to disappear as if by magic.

The search for unity continues and Constantinople intends to pursue it still more actively within the World Council of Churches, in which all the Orthodox Churches are united today. This presence, Patriarch Athenagoras was to say in his Christmas message of 1962, is a sign of the wisdom and providence of God. And then, speaking of the Council, the Patriarch continued:

We consider as an analogical manifestation of the wisdom of God this Second Vatican Council of the ancient and venerable Roman Catholic Church, which has just begun and which is being carried on with great expectations. To this Council we have accorded the attention and esteem which it deserves, and we hope that there will emerge from it, by the grace of the Most High, new and more positive promises of mutual understanding, theological encounters, and fruitful contacts.[15]

Orthodoxy was preparing to celebrate in March and April, 1963, the millennium of the monastic establishment of Mount Athos. This was for all Orthodox Churches an occasion to meet at the very spot where the unity of Orthodoxy and loyalty to its tradition have always been forcefully affirmed, which has been the central purpose and mission of the Athos community. Orthodoxy is one in faith, liturgy, fundamental canonical rules, and one in love of Christ and men. As a result of political vicissitudes and the weaknesses of men, this unity could not find expression in a common attitude towards the Council. However, this practical matter is linked neither to faith nor to the fundamental laws of Orthodoxy. Nevertheless, for the sake of unity and for complete agreement among the Orthodox Churches themselves, it is highly desirable that Orthodoxy adopt a common attitude toward Vatican II.

As Patriarch Athenagoras said one day: "The door is open; no one can close it. It is for the heads of the Churches to assume their responsibilities." It is certain that Rome, Constantinople and Moscow will want to undertake everything possible to bring about this unity.[16]

NOTES

[1] By the three Churches is meant the theory of the three branches: the Catholic, Orthodox, and Protestant Churches.

[2] From the newspaper *Kathimerini,* Athens (October 29, 1962).

[3] The Cardinal stressed this word, saying, "And I mean *temporary."*

[4] The interview was also published in English in the magazine *The Catholic World* (February, 1963), pp. 273–278. The author, Berlin-born, is a specialist in ecumenical matters. Married to Mr. Inglesis, she has published in collaboration with him, a biography of Cardinal Bea, *Kardinal der Einheit* (Paulus Verlag, Recklinghausen, 1962), 152 pages.

[5] It is important to understand this principle in ecumenical relations. The Russian Church was determined to treat the question of observers only on an equal footing with Rome. At Paris, we witnessed the disappointment of the Orthodox bishops in noticing that at the various receptions which took place in honor of the Central Committee of the World Council, of which they were a part, the Catholic bishops of the local hierarchy were never present.

[6] Cardinal Bea's telegram left Rome on October 4, at the same time as the official invitation.

[7] This is the most obscure point. *Les Informations Catholiques Internationales* (March 15, 1963), pp. 27–28, presents the Phanar's point of view in response to the interview of Archpriest Borovoi. An Orthodox clergyman, who followed the preconciliar contacts closely, specifies that the decision, taken by Constantinople in the name of all the Orthodox Churches which had been consulted and had given their answer, was communicated to Moscow on Monday, October 8 at 3:00 p.m. by urgent telegram. "Knowing this," the clergyman said, "it is really odd to explain the 'disappointment' of the Russian observers on their arrival in Rome in finding themselves alone there. I believe," he added, "that at the end of October, there was an attempt to bring round the Churches of Bulgaria, Yugoslavia and Romania to Moscow's decision. They refused—precisely to keep intact the unanimity of Orthodoxy."

[8] The succession of events concerning Metropolitan Slipyi confirms this version. The *France-Presse* Agency did announce that the two observers let Soviet governmental channels know about the bad impression and sadness that Rome and Catholics felt regarding the confinement of Slipyi.

[9] On the occasion of the visit by American Christians to Russia in September, 1962, Archpriest Borovoi gave a lecture on the unity of the Church. The Orthodox

Church, as a Church that is one, holy, universal (*sobornia*) and apostolic, does not deny the historic importance of the other Christian Confessions and it strives to reach along with them, an "empirical" unity. With this hope, our Church has always been ready to discuss these problems in friendship with brothers in Christ of other Confessions, to explain its point of view to them patiently, to show untiringly before them the great heritage of the undivided Church, loyally preserved by the Orthodox Church, which hopes to conduct an honorable dialogue with them on a basis of equality. With this purpose, the Russian Orthodox Church joined the World Council of Churches and supports all its enterprises for Christian unity.

[10] The Athenian newspaper was, therefore, first to report the rumors which the Western press was to complacently cover concerning the contacts between the Vatican and the Soviet Government, notably on the occasion of the stay in Rome in February-March of Mr. Adzhubei, editor-in-chief of *Izvestia* and son-in-law of Mr. Khrushchev.

[11] However, this is what Patriarch Alexis' spokesman had declared, during his visit to Patriarch Athenagoras at Christmas, 1960.

[12] See above, p. 241 (in original French text).

[13] The expression is not clear in the Greek text.

[14] The Pan-Orthodox Conference of Rhodes decided upon the idea of a pre-synod and drew up a rough draft of questions. The Synod (that is to say the Council) could only be held afterwards.

[15] *Apostolos Andreas,* weekly paper of the Ecumenical Patriarchate (December 26, 1962).

[16] *The Journal of the Patriarchate* (February, 1963), published a new article on the Council and more particularly on the presence of the observers of the Russian Orthodox Church. The article affirms that those who saw in the presence of the Russian observers a symbol of a betterment of relations among Christians have interpreted the situation correctly. The observers, writes the magazine, wanted to be heralds of a new closeness among Christians of the entire world, and particularly between the Russian and Roman Churches. Giving a historical account of the negotiations which preceded the departure of the two Orthodox observers for Rome, the magazine indicates that Patriarch Alexis had hesitated to accept the Vatican's overtures. The Patriarchate, "remembering past difficulties," was anxious to understand the Council's purposes clearly before preparing this trip, and it was the declaration made by Pope John XXIII before the Council which opened perspectives appearing to be in accord with the Orthodox point of view.

At the time when this book was published, this issue of the magazine had not yet arrived in Paris. Therefore we do not know to which declaration it alludes. It does not refer to the opening discourse, since that was made on October 11 only, while Moscow's acceptance came on the 10th. Therefore, it probably refers to the radio broadcast of September 11.

IV

The Ecumenical Dialogue

Ecumenical "Conditioning"

SOME PEOPLE HAVE SPOKEN AROUT A CONDITIONING OF THE
Council by the press.[1] From what we could observe—and we have
followed the development of the Council from the closest possible
vantage point—we had the impression that the Fathers actually were
subjected to a conditioning. This was not the doing of the press, but
resulted from the presence of so many observers from the Christian
Churches. This conditioning was inevitable. Anyone who had desired
the presence of the observers could not be unaware of the consequences.
Without changing the nature of the Council, which is not a "reunion"
Council like those of Lyons in 1274 and Florence in 1439, the presence
of observers profoundly influenced the course of the proceedings.

As the Council progressed, one could sense the Fathers becoming
increasingly preoccupied with ecumenism, to the point that one day a
bishop deemed it advisable to put the assembly on its guard against
what he considered an excess. He tried to remind the assembly of the
first goal of the Council, namely, the internal reform of the Church.
He adjured the Fathers to return to these perspectives and to discuss all
subjects freely. "There are those here," he remarked, "who say, 'Let us
not talk about the primacy of the Pope, so as not to displease the Orthodox; let us say nothing about Tradition or the Virgin Mary, so as not
to offend the Protestants; let us not speak about the demands of morality,
since the world does not like to hear this kind of talk.' "[2]

The Council did not share these apprehensions. All the Fathers,
doubtless, did not understand the ecumenical dialogue in the same way,
but they are unanimous in saying that the "ecumenical" dimension was
one of the characteristics of the first session.

The Christian Churches or denominations that had sent observers to the Council were careful not to engage in official conversations, for the observers had no mandate to do so. However, they did not intend their delegates to be purely passive. They were there primarily to follow the proceedings, but also to express their views. To the extent that the Council took their views into consideration, the Catholic Church would prove to separated Christians that she is resolved to take up the dialogue with them.

Significance and Import of the Dialogue

Dialogue is the word in vogue today. Ecumenical dialogue appears to be the remedy for all evils. It is quite true that there could be no meeting of minds without dialogue. It is therefore important to understand this clearly.[3]

Mr. Visser't Hooft proposed to the World Council a definition of dialogue that suits our purpose very well. In attempting to define dialogue, he said:

The great philosopher of dialogue, Martin Buber, gives us a definition which I shall translate freely:[4] "There is true dialogue when each participant is really concerned with others in their existence (*Dasein*) and individual nature (*Sosein*), and turns toward them with the intention of seeing a living reciprocity develop. In other words, dialogue does not mean abandoning principles or convictions or becoming indifferent to truth, but showing concern for others, listening to them, desiring to communicate with them for mutual enrichment. This holds true all the more for those who believe in the same Jesus Christ."[5]

This dialogue, according to Mr. Visser't Hooft, must be instituted not only between persons, but at the level of the Churches, for only when the Churches themselves are engaged in dialogue will reconciliation be possible. And he concluded by formulating the hope that Vatican II might finally provide this possibility to Christians.

Did the Council justify this hope? Yes, to an extent that has exceeded expectation. The observers are unanimous in stating that they obtained more chances for dialogue than they had hoped for. The conversations were not conducted within the Council Assembly. Vatican II is not a reunion Council. However, the observers very often heard from the mouths of the Fathers what they themselves would have wished to say in the Council. They were, as Pastor Hébert Roux said, by their very presence evident and visible witnesses of an absence, but also witnesses of an interrogation and a demand. He acknowledged that this presence was for the Catholic Church the occasion for an *"effort of spiritual understanding, humility and loyalty"*; it led the Church *"to consider herself ready for and wanting to participate in the dialogue in faith, charity and hope (therefore in truth, mutual respect and prayer) with all those that she henceforth recognizes as 'believers in Christ,' even though they contest her major claim of possessing for herself alone the plenitude of catholicity."*[6]

Professor Cullman, speaking to newspapermen about his experience as observer, noted that it was impossible for him to remain neutral in the debates; he took sides pro or con. He warned us against ill-considered enthusiasm and attempted to define the real nature of the ecumenical dialogue. "Catholics are in agreement," he remarked, "with most of the positive truths that we believe and preach, basing ourselves on the Bible. But what separates us, aside from the concept of unity, is not the positive elements of our faith, but, precisely, the *plus* factors in Catholicism (in our perspective, the *superfluous* factors) and conversely, our own minus factors (in the Catholic perspective, *what we lack*)."

According to Professor Cullmann, the interconfessional dialogue will make headway when Catholics cease considering this minus as a deficit, but consider it instead as a concentration, inspired by the Holy Spirit, on what appears to be the essence of our faith in Christ; on the other hand, Protestants should consider whether there has taken place among them "a narrow constriction with regard to the Bible and whether there are not some biblical elements that they have wrongly omitted."[7]

The meetings between the observers and the members of the Secretariat were actually meetings of the mind. The dialogue begun in these meetings was echoed in the Council, as usually a member of the Secretariat, often Cardinal Bea, intervened in the discussion to call the attention of the Fathers to the difficulties that certain formulas presented from the viewpoint of the separated Christians.[8]

On the occasion of an intervention on the schema of *Sources of Revelation,* Bishop de Smedt of Bruges, speaking in the name of the

Secretariat, made the celebrated intervention on November 17 on ecumenical spirit and style. *Les Etudes, La Documentation Catholique,* and *La Civiltà Cattolica* published this statement in its entirety.[9] The substance of the bishop's intervention follows here:

We must take into consideration at the outset that all Christians acknowledge and confess Jesus Christ.[10] We do not agree on the manner of approaching Christ. We have been divided for centuries and these divisions have only become more marked, each affirming his own conception of the truth against the other's "truth." Now, we must distinguish between the truth and the expression of truth.

The ecumenical manner in no way presupposes any mutilation of doctrine, which would be depriving one another and would be completely anti-ecumenical. Therefore, ecumenical style and the complete exposition of truth must not be set against each other. But the ecumenical perspective takes for granted that we have current knowledge of the Orthodox and Protestants: their faith, their liturgy, their theology, and their history. It also assumes that we know what they think of our doctrine and which points they understand or misunderstand, and what they consider as not sufficiently clarified or as deficient.

We must consider whether, in the place of scholastic formulas foreign to their way of thinking, there may not be biblical or patristic language common to all Christians and understood by all in the same way. We must think about the psychological reactions that our formulas, words, images, customs, and judgments will produce. Moreover, we must forego any polemics, and in the refutation of errors we must carefully avoid offending those who hold these erroneous beliefs.

And the bishop concluded:

The time is providential. But it is critical. If these schemata of the Theological Commission are not rewritten, we shall be responsible for the fact that the Second Vatican Council has destroyed a great and immense hope. I mean the hope of all those who, with John XXIII, are now waiting in fasting and prayer for a step to be made toward fraternal union of all those for whom Christ Our Lord prayed "that all may be one."

Enthusiastic applause greeted this intervention. As a matter of fact, it constitutes an outline of the ecumenical dialogue and determines the starting point for reconciliation. Certain practical consequences are inherent in this intervention. Bishop Schmitt of Metz formulates some of them in a pastoral letter that is like an echo of what he himself had said in the Council.

The Catholic Church will not be truly itself and totally ecumenical unless she makes a greater place in her theology for certain aspects of Revelation that the Orthodox Churches, and in part the Reformed Churches, have emphasized:

1. The Holy Scripture is the standard to which Christian thought must constantly refer.

2. Jesus Christ, as much by what He is as by what He teaches, is the ultimate foundation of the faith of the Church. Christianity, far from being a value in itself, is the present form of the Covenant until the day of the second coming of Christ.

3. The Holy Spirit is the only true way to Christ. Those who claim that, in the Catholic Church, ecclesiastical organization too frequently obscures the Holy Spirit, doubtless are judging only by deceptive appearances. We must therefore recognize that these appearances can be deceptive. In truth, the Church is the great sacrament that the Holy Spirit uses to enable us to understand Jesus Christ in His mystery and message.

4. The laity are not Christians of a second order; they constitute the faithful people whose members, through baptism, form a "royal priesthood and a holy nation."[11]

The Dialogues

These conciliar texts deal directly with ecumenical problems:

The schema on Catholic ecumenism, prepared by the Secretariat for the Promotion of Christian Unity, not yet published;

Chapter XI of the schema on the Church.

We explained in the first part how and why Cardinal Bea called for a vote on a resolution decreeing that these three texts would be studied in a single document in the course of the second session. Consequently, this document is the equivalent of Schema XX of the new agenda: on reunion to be furthered among Christians. It will also deal with religious freedom. But actually, the ecumenical problem cropped up everywhere. It appeared during the discussions on the sources of Revelation, on the Church, and on the Liturgy.

The problem that concerns all Christians and that is basic for ecumenism is the doctrine of the Church. In the text proposed to the Fathers, membership in the Church was defined in excessively juridical terms. The unity of the Church is derived from the profession of a single faith, the reception of the same sacraments, submission to a single hierarchical authority in communion with the Pope. Consequently, all those are members of the Church who profess this one faith and share the same worship, under the authority of a single hierarchy united with the Pope of Rome. To begin with, is this not making membership in the Church and through her to Christ, dependent upon an extrinsic and juridical action (submission to the authority of the Pope) and not upon spiritual realities like the sacraments or faith?

To answer these difficulties, at the recent prompting of Cardinal Bea, the theology that teaches radical membership in the mystical body of Christ through baptism has become current again. All those who have received a valid baptism belong to the Church, mother of all the baptized. Certainly, rejection of the authority of the Roman Pontiff or the bishops, successors of the apostles, or refusal to profess any article of faith defined by the Church can strain these ties to the point of breaking membership in the visible body of the Church. They cannot destroy the fact of being a Christian, nor faith in Christ as God and Savior.[12]

I have been struck by certain constant themes in the interventions of the Fathers on this subject. They would say, "We must not reduce membership in the Church to exclusively juridical notions. When we speak of the Mystical Body, we must avoid keeping only the juridical aspects of the head and body and submission of the limbs to the head." Someone suggested,

We must consider membership in the Church not in a univocal but an analogical way. For example, the Orthodox have the same baptism, profess the same faith, practice the same sacraments as we. Are they completely outside of the Church simply because they do not acknowledge the authority of the Pope of whom they have known so little for long centuries, and of whom many know nothing still. We must not express the doctrine of the Church in terms of scholastic theology, but rather we should take into account both Scripture and Tradition. This mystery is not simple, and in order to express it, inspired authors have had recourse to multiple formulas. Why do theologians want to express everything in a single formula?

I admit that certain Fathers questioned these statements. "Claiming that one belongs to the Church through baptism alone," said Cardinal Ruffini, "is not sound theology. The Church is founded on Peter and all those who do not acknowledge Peter are outside the Church."

The problem was merely touched on during the first session, since only five general Congregations were devoted to discussion of the schema. But the criticism was so intense, and so much of it was alike, that a complete revision of this schema for the purpose of a more ecumenical formulation must be anticipated.

For the Protestants, there was one subject which would be especially revealing and pertinent: the sources of Revelation. They were inclined to judge the Council by the attitude it would take on this question.[18] The crux of the matter was whether the Fathers were going to emphasize the authority of Tradition to the point of admitting two distinct sources of Revelation, so that there could be some truths in Tradition which would not be found in Scripture, or whether they were going to show that the truths contained in Tradition are themselves also in Holy Scripture, from which they receive their illumination.

With regard to understanding the Word of God, the Protestants wondered whether the Council was going to approve and consecrate the efforts of the exegetes, which were often carried out jointly by Catholics and Protestants, in many cases efforts that have permitted understanding of the Scripture in the same way. Now those who understand the Word of God in the same way are quite prepared to profess the same faith, since the Word is the rule of faith.

We already know what became of the schema on the sources of Revelation. On November 14, nine Cardinals sharply criticized the formula and the spirit of the schema, while only two found it good. On the 19th, 1,386 Fathers refused to discuss the details of the chapters. Only 822 favored discussion. On the 20th the Pope decided to refer it to a mixed Commission.

Collegiality in Unity

The Orthodox are particularly concerned about the matter of episcopal collegiality, and Catholic bishops and theologians are now unanimous in recognizing that one of the most tangible results of the first session was the discovery of this collegiality. The Church, on the occasion of the Council, has experienced in action a collegiality that belongs to the institution, but which during recent decades, not to say recent centuries, had remained merely potential and theoretical.

The dialogue with the Orthodox seems to require the Council to provide a definition of the role and powers of the collegial episcopate. This same question, moreover, was scheduled for consideration by the First Vatican Council. It could not be examined, however, due to the war which abruptly ended the conciliar proceedings. A certain imbalance has resulted from this. While the powers and prerogatives of the Pope of Rome were put in a definitive light, those of the bishops were left in shadow. The privileges appertaining to a single prelate seemed to eclipse the power that tradition recognized as belonging to all the bishops, both as individuals and in their collegiality.

However, this image is false and is due to historical circumstances as well as abuses of language on the part of some Catholics. This is proved by the very fact that the Popes have always made the bishops a party to decisions of faith, as the definition of the Assumption of Mary clearly shows. They have also had their part in all the important activity of the Church, as the encyclical *Fidei donum* proves, in which Pius XII reminded the bishops that they are jointly responsible with him for the evangelization of the world.

Besides, the very fact of convoking a Council, especially after the definition of the Pope's infallibility, shows that the privilege of the Roman Pontiff does not abolish the prerogatives of the apostolic college represented by all the bishops in communion with the Apostolic See.

The Orthodox Church cannot help but be deeply interested in this Second Vatican Council. There was a period in Eastern theology, especially after the definition of Papal Infallibility, when the Orthodox readily called their Church the conciliar Church or the Church of the Seven First Councils, as contrasted with the papal, monarchical Church of Rome. They believed that a Council was a distinctive sign of the true Church of Christ. And now the monarchical Church of Rome is celebrating an Ecumenical Council, showing by her actions that she has not lost the usage of that ancient institution or that solemn and collegial form of teaching and government.

And the Pope himself, accused of having reduced the powers of bishops in the Church, took the initiative in this matter, although no pressure was brought to bear upon him by the bishops or the faithful. John XXIII restored to honor the collegial principle in the Church. This restoration is a factor of prime importance in bringing about the unity which all desire.

It is the Council's task to translate this theology into action and to organize the Church so that she will be recognized by all men not only as their spiritual home, but also for what she really is: the true Church of Christ, one, holy, Catholic and Apostolic.

The difficulty, for Eastern Christians, will be in failing to blend unity with collegiality; and for Western Christians it will be in giving insufficient effectiveness to collegiality, which includes a head in whom a real primacy and infallible teaching are recognized. The Council itself, however, has shown how to proceed. There was constant interaction between the two authorities. The authority of the Pope, far from hindering the sovereign and free discussion of the Council, has been a principle of effective action. If the Pope had not exercised his sovereign authority at times, it seems that the Council would have bogged down or would have been divided into a majority and minority with all the formidable consequences of such a rupture. The apostles were twelve, and Christ put a chief at their head. Their successors are spread in thousands today over the entire earth. How could they not need a head to express, carry out, and preserve the visible unity of the whole body?

Protestant Reactions After the First Session

The first session of the Council evoked numerous reactions in the Protestant world.[14] In Orthodox circles, except for the statements of the Russian observers, which we shall analyze farther on, the reactions have been practically nil up to the present. As the Churches of Greece and Constantinople sent no observers to Rome, they have remained silent. The theologians and the press model their attitudes on that of the hierarchy—they have, up to the present, maintained great reserve.[15]

The multiplicity of Protestant reactions is explained by their very keen interest in ecumenism and the great theological activity that is characteristic of Protestantism. In general these reactions have been critical, but on the whole benevolent. It is not possible to present a complete summary of them, so we shall confine ourselves to presenting a few of the positions taken by persons whose thought or function seems to be representative.

Speaking at Dijon on the "Council and Unity," Pastor Marc Boegner, Honorary President of the Protestant Federation of France and former president of the World Council of Churches, was pleased with the results of the first session: "I deeply feel that this first session of the Council has marked, by its development and the general tenor of its debates, a change of climate and the opening up of admirable perspectives because of its interest in ecumenism which seemed to become increasingly earnest in the hearts of the conciliar Fathers."

In expressing satisfaction with the welcome accorded to the non-Catholic observers, Pastor Boegner described the creation of the Secretariat for the Promotion of Christian Unity, presided over by Cardinal Bea, as a "stroke of genius that we have welcomed with gratitude, confidence, and the hope of seeing the dialogue established under his aegis."

According to Pastor Boegner, this dialogue could be engaged in on three principal points: the sources of Revelation, for which a basis for understanding can be found in the Bible; Marian dogmas which according to non-Catholic Churches do not rest upon incontestable foundations; lastly, the primacy of Peter, the subject of various positions which are susceptible to reconciliation through more extensive study.[16]

At Paris, Prof. Oscar Cullmann, who participated in the proceedings of the Council as a guest of the Secretariat, gave a lecture at the Sorbonne entitled, "Between Two Council Sessions: Experiences and Hopes of a Protestant Observer." The Council proposes, he said, to distinguish in Catholic doctrine between what is immutable substance and what is variable form of expression. Vatican II has revealed that there is within the Church—behind the Pope—a manifest desire to clothe doctrinal substance with new forms. This step is decisive in the opinion of Mr. Cullmann, who expressed the hope that "the question of mixed marriages, which is at present poisoning the atmosphere," will receive a more satisfactory solution.

However, he added, even if efforts toward renewal were to prevail, which is likely, it does not mean that union between Catholicism and Protestantism would be possible. "I do not see," said Mr. Cullmann, "any theological solution in view of the fact that the Roman concept of authority is not part of the variable form of Catholic doctrine, but rather to its substance." The difficulty of "the primacy by divine right" of Peter's successor must be added to the problem of biblical interpretation and the normative value to be accorded to tradition in the history of the Church. Consequently, what is to be done? "Let us each remain faithful to our faith," Mr. Cullmann concluded, "but let us shake hands with each other. The Council created the climate necessary for that. If each Church fulfills its own task and makes an effort to renew itself through the Holy Spirit, the principle of unity may some day ensue."[17]

In Marseilles, Pastor Lukas Vischer, an observer-delegate of the World Council of Churches at the Council, made a speech in the presence of Bishop Lallier. He made a positive evaluation of the results of the Council, at the same time warning Catholics against a wrong appraisal of its repercussions among Protestants. He remarked:

A spirit of authentic ecumenical opening was manifested at the Council and we cannot be too thankful for that. The Council was visibly characterized by a desire for renewal. The observer-delegates of the non-Roman Churches can testify how greatly readiness was shown in the Council to open their hearts to the convictions of other confessions. The coming months will be of decisive importance, as they will show what results can be obtained in the atmosphere created during the first session.[18]

Mr. Vischer dwelt upon the importance of the year 1963 for the ecumenical movement. He mentioned the fourth World Conference of Faith and Order, scheduled for July, stressing the fact that the subject matter of that conference would be almost the same as that engaging the conciliar Fathers. Even if this convergence is not synonymous with agreement, it is still of considerable importance for the dialogue of the Churches.[19]

Mr. Vischer then asked:

What then is the hope aroused at the present time by the ecumenical movement? It is evident that the Churches are still very far from unity and it is a mistake to speak as though it were about to be realized. However, a parallelism may be establishing itself between the Roman Church and the other Churches, like that which already exists within the World Council of Churches. Without eliminating our differences, perhaps we shall arrive at a common orientation to the extent that we are capable of turning our eyes away from the problems that separate the Churches, and then turn together toward the mission and task of the Church of Christ in today's world.

Great care and attention will be necessary to establish and maintain such a parallelism between the Churches. It will be understood how important it is, in this perspective, that the Council, in the course of its debates on the Church, has defined the Church as a servant and categorically rejected any form of "triumphalism" whatsoever.[20] However, after the Council, there is the risk of seeing a sort of "ecumenical triumphalism" develop which would block the road toward unity.[21]

Fear of a Catholic "Triumphalism"

Finally, on the occasion of a session of the Executive Committee of the World Council, which was held at Geneva in February of 1963, Mr. Visser't Hooft drew up a kind of ecumenical "balance sheet" of the first session of Vatican II. The debates showed that the Roman Catholic Church is in process of emerging from a period of pure monologue. It is beginning to realize that other Christian Churches exist, Mr. Visser't Hooft said, but he immediately added, *"We could not yet say that the Roman Catholic Church recognizes them ecclesiastically, nor that it has initiated an authentic dialogue with them."*

The principal problem that now arises for all concerned, according to Mr. Visser't Hooft, is to determine whether

the ecumenism of the Roman Catholic Church will only assume the form of a different terminology and a more friendly attitude, or whether it will lead that Church to show itself ready for a real dialogue in which the questions of the other participants are taken seriously and in which concrete changes modify one or another of the Church's tendencies that make it difficult for the Roman Catholic Church and the other Churches to maintain good relations with one another.[22]

Speaking of the modifications that the Vatican Council is making probable, the Secretary General of the World Council of Churches stressed that "the Roman Catholic Church is in process of becoming aware of its real situation in the modern world and taking seriously the exigencies of contemporary circumstances."

The Council, he added, certainly demonstrates that the Catholic Church possesses "a greater capacity for renewal than most non-Roman

Christians and even most Roman Catholics ever thought possible." Particularly, what he calls "the new theology" received much greater support than its proponents had anticipated. Until recently, Mr. Visser't Hooft stressed, the Roman Catholic Church had "left the ecumenical initiative up to the World Council and other ecumenical organizations." But the Church has now become "a center of ecumenical initiative." Care must be taken, however, that this fact does not open the door to the type of propaganda that claims "that shortly all Christians will be returning to Rome."

Mr. Visser't Hooft found that relations between the Vatican Secretariat for the Promotion of Christian Unity and the World Council of Churches are growing and becoming increasingly fruitful. They facilitate not only "a substantial exchange of information" but also "regular discussion of subjects of mutual interest."

Regarding the attitude of the World Council toward the Roman Catholic Church, Mr. Visser't Hooft stated, "The Council must continue requesting that ecumenical relations be in the form of dialogue. That is equivalent to saying that ecumenism consists not solely in adopting an irenical attitude, but also in acknowledging that the other Churches in some way possess the attributes of real Churches whose fundamental questions should be listened to when put forth." This applies particularly at present to the problems of mixed marriages and religious freedom which are not only important in themselves but also constitute "tests of the reality and earnestness of the ecumenical attitude."

"The World Council of Churches must furthermore resist any temptation to consider the relations between itself and the Roman Catholic Church from the aspect of competition or prestige." Lastly, he said, "The task and the nature of the World Council, which includes Churches of diverse traditions, are in no way comparable to those of a particular Church, however large the latter may be."

The Unity That Christ Desires for His Church

Mr. Visser't Hooft and Mr. Vischer, in emphasizing the risk of a certain degree of post-conciliar triumphalism among Catholics, alludes to an article in the *Herder Korrespondenz* in December, 1962. This article commented on the general intention of the Apostolate of Prayer for the month of January 1963: "May the desire for ecclesiastical unity that prevails among Protestants lead them to the knowledge of the true Church of Christ."[23] Cardinal Bea drew up a commentary on this intention of the Apostolate of Prayer[24] which was printed in *la Documentation Catholique* of January 6, 1963. The columnist of the *Herder Korrespondenz* remarked that the Catholic Church, which formulates these intentions, has no doubt concerning the identity of the true Church of Christ, praying only that Protestants may discover this true Church.

This is exactly the goal of the World Council. It would have been more ecumenical to show the progress made in the quest for unity by the Protestant Churches, thanks to the action and efforts of the World Council of Churches. The article, on the contrary, goes to great lengths to show that Vatican II has become the place for seeking unity, for both Orthodox and Protestants. If Catholics have many reasons to be surprised at what happened at the Council—openness, freedom, opposition to the Curia—Protestants are even more surprised. Too often, from their viewpoint, the basic visible structures of the Roman Catholic Church consisted of a lack of freedom, excessive uniformity, and the omnipotence of the Curia.

The article then formulates a conclusion with regard to Protestants that Catholics may draw for themselves, but which is nevertheless a subject of reflection for both. The article states that the definition of unity proposed by the World Council of Churches at New Delhi was exactly the one achieved by the Vatican Council.

In fact, if this description of unity is ready and then projected upon Vatican II, no difference will appear except in a negative way omitting the authority of the Pope and the hierarchy, which, of course, is an essential point.

We believe that unity, which is at the same time the gift of God and His will for His Church, is made visible when, in one place, all those who are baptized in Jesus Christ and confess Him as their Lord and Savior are led by the Holy Spirit to form a community, confessing the same apostolic faith, preaching the same Gospel, breaking the same bread, uniting in common prayer and living a communal life which finds expression in witnessing and service by all; and when, furthermore, they are in communion with the entire Christian community in all places and at all times, in such a way that their ministry and membership are recognized by all, so that all may, as circumstances require, act and speak in common accord to perform the tasks to which God calls His people.[25]

Protestants everywhere have been stressing the two questions of religious freedom and mixed marriages. It was not possible for us to anticipate the conclusions of the Council, but it was certain that the second session would consider these problems.

The Secretariat for the Promotion of Christian Unity prepared a schema on religious freedom, which the press release of the Central Commission handled very discreetly:

The Secretariat for the reunion of Christians presented to the session of June 1962, four schemata: on Catholic Ecumenism, on the necessity of praying for unity, on the Word of God as a basis for unity, and on religious freedom. On this point in particular the Secretariat dealt with the right of man to follow, even in religious matters, the dictates of his own conscience, and with the rights and duties which this entails for civil society (the State), namely the duty of respecting in practice this right of its subjects.[26]

In Spain, especially, and in Colombia, the Catholic Church is accused of intolerance with respect to non-Catholics. On the situation in Spain, Bishop Pedro Cantero Cuadrado of Huelva at the beginning of February, 1963, made the following statement:

The Catholic unity of Spain and the established status of the Catholic Church are completely compatible with the exercise of all natural rights and legitimate religious liberties of Spaniards who are not of the Catholic Religion. As regards the legal status of Protestants in Spain, the Spanish State has imbued its legislation with the principles of the Catholic Religion, interpreted in the light of the magisterium of the Church, in conformity with the exigencies of the common good of the Church, the people and the international community. But today these exigencies have changed both in Spain and in the world and, consequently, it is essential that applications of the permanent principles of the Church be modified with relation to freedom of conscience and the individual's self-expression and actions in modern society.[27]

The Council must surely be determined to dissipate ambiguities. In fact, it is essential to distinguish in actions of intolerance between what was the Church's part and what was the State's part, and from what ensues, to establish principles or what is simply the action of a will to power or of the activity of men. On this point, the Churches all have to examine their consciences.

As to mixed marriages, the Protestants, as a whole, judge the present legislation of the Catholic Church rather harshly. They consider the problem of mixed marriages as a test of the Church's good will. It will be remembered that at New Delhi, Bishop May of the Reformed Church of Austria provoked an incident with regard to this problem on the part of the Catholic observers. The Protestant bishop had been saying that this question is the touchstone that will permit finding out whether the Catholic Church intends to dominate other Churches or whether she has decided to collaborate with them. The solution of this problem, which causes spiritual distress among thousands of Christians, would be a positive action. Some way had to be found to ask to modify canon law and at least return to the broader legislation that obtained before 1918.[28]

During an encounter between German Catholics and Protestants who were responsible for public opinion, in May, 1962, at Bad Boll,[29] a spokesman for the Protestants stated that Catholic legislation on mixed marriages was untenable for them. In the new ecumenical climate, it is like a late frost on a spring flower. The Catholic Church is legislating on mixed marriages without taking the Protestant partner into consideration. But the latter is also involved. A kind of denial of his faith is asked of him, since he must pledge himself to have his children brought up in the Catholic faith. His own faith is threatened in this marriage, since canon law urges the Catholic to win the spouse over to the Catholic faith. The Protestant spokesman went on to say that canon law cannot be imposed indirectly on the Protestant partner. Would it not be possible to return to the legislation that prevailed before 1918 by which, for German-speaking countries, mixed marriages contracted outside of the Catholic Church were considered valid? The spokesman expressed the hope that some day both spouses might decide on the form of marriage (Catholic or Protestant) and the education of the children. This right, he thinks, is not excessive for adult Christians. The result would be the decline of civil marriages and an increase of religious marriages in both Churches.[30] The present legislation is based on fear. May the future law be inspired by confidence and love.

His Excellency, Archbishop Jaeger of Paderborn, who attended the meeting, warned against anything resembling a summation to the Council, which, for a Catholic, would be like giving orders to the Holy Spirit, the master of all. If the Catholic Church is strict regarding mixed marriages, it is because it considers the Catholic faith as the most precious possession of her members. To preserve personal religious instruction, in this matter, the Council can set forth only general laws and principles and leave to episcopal conferences the formulation of concrete legislation because of the diversity of situations.

NOTES

[1] *Itinéraires,* n. 68 (Dec., 1962), p. 24. "The ideological conditioning brought about by the press is carried out with regard to the Council in order to impose upon it the wishes of a prefabricated self-styled 'public opinion.' . . . It has by no means been proved that all the conciliar Fathers are as easily fooled by the newspapers as is hoped or that they take at face value and as a faithful translation of the aspirations and thoughts of the nations what is written in a press which has more than amply shown that it is neither qualified nor representative. It has by no means been proved that conciliar Fathers will let themselves be intimidated, impressed, or influenced by press campaigns which are admittedly waged for precisely such ends. In any event, this is the first Council in history held in the atmosphere of an unreal universe of rumors and inaccuracies manufactured by the newspapers."

We are far from agreement with Mr. Madiran when he adds that "the press polemics that accompanied the First Vatican Council were practically nothing in comparison with the formidable conditioning of minds systematically organized throughout the world by means of so-called *news*papers." If Vatican Council II in its first session was reserved with regard to the press, it is precisely because the Pope was disturbed about the role that the press had played at the First Council. It is known that the Pope, before Vatican II, read *Rome pendant le Concile* by Louis Veuillot, 2 vol. (Paris, 1872).

[2] We wish to note that the Press Bureau release did not call attention to this intervention. It seemed evident to the authors of the release that it did not reflect the sentiment of the great majoriy of the Fathers.

[3] Jean Guitton has given definitions of it in his fine volume *Dialogue avec les précurseurs: Journal oecuménique 1922–1962* (Paris, 1962), especially pp. 251–261, *"Le dialogue oecuménique, méditation et confrontation."*

[4] Martin Buber, born in 1878, Jewish philosopher, Professor of Religious Science in Frankfurt until 1933. In 1922 he wrote an essay: *Ich und Du,* and in 1954 a collection: *Die Schriften über das dialogische Prinzip.*

[5] Report of the Central Committee, Paris, August 1962.

[6] *Réforme,* Jan. 6, 1963.

[7] Prof. Cullmann's press conference, which took place Nov. 23, is published in *Documentation Catholique,* Dec. 16, 1962, col. 1619–1626. See col. 1623.

[8] There were other occasions for meeting privately or with small groups. In the opinion of the observers, these were no less fruitful than the official meetings.

[9] All these publications used the Swiss news agency KIPA as their source. This agency, for the duration of the Council, published a considerable number of documents.

By providing service to the newspapers in this way, the agency at times placed them in delicate situations.

[10] It is possible that the Bishop wanted to allude to what is called the basic purpose of the World Council of Churches: "The World Council of Churches is a fraternal association of Churches that confess the Lord Jesus Christ as God and Savior, according to the Scriptures, and strive to respond to their common calling for the glory of the one God, the Father, Son, and Holy Spirit."

[11] *Eglise de Metz* (Jan. 16, 1963), pp. 8–11.

[12] The various writings of Cardinal Bea on unity are collected in a volume: *l'Unione dei Cristiani* (Civiltà Cattolica). Also see *op. cit.:* E. M. Jung-Inglesis, *Augustin Bea, Kardinal der Einheit.*

[13] Pastor Richard-Mollard writes, with a touch of severity, in *Réforme* (Nov. 17, 1962): ". . . From the very beginning of the Council, certain 'observers' had been telling us that if this theological schema was adopted, they would have no alternative but to quit the Council. . . . If Tradition is put on the same level as Scripture or the Gospel as a source of Revelation, obviously no great renewal can be expected in the Council by means of any schema whatever. . . . Perhaps from the written expression of Catholic thought and also Catholic ethics in their most unacceptable form, the most authentic hope, God willing . . . or the most inexorable break, will emerge."

[14] Consult *Service oecuménique de presse et d'information* published by the Information Service of the World Council of Churches, 17, route de Malagnou, Geneva. This is indispensable to ecumenists and theologians, who are quickly alerted to actions and events relating to the reunion movement. *La Documentation Catholique,* March 17, 1963, col. 383–404, gives an excellent survey of Protestant reactions.

[15] The hierarchy (the body of Greek Bishops), during its Assembly in February, 1963, did not express any reactions with regard to the Council. Mr. Alivisatos, one of the proponents of the ecumenical movement in Greece, has just been named Government Procurator (that is, basically, the representative of the government Ministry of Religion) for the Holy Synod. This is an auspicious omen for ecumenical openings. Mr. Alivisatos, in addition, is preparing a study on the Council. Mr. Joannidis, whose articles appear in the review *Ekklessia,* is doing the same. Up to now only a few lines have been found in *Ekklessia* (Dec. 20, 1962 and Jan. 15, 1963). The review reports that "the essential results" and "the signs of good omen" of the Council are that the Roman Catholic Church feels the need of strengthening the synodal institution which had been suppressed. This is a condition for the dialogue with the Eastern Church. *Anaplassis* (January, 1963) reports that the Council is even considering communication media—theatre, cinema, and television—because the Church, as the mother of the faithful, wishes to take advantage of all legitimate media for the good of her children; and, on this score, the Church is appealing for the collaboration of the laity. (*Anaplassis* is a review directed especially to the laity, which often defends the role and position of the laity in the Church.)

[16] S. OE. P. I., n. 5 (Feb. 8, 1963), p. 6.

[17] S. OE. P. I. *ibid.,* p. 5. Cf. *La Croix* (Feb. 2, 1963).

[18] S. OE. P. I., n. 4 (Feb. 1, 1963), p. 1.

[19] The proceedings at Montreal dealt particularly with the various concepts of baptism, Holy Communion, rites, and the ministry and government of the Church. The delegates were divided into five sections for study: a) The Church in God's plan; b) The Scripture, Tradition and traditions; c) The redemptive work of Christ and the ministry of His Church; d) Worship and unity of the Church of Christ; e) "All in one place," the common path of the Churches.

The preceding Conference of Faith and Order had taken place at Lund (Sweden) in 1952. A consultation at the Ecumenical Institute in Bossey (Switzerland) which was held March 18–26, 1963, brought together 15 Catholic theologians and 15 Orthodox, Anglican and Protestant theologians, who were invited by the Faith and Order Division to examine the reports of the Theological Commissions on Faith and Order covering the following subjects: Christ and the Church, Tradition and traditions, rites and institutionalism.

20 Mr. Vischer is obviously alluding here, not to the first intervention of Bishop de Smedt of Bruges on ecumenism, but to his intervention on the Church. This schema, the Bishop said, was triply at fault through triumphalism, clericalism, and legalism.

21 S. OE. P. I., n. 4 (Feb. 1, 1963), p. 2.

22 S. OE. P. I. n. 6 (Feb. 15, 1963), p. 1.

23 This is our translation of the Latin formula: *Ut desiderium unitatis ecclesiasticae inter protestantes vigens ad cognitionem verae Ecclesiae Christi perducat.* (*Herder Korrespondenz,* December 1962, 115).

24 Apostolate of Prayer; monthly intention, commentaries, documentation (January, 1963, Borgo S. Spirito, 5, Rome).

25 *New Delhi, 1961, World Council of Churches.* Report of the Third Public Assembly published under the direction of W. A. Visser't Hooft (Editions Delachaux et Niestlé, Neuchatel, Switzerland, 1962), 412 pp.

Herder Korrespondenz notes that Professor Schlink had found the definition made at New Delhi too formal because even though it does mention the Creed, Gospel, sacraments, ministry etc., it does not explain sufficiently the content of these terms or what they mean. However, it is essential for union of the Churches that a consensus of opinion be reached on the content and meaning of those words. (*Op. cit.,* p. 131).

Herder Korrespondenz notes further: Everybody admired the liberalism of the conciliar debates. If this spirit were contagious and were to extend to the relations between the Council and the press, through the General Secretariat of the Council, it would have a considerable repercussion. . . .

26 Press Service of the Central Commission, Communiqué, n. 97.

27 *S. OE. P. I.,* n. 6 (Feb. 15, 1963).

S. OE. P. I. (Feb. 22, 1963), stated that ten Protestant Churches in Spain were reopened with the consent of the authorities. Mr. José Cardona, Executive Secretary of the Juridical Commission for defending the Rights of Protestants (Comisión de defensa Evangélica), stressed the fact that he found on the part of the Spanish authorities "a more positive attitude with regard to the requests of Protestants; however, the Protestants in Spain lack a legal basis to support their petitions."

28 See our report on the New Delhi Assembly in the review *Unitas,* n. 59 (1962), 161–203, 174–175.

29 Cf. *La Croix* (May 13–14, 1962).

30 A special difficulty arises from the fact that the Protestants do not consider marriage as a sacrament, although the Scriptures and St. Paul ascribe a sacred character to it. According to the most common Protestant doctrine, marriage is an earthly reality of the order of nature. A reaction is taking shape today against this tendency. Hans Asmüssen, in his book *Das Sakrament,* (Evangelisches Verlagswerk, Stuttgart), devotes a chapter to marriage: "The Church and Marriage" (*Die Kirche und die Ehe*) pp. 102–114. A sentence of Luther is often used for reference. "Marriage is a thing of this world (*ein weltlich Ding*). "If Luther's sentence," writes Asmüssen, "that marriage is a secular thing has any meaning, it can mean only this: that Christian marriage in the name of Jesus Christ takes possession of a portion of creation and transforms it. The essential features of a Christian ordination of marriage are, among others, that it be treated as a gift of God and a mission of God; furthermore, that it is

indissoluble until death separates the spouses. Civil marriage laws have need of neither feature, for civil marriage is not in itself a Christian marriage. Luther could not have thought differently; otherwise what meaning would his *Traubüchlein* (booklet for marriages) possess?" (*Das Sakrament*, p. 114.)

conclusion
The Council and the World

THE POPE HAS ALWAYS VIEWED THE COUNCIL ACCORDING TO three levels of reference: (1) the Catholic Church, (2) all the Christian communities, and (3) the entire human family. It is less a question of juxtaposed levels than of concentric circles or chain reactions. From the internal reform of the Church flows a stronger aspiration for unity among Christians, and for all of humanity a supplementary abundance, "like great wealth, *'de rore caeli et de pinguedine terrae'* (Gen. 27: 28)," as expressed by the Pope in his discourse at Saint Paul-Outside-the-Walls.[1]

The Bull *Humane salutis* reveals the same progression of levels. The Council will bring new youth to the Church; this renewal will promote a greater desire for unity among all Christians; and as for the whole of humanity, the Pope expressed the hope that the ensuing Council would promote in all men thoughts and resolutions of peace. *"We are confident that the questions discussed in the Council will be of such pertinence that they will not only instill in the hearts of men fervent energy and the light of Christian wisdom, but will also influence the whole of human activity."*[2]

The message of September 11, 1962, as we have already noted, is almost entirely dedicated to temporal problems. *La Croix* could also have placed in headlines, to the astonishment of many, but with perfect fidelity to the text: "The Church Takes to Heart All Human Cares: Happiness, Daily Bread, Peace, Salvation." The Pope enumerated several more pressing problems: the fundamental equality of peoples in exercising rights and duties toward the whole family of nations, the preservation of the sacred character of marriage, a religious and moral outlook on the procreative mission of couples, religious faith and unbelief in all

215

its forms; and the problem of poverty: "To underdeveloped countries, the Church presents itself—and strives to be—the Church of everyone and, particularly, the Church of the poor." Finally, the problem of peace:

> The bishops, as shepherds of Christ's flock in all nations, will again interpret the concept of peace, not in its negative aspect alone, as forbidding armed battles, but in its positive requirements as well. Peace demands of each man the constant recognition and performance of his personal duties, respect for the hierarchy and harmony of values, the serving of spiritual values which must be accessible to all, and the possession and application of nature's forces and technical means for the sole purpose of raising the standard of spiritual and economic life of the nations.[3]

The opening address also stresses the Church's contribution to the perfection of mankind and the peace of the world, as we have already pointed out.

To journalists, who by nature tend to consider the exterior and the temporal, the Pope stressed the religious character of the Council. Nevertheless he emphasized that "it can also, in the long run, exert a favorable influence on human relations in the social as well as in the political domain."[4]

The Council: Its Labor for Peace

The French public reacted rather indifferently to these various addresses. But in Italy it was a completely different matter because the "opening to the left" had already influenced public opinion. Some found in this orientation of the Council a confirmation of this trend. The liberal press wondered if, on the occasion of the Council, the Church, too, was not going to make an opening to the Left.

Il Messaggero, on the day following the September 11 message, expressed fear that the Church would fall into step with Communism. This newspaper also wrote: "Nevertheless, Communism is neither resolved nor dissolved through social reforms. It is the supreme heresy, being the negation of religion."

The Communist press, on the other hand, took the opportunity to emphasize that in this address there were highly praiseworthy affirmations of peace and justice. However, according to Communists the merit of these propositions was more the result of pressure exerted by the masses than attributable to the sincere intentions of the Catholic Church.

Osservatore Romano then noted that the social doctrine of the Church, in relation to Communism, is not merely a higher bid, but is founded on the Gospel and the dictates of moral conscience, the latter being constantly confronted by economic and social conditions that are constantly changing.

During the Council's deliberations, it was the liberal press of Italy, and afterward the progressive press of East Germany, Poland and, naturally, the Communist press of the Soviet Union which persistently tried to make the Council consider political matters. There was a resolution addressed to the Fathers by the first group, to condemn Communism, and by the second group, to take up the cause of peace, which they identified with Communism. The Soviet press, hostile toward the Council before it began, particularly appreciated the calls to peace made by Pope John XXIII in his speeches of October 11 and October 25, at the time of the Cuban crisis. This will be fully analyzed in a later chapter.

Because the work of the Council in favor of peace received the interested approval of the Communist world, a certain newspaper in Italy, and perhaps newspapers elsewhere, expressed concern. *Osservatore Romano* on February 2, 1963, stated that these journals, today, have discovered the "Church of Silence." If the purpose were to record a fact that has existed for forty-five years, as Mr. Alessandrini remarked, then we can rejoice. A simple exhibit (like the one devoted to the "Church of Silence") would have succeeded whereas all the campaigns to disburse information had remained without result.[5]

In reality, these articles were less concerned with defending the oppressed Church and sympathizing with its difficulties than about developing charges against alleged "betrayals." In short, they wanted to retaliate for a certain "policy" attributed to the Holy See which did not correspond to preferences or interests of a non-religious nature.[6] Toward that end, they affirmed that all the efforts from Pope Pius XII to Father Lombardi, and from Gedda to Don Sturzo and Gasperi to construct a barrier against Communism were annihilated by an irrational force!

But what is the Council then, if not a work of truth? When the Pope assembled the bishops of the entire world so that truth, without mutilation, might be disseminated more widely and might penetrate further into a disoriented and errant society, was he not solidifying this very bulwark by imbuing the Church with new zeal for spiritual conquest or reconquest?

To speak of the Church of Silence, Communism and peace, the Pope and the Council utilized language transcending political controversy—language derived trom the Gospel and inspired by the universal love of men.[7]

This intent of the Church and this language were clearly understood by the people. The Pope emphasized all this in his speech of February 2, 1963. He recalled on this occasion that a year previously he had announced to the world that the Council would open on October 11, 1962. "The work of the Council," he declared, "will be to represent the Church as the light of the nations, so that Christian peoples may finally enjoy true peace in the respect of mutual rights and duties."

The Pope stated later:

The reality has surpassed Our expectations. We have heard it said that the Council has been received as a contribution to peace and has effectively furthered the cause of peace. This opinion has been expressed not only in Catholic assemblies but also throughout the world, and with such evident sympathy that We are encouraged, on Our part, to continue this apostolic service and Our efforts in this respect.[8]

International opinion has recognized the services rendered by the Pope in the interests of peace. On March 1, Pope John XXIII received the prize of the Eugene Balzan Foundation "for his activity in the interests of brotherhood among men and all nations, because of his appeals for peace and good will and his recent interventions in the political realm."[9] To the two reasons mentioned by the press, *Osservatore Romano,* on March 2, also named the Council as the "culminating point" of activity in the interest of peace:

The unanimous testimony of the representatives of twenty nations composing the board of the "Balzan International Federation" is supported by the universal sentiment of recognition and admiration accorded Pope John XXIII for the devoted and effective work in defense of peace which characterized his pontificate.

In particularly serious and tense international situations, an anxious humanity has always felt the watchful presence of the Pastor of the Church, who has touched the hearts and penetrated the souls of statesmen and people by his expressive and noble interventions, speaking in a language of truth, responsibility and historical realism (*concretezza*), through which reflections of spiritual charity and human loyalty shine forth.

To his peace messages, Pope John XXIII added a wise diplomatic action, understood and appreciated by all, increasing the consideration and the prestige of the Church which elevates and sanctifies all humanity.

The Council represents a culminating point in these efforts for peace because of its universal proclamation of the doctrine of love and charity of Christ and the Church, its renewal of hearts and minds in the faith and in the virtues inspired by the Gospel which, alone, can reduce opposition between men.

The Council, also attended by representatives of other communions, kindles new reasons to hope for an ideal coexistence of all peoples in truth and charity.

Indeed, it seems quite apparent that the Council itself was one of the reasons why members of the Balzan Foundation bestowed the peace prize on Pope John XXIII. President Gronchi, at the time of the presentation of the prize on March 7, 1963, read a statement of motives, and it seems that the following text clearly expresses the sentiment of the entire group:

For peace among men and nations, in his tireless concern to contribute toward the maintenance of peaceful relations between governments by his appeals to the good will of men and by his recent diplomatic interventions.

For brotherhood between men and peoples by reason of his major contribution made to this brotherhood, most particularly in the course of this past year: by inviting the representatives of other Christian Churches, Orthodox and Protestant, to attend and take special part in the Ecumenical Council;

. . . by thus inspiring in members of these non-Catholic communions as well as in members of the Catholic Church, an attitude of the greatest mutual understanding, whose effects will be numerous and important;

. . . and by establishing contacts extending well beyond the Christian community.[10]

This text bears emphasizing. Expressing the thoughts of eminent men of the most diverse political and spiritual outlook, it is a kind of recognition by competent representatives of public opinion that the Council has effectively contributed to world peace and reconciliation among men.

May all peoples understand this clearly. The action undertaken by the Pope and the Council, which will be undertaken again in the interest of peace, should not be confused with political activity. Pope John XXIII appropriately recalled, on the occasion of the awarding of the Balzan Prize, the doctrine of the supranational nature of the Church vigorously formulated by Pope Pius XII. It would be astonishing, even scandalous, if these events were interpreted other than as intended by the Church. The neutrality of the Church does not extend to the moral principles that shape the conduct of statesmen. The peace proclaimed by the Church is a Christian peace. "It is rooted in theological virtues of faith, hope, and charity; it is affirmed and advanced by the generous and voluntary exercise of prudence, justice, fortitude, and temperance."[11]

Lo, I Am with You. . . .

One thing is now clearly apparent: the Council has proved to the world that the Church is not dead and that Christianity has not succumbed to the materialism which threatened to smother it. Even those unconcerned about spiritual problems now understand that the Church is still existent and alive. The Pope, who made this remark to pilgrims on February 20, 1963, revealed something of his own personal experience of the Council. For him, the Council demonstrated that the Master's declaration to the Prince of the Apostles is now more valid than ever: "You are Peter, and upon this rock I shall build my Church."

In Rome, this statement finds its permanent fulfillment, for this is the center of the Church, against which the gates of Hell cannot prevail. This saying is a source of consolation and hope. "Insufficiency, difficulty, injustice—sometimes even violence, which in certain countries of the world seems to prevail—rather than weakening the statement, increases its power."

The Pope's line of thought then took an unaccustomed turn; from an informal tone it became solemn, culminating in prayer. "We believe in Thee, O Christ, and adore Thee because through Thy Incarnation, Suffering, and Death, Thou hast redeemed us and hast remained with Thy Church down through the centuries, and thus we know that Thou willst continue always to give it life and sustenance, until some day it attains to plenitude in the Church triumphant."[12]

Indeed, Christ is always present in His Church, in the same way that the command given to the Apostles is given permanently to the bishops; the two are bound together: "Go therefore and make disciples of all nations, baptizing them in the name of the Father and of the Son and of the Holy Spirit, teaching them to observe all that I have commanded you; and lo, I am with you always, even unto the consummation of the world." (Matt. 28:19–20)

The Council has manifested Christ's presence in the Church, and will manifest it again.

NOTES

[1] Address at St. Paul's-Outside-the-Walls, *Documentation Catholique* (March 29, 1959), col. 385–388.

[2] *Documentation Catholique* (January 21, 1962), col. 102.

[3] *Documentation Catholique* (October 7, 1962), col. 1220–1221.

[4] *Documentation Catholique* (November 4, 1962), col. 1392.

[5] Mr. Alessandrini refers to the exposition organized by the Jesuits, at the Piazza Pilotta, and dedicated to the Church of Silence.

[6] Reference to the "opening to the left" attempted by the Fanfani government.

[7] Let us cite, for example, the manner in which the Encyclical *Mater et Magistra* speaks of erroneous ideologies. Error carries its own condemnation; this reappears in the opening address. Atheistic materialism is thus designated without being named in *Mater et Magistra:* "The most radical error of the modern era is certainly that of considering the religious exigency of the human spirit as an expression of sentiment or imagination—or even as a product of historical chance—which must be eliminated as anachronistic and an obstacle to human progress . . ."

"However great technical or economic progress may be, unless men recover their sense of dignity as creatures and sons of God—the primary and ultimate purpose of all creation—there will be neither justice nor peace in the world. Man separated from God becomes inhuman toward himself as well as toward others, because harmonious relations between men presuppose harmonious relations of the soul with God—the source of truth, justice, and love." (*Mater et Magistra,* in *Les encycliques sociales* [Editions Bonne Presse, 1962], p. 380.)

[8] *Osservatore Romano* (February 3, 1963).

[9] The Balzan Foundation was created in 1961 in memory of Eugenio Balzan, director of the Italian newspaper *Corriere della Sera,* a powerful adversary of the Mussolini regime. His daughter, Miss Angela Lina Balzan, who died in 1957, left her inheritance to fulfill her father's dream: to create a foundation similar to the Nobel Prize. Thirty-eight persons (all members of the International Commission for awarding the prize, including four from the Soviet Union), unanimously chose the Pope.

[10] *Osservatore Romano* (March 8, 1963).

[11] At the close of the ceremony for the awarding of the Balzan Prize, Pope John XXIII held a private audience with Mr. and Mrs. Adzhubei, editor of *Izvestia* and son-in-law of Mr. Khrushchev. This visit resulted in much speculation. It is significant to note that the audience was requested by Mr. Adzhubei. Some interpreted the Pope's gestures of courtesy as an abandonment by the Pope of basic principles. On the other hand, others were quick to criticize papal procedure or even seem scandalized when the attitude of the Holy See did not correspond to their own political preferences.

[12] *Osservatore Romano* (February 22, 1963).

appendix II
The Council and the
Soviet Press

COMMUNISM MAKES NO MYSTERY ABOUT ITS ULTIMATE PURPOSE. It aims to eliminate religion and, consequently, to suppress all churches. In this struggle, which Communists are certain will culminate in victory for themselves, Communism depends upon the dissemination of the natural sciences that make recourse to an "irrational" power unnecessary, and counts upon the establishment of atheistic social structures which, unobtrusively, will form an atheistic thought and outlook in the minds of many.[1]

Atheistic materialism would apparently consider it advantageous to find itself confronted by a petrified Church, unable to reform itself and excessively centralized, which would somehow constitute the last stage of religion, just as imperialism is the ultimate form of capitalism. In fact, the Soviet press unconditionally supports the reforms that proceed from the base and are directed against the center. It favors the reformers as a matter of principle, simply because this tension accelerates the internal disintegration of the Church, as Marxist dialectics affirm.[2]

If Communism is now rather disconcerted because of the Council's accomplishments, it is because the efforts made to effect renewal and adaptation are occurring not only at the base but also at the summit of the Church, and they seem highly capable of renewing the spiritual vigor of the Catholic Church throughout the world. This possibility, which we need not hesitate to mention, can only serve as a warning to Communism. The resulting fear would justify a hostile reaction in the Communist camp everywhere. Paradoxically, however, since the Council has taken to heart the cause of world peace, and has manifested a constant concern to dissociate itself from all political groupings or movements, Communists believe that this has disarmed the professional militants engaged in political anti-Communism who claim religious motives for their activity. This explains the increasingly greater interest in the Council on the part of Communists in the Soviet Union and elsewhere.

There is, of course, but little mention of the Council in the daily newspapers of the Soviet Union. Obviously, Communist policy would oppose the dissemination of news concerning events that attest the vitality of the Catholic Church. Articles devoted to the Council appear in periodicals intended for an intellectual or political élite as, for instance, *Litera-tournaïa Gazeta, (New Times)* and the atheistic review, *Naouka i Religia (Science and Religion)*.

The first news reports published in *Science and Religion,* in 1961 and 1962, tended to disparage the Council and the Catholic Church. A brief notice in the March issue commented ironically that the Council's agenda included "such contemporary questions as holy Scripture, prayer, ecclesiastical discipline, missions, communion, etc. And yet we still do not know what place will be given to questions that concern all mankind as, for example, the struggle for peace, general and complete disarmament and the liquidation of the colonial system."

The first real article on the Council appeared in the issue of July, 1962. The author described the Council as an alliance of religious forces against Communism. "One of the most acute problems," he wrote, "will be the question of the relations between the Catholic Church and Communism." He quoted a news item attributed to *Agence France-Presse* reporting a statement by Bishop Castellano, then assistant director of Italian Catholic Action, who said that Communism, the fundamental heresy of all times, would be anathematized in the most formal and solemn way by the Council which he described as the most important ever convoked by the Church. The bishops of all countries would proclaim the eternal truth of Christianity in opposition to Communism, and the certainty of Christ's triumphant victory over His enemies. Similarly, a declaration made in November by Archbishop Felici, the future Secretary of the Council, was also quoted: "The Council will renew the anathema against the principal errors of our time and will strengthen the fundamental points of Christian doctrine."

The author made a remark in regard to these statements which denotes a perspicacity that is sometimes lacking in theologians and Catholic journalists: "We may wonder," he said, "whether the Council will also concern itself with the maintenance of world peace. This question, apparently, has not been given consideration in any preparatory Commission, but if we may judge by certain interventions of Pope John XXIII, in which he asked that the use of atomic weapons as a means of settling international problems and disputes be condemned, we may suppose that the question of peace, in one form or another, will certainly be raised."

The article, moreover, lays great stress on the psychological mobilization of all Catholics. In efforts to bring about the reunion of Christians it sees only an attempt to establish a Christian "front" against Communism. This would mean that it is less a matter of achieving unity in the faith than determining the lines of a parallel political activity ensuring the united action of all Christian Churches. The decision to convoke a Council indicates that the Catholic Church took the initiative in preparing a political coalition of the Churches. The Vatican would like, on the one hand, to bind the so-called Christian governments of NATO by a supplementary bond, provided by religion, and on the other hand, to create obstacles to the peace movement by attracting Protestants and Orthodox into this alliance.[3]

The September issue, 1962, of the same review, published an article by Scheinmann, the author of many books and essays against the Vatican, including *"The Vatican on the Eve of the Council, or the Quest for Adaptation."* The author expressed fear that efforts to bring about the reunion of the Churches really mean that "the Papacy is attempting to take the initiative in the cause of the reunion of the Churches and even in the reconciliation of Christians with the non-Christian religions" (Moslems, Jews, and others). Successes in this domain, he believes, would increase the authority of the Papacy and would facilitate the establishment of an international ecclesiastical alliance against Communism, which many prelates and political leaders of the bourgeoisie approve and desire.

To achieve this kind of unity, the Papacy is ready and willing to make concessions to the non-Catholic Churches, respecting their own traditions and customs. On one point, however, the Vatican is determined to stand fast: "the dogma of the sovereign power and infalli-

225

bility of the Pope, which is precisely one of the most serious obstacles to unity."

In conclusion, Scheinmann threw down a challenge to the Fathers of the Council:

The Second Vatican Council is meeting in a time of immense changes in the world. Whether the Vatican prelates like it or not, the Socialist system exists and is developing successfully. The aim of the Socialist countries is the construction of Communism. Communists and people belonging to no party, atheists and believers, and among them millions of Catholics, are participating in this construction. Communism has won enormous victories and millions of people are supporting it. Anathemas and threats directed against Communism can only discredit the Church and deepen its own internal crisis. In arousing anti-Communist sentiment and inciting the cold war, the only ones to gain will be those who make millions from the blood and suffering of the peoples. To the great mass of workers, whether believers or atheists, it is wholly irrelevant and immaterial that the Council be utilized by the defenders of political and warmongering adventures for propagandizing such a crusade.

Volume VI (1962) of the *Yearbook of the Museum of the History of Religion and Atheism,* published by the Academy of Sciences of the Soviet Union, contains two articles on the Council. Although this volume was not available until February, 1963, it was printed before the Council was in session. The two articles, therefore, were anterior to the event.

The author of the first article, *The Papacy and Reunion of the Churches,* is Edward Winter, a member of the East German Academy of Science, who also wrote an essay on the relations of Russia and the Papacy (*Russland und das Papsttum,* 2 vol. [Berlin, 1960–1961]). Another book by the same author, scheduled for publication, is *The Soviet and the Vatican.* "The Roman Church," he wrote in the conclusion of his essay, "hopes that the Second Vatican Council will establish a common front against Communism and the Socialist countries. This Front would be supported by the powers of the so-called free world, to which, in its turn, the Church will provide ideological backing. Acknowledging this fact is to acknowledge at the same time the weakness of the Christian slogan *ut omnes unum sint.*"[4]

The second article, *The Ecumenical Council of 1962 and the Catholic Dogma of the Unity of the Church,* was written by B. Ramm.

226

This long essay is more of a historical study.[5] The author, however, considers the idea of unity as nothing more than the establishment of a religious front for the struggle against atheistic Communism. Such a policy, he concludes, is directly contrary to the deepest aspirations of the peoples of the world. Consequently, it is destined to fail. The peoples, regardless of their political preferences, their race, or even their religious adherence, all aspire to peace. Anything that is contrary to peace receives no popular support.

As a matter of fact, the convoking of the Council and the orientation that it took preoccupied the Communist leaders much more than they wished to admit. The two observers of the Russian Orthodox Church could not come to Rome without the authorization of the Soviet government. Therefore, if the latter allowed the Church to take this initiative, it is because it was considered advantageous that two Soviet citizens attend the Council. The Soviet Union could only gain by this in public opinion everywhere, and leaders assumed that there would be greater circumspection whenever mention was made of Communism or atheism during the conciliar sessions.

Mr. Krassikov, the correspondent of the *Tass* agency in Rome, wrote a very benevolent description of the Council's opening ceremonies and the Pope's address to the Fathers. He did not conceal from his colleagues that the deeds and gestures of Pope John XXIII had favorably impressed him. A considerable part of the *Tass* bulletin was published in *Izvestia* on October 12th:

> The members of the Council will discuss a large number of questions principally concerning dogmas of the Church and ritual. At the same time, however, they will doubtless take up problems connected with the present international situation. It is this aspect of the proceedings which most attracts the attention of the many observers now gathered in Rome. As we know, the present Pope, John XIII, has on more than one occasion spoken out in favor of peace and against the atomic armaments race, and for the settlement of international disputes by means of negotiation. What position will be taken on all these questions by the most authoritative assembly composed of leaders of the Catholic Church?[6]

The newspaper left this question unanswered, and *Pravda,* for its part, simply kept silent.

Komsomolskaïa Pravda (the journal of the Young Communists), however, published a violent pamphlet on the Catholic Church and the Council, which was titled *"What Will the New Syllabus Be Like?"*

What is the real purpose of such a considerable gathering? This is the question posed by I. Lavretski. "Although the preparatory proceedings are wrapped in secrecy, the purpose can be surmised from the numerous statements of princes of the Church demanding, like the bishops of the United States, a solemn condemnation of Communism."

The Church had counted on Fascism to put an end to Communism. But these hopes were not fulfilled. And for the sake of survival, the Church is ready to sacrifice its orthodoxy. Today it proclaims itself as the friend of science and progress, although it does not abandon its anti-Communism, of course. "In a fit of hysteria, Pius XII excommunicated all Communists, the adversaries of NATO and adherents of the peace movement." But this attitude merely aggravated the crises within the Catholic Church. On the death of Pius XII, wary Cardinals decided that it would be best to elect a successor known for softness. But "the present Pope is just as fiercely anti-Communist as his predecessor. He simply manifests greater political ability." He intervenes in favor of peace and against nuclear experiments; he pleads for general disarmament. He even congratulated the cosmonauts Nikolaiev and Popovich. "For the head of a Church that condemned Galileo and sent Giordano Bruno to the stake, and which, for many centuries, taught that the earth is the center of the universe, it certainly was a rather audacious act to congratulate the cosmonauts who, moreover, were Communists as well."

But that is not all! The opening to the left, the collaboration with Socialists, the development of a "popular" capitalism (an allusion to *Mater et Magistra*) were sufficient to alarm the conservative right wing of the Vatican, Cardinal Ottaviani and his cohorts: Adenauer, Franco, Salazar, the fanatics of the French O.A.S. with Bidault, Cardinal Spellman and other American prelates in whose eyes even Kennedy was a progressive. We may expect, Lavretski concluded, more than one battle in the Council between the liberals and the ecclesiastical extremists. It is difficult to foresee which tendency will finally prevail. But whatever the outcome may be, it is a time of crisis for the Church which now resembles a living corpse. No matter what garb is chosen to clothe her, and regardless of the chants that accompany this action, nobody has the power to resurrect the dead!

One could only wonder whether the likable and objective correspondent of the *Tass* agency or the militant atheistic dogmatist would succeed in forming public opinion in the Soviet Union. The proceedings of the Council and the Pope's successive appeals for peace served to justify Krassikov's point of view rather than Lavretski. And we can be glad of that! The article in *Komsomolskaïa Pravda* was the last of its kind. The tone would hereafter be set by Krassikov. The Soviets quickly sent four more journalists to Rome, including Mtchedlov of the *Literatournaïa Gazeta;* Brajnik and Galdikas, of the *Novosti* agency; Kolonitski, editor-in-chief of the atheistic review, *Naouka i Religia* (*Science and Religion*). The first three received their accreditation on the same basis as other journalists. Kolonitski was told that he would have access to documents and to the same information, but it had not seemed possible to give him an accreditation card because the review for which he was responsible existed primarily to foster the struggle against religion.

During the Council, these journalists published nothing about the proceedings. They were waiting for the final outcome. The first reaction was expressed by Mtchedlov in an article that appeared in *Literatournaïa Gazeta* on December 8th: "The 21st Ecumenical Council." Describing the departure of the Fathers after a general congregation, the author commented, "They are the general staff of a Church that numbers about 500 million believers, scattered all over the world. Although they are far from constituting a monolithic bloc (there are workers and capitalists, men of the left and inveterate reactionaries), all, however, are subject to the influence of the Church." That is why men of good will cannot remain indifferent to the instructions they receive, nor to the position that will be taken in the Council in relation to the vital questions of our time.

The author thus hopes to justify the interest shown by the Soviet press in regard to the Council, whereas ordinarily it is contemptuous in reporting religious events.

How should the Council be judged? First of all, the event should not be overly magnified. A certain bourgeois propaganda seeks to exaggerate the significance of the Council by referring to it as a decisive fact in contemporary history. To properly understand the real purpose of the Council, the author says, it should be remembered that it was desired primarily as an internal action of the Catholic Church to enable Catholicism to preserve its influence in the modern world. Some of the problems under consideration have no connection with matters that greatly concern the world of today as, for instance, the discussions on the sources of Revelation, the long quarrels regarding the use of Latin in the liturgy or the necessity of restoring communion in two kinds.

The important issues today are the elimination of war, the strengthening of peace, and the ending of international tension by means of negotiation. These questions are not expressly included in the agenda of the twenty-first Council. They are so serious, however, that they cannot be avoided. In this area, Mtchedlov observes, it is fitting to acknowledge the merit of John XXIII who adopted a realistic position. When he became Pope, new tendencies made their appearance in the Vatican. The encyclicals no longer openly or violently condemned Communism. Nor was there any unconditional support granted to NATO or CENTO, nor any new encouragement of the cold war. It would be incorrect, the author continued, to attribute these changes exclusively to Roncalli's character. There are deeper and more objective factors. "For the Catholic Church, the primary problem is to maintain her influence among the masses." To achieve this, she must take into account the objective transformations of society. Consider, for example, the question of Communism. The author says that the open condemnation of Communism has failed owing to the triumphant progress of Communism. Sympathy for Socialism in Catholic circles obliges Church leaders to elaborate new methods when relations between Communists and Catholics are concerned, i.e., "between those two ideologies that exclude each other, Catholicism and Communism."

There is also a new attitude with regard to the problem of peace. The Pope's address to the official delegations of the Council on October 12, 1962, and the appeal for peace during the Cuban crisis were real contributions to the cause of world peace. The Council's message to the world is considered a victory of the bishops over the Curia. According to Mtchedlov, the bishops are nearer the people than the Curia and, consequently, they have a better understanding of the signs of the times, whereas in Rome there is a continuous slandering of Communism.

The article then mentions the Ukrainian bishops and the press conference in which the representatives of the Uniate Churches alluded to "persecutions, shootings and repressions that victimized Ukrainian believers, simply because of their faith." In conclusion, the author says, "These slanders could not be disseminated if they were not inspired by members of the Roman Curia."

Osservatore Romano published a critical reply to Mtchedlov who then wrote another article in a more polemical vein. *Osservatore Romano* had affirmed that the Church, being insensible to the winds of history, is now and will always remain unchanged. Mtchedlov, however, insisted on taking a closer look. Pope John XXIII convoked the Council while under the effect of a heavenly inspiration. And the Church emphasizes the supernatural character of this event in order to persuade everyone that his house was not on fire. However, we need only open our eyes to discover many reasons for convoking the Council. The Catholic Church wants to adapt her doctrine and organization in such a way as to avoid open conflict with the modern mind and the materialistic outlook of contemporary man. In a word, the Church wants to identify herself with this day and age.

Liturgical reform is quite revealing in this respect. For example, public worship requires time, energy, and means from both the clergy and the faithful. Consequently, the faithful drift away from the Church. And to retain her hold upon them, the Church will now simplify public worship, making it accessible to the peoples of Africa, Asia, and Latin America where intensive missionary activity is carried on. Finally, Mtchedlov comments upon the press conference of October 25th given by Fr. H. Schmidt: "He speaks very well and is certainly a good theologian. He lays stress upon the analogy between worship and culture."

I also remember that press conference. I had noted the passive and rather absent-minded attitude of Mtchedlov, seated at the rear of the room and surrounded by his Soviet colleagues. He did not understand English and seemed to be daydreaming. But the article in *Literatournaïa Gazeta* proves that he carefully studied the text and understood its meaning. Communists do not like the efforts of adaptation being made by the Church with regard to the younger Churches in the new countries. And Father Schmidt's conference (unrelated to the Council) was remarkable in that it pointed the way to great possibilities for openness and adaptation in liturgical reform.

Mtchedlov is convinced that high-ranking prelates of the Church are now advocating ideas for which the Church would have condemned them to the stake during the Middle Ages. The Council has made a sweeping self-criticism. The advantages and disadvantages of Latin, ceremonial details, fasting, burials and the sacraments have all been carefully re-examined. The Church is tending toward democratization everywhere.

But why are such efforts being made now? Because the dictatorship of the Church is retreating. It has lost the working class. "The search for efficacious measures against the progress of atheism and against the growing influence of ideas of social progress and Communism, and the search for suitable steps to be taken in preserving and strengthening their positions, preoccupy and deeply concern all Churches today, and Catholicism most of all." The article concludes: "This is what primarily troubles the successors of the Prince of the Apostles who nostalgically remember a happier past that they will never find again."

The issue of *Science and Religion* for January, 1963, contains two articles on the Council. One of them, signed by Inga Kitchanova, is written in a pleasant and satirical tone, and is titled *"The Catholic Church Confronting the Problems of Men."* The other is by P. Kolonitski, editor-in-chief of the review, with the title: *"Under the Pressures of Life's Demands."*

The first speaks of the Council in a very superficial way. According to the author, the Catholic Church, in attempting to cope with the grave problems confronting men today, which could lead them away from religion forever, has only come up with solutions that are too old to be efficacious any longer.

The second article was written in another vein. It represents the most serious essay on the Council that has yet appeared in a Communist country. And while judging the Council in accordance with Marxist criteria, Kolonitski described the event with objective veracity. A detailed analysis is presented here, because it is important to know exactly what millions of Marxist men, or those influenced by Marxism, really think of the Council. After all, the Council concerns them too, and not merely because it is laboring for world peace. The quest for truth is of interest to all mankind. The Council makes it possible for the Church to "open to all men the source of the life-giving doctrine which enables them, in the light of Christ, to fully understand what they really are, as also their high nobility and final destiny," as John XXIII declared in the opening address.

Kolonitski analyzed the Council's action in the fostering of world peace, and then the liturgical reform. In conclusion, he asks whether the Council will mark the end of anti-Communism.

"Although most of the work remains to be done, it is possible at the end of the first session," the author says, "to form some idea about the Council's nature and purpose. It was convoked at a moment in history that was particularly grave." The Cuban crisis, provoked by American "imperialists" during the first days of the Council, which placed mankind on the very brink of atomic catastrophe, is sufficient evidence. Although the Council is primarily concerned about heavenly things, there is nobody who can remain indifferent when world peace is threatened. With regard to world peace, "the most important and most urgent problem, concerning all mankind, the Council addressed itself, not to God, but to all men, the heads of government and the peoples everywhere." It was clearly understood that trusting in God alone, in a matter of such importance, without taking appropriate steps, is very dangerous and might easily lead to the holocaust of thermonuclear war!

"Men of good will, including both believers and atheists, gladly welcomed the peaceful declarations made by John XXIII at the opening of the Council, and his remarks during the audience accorded to the heads of official diplomatic missions, and at the reception for journalists, as well as the Council's appeal to all mankind."

These statements and messages, in Kolonitski's opinion, constitute a victory of good sense and realism. They are, as he believes, substantially different from the wind that was blowing in the Vatican before the Council, and particularly different from the things that were said by Pope Pius XII, the predecessor of John XXIII.

The author adds that it would be imprudent to exaggerate the significance of these various manifestations. The Vatican, he claims, bears a very heavy responsibility in the face of social progress, the democracies and world peace, and consequently one must not allow oneself to be seduced by peaceful declarations without giving further thought to the

233

matter. In the light of the past, it is necessary to judge whatever is said, and then whatever is done. The words have been spoken, and the future will show what they are worth. It is quite possible that they define the Vatican's line of conduct for some time to come. And the tone of the article suggests that the author is of that opinion.

Does this not attribute excessive importance to a religious event and to the Catholic Church? Kolonitski provides his own explanation:

Nobody likes war. Consequently we can expect action in favor of peace on the part of people whose activity is ordinarily of a wholly different kind. Now the question of world peace is so important that it is quite fitting to welcome, however circumspectly, any steps leading to peace, as well as any declaration in favor of peace, even though we approve it with reservations.

For the support which the Church seems determined to bring to the cause of world peace will, to the same extent, weaken the efforts of those who favor war. Will the Council that was heralded as an instrument of war against Communism be constructed at the expense of capitalism? The author does not ask himself this question in such clear terms. But that is the problem he poses and he suggests a possible explanation.

The Council was convoked to discuss problems pertaining to the interior life of the Church. The official declarations and the broadcasts of Radio-Vatican lay great emphasis upon the purely religious character of the Council. The Council, it has often been said, was not convoked against anyone. Kolonitski remarks that it is not connected with any political faction. It is free from all external influence. Not only does it refuse to condemn, but it does not even want to touch upon political problems that are not properly within the domain of the Church.

Radio-Vatican criticized the erroneous information of the Soviet press concerning the significance of the Council, more especially the articles published in *Komsomolskaïa Pravda* and in *Science and Religion:* "We would be very glad if certain forecasts expressed in the organs of our press proved to be untrue. The Council would greatly increase its prestige in the eyes of believers everywhere if it seriously broke with the policy of anti-Communism which the Vatican, until quite recently, was supporting so actively and openly."

We may now wonder in what direction the Church is leaning. Before all else, of course, it is concerned about itself. It is still the enemy of Communism, and if it now seems to be forsaking capitalism, it is because it wants to retain its hold upon the masses who are themselves turning away from capitalism more and more. The principal concern of the Council, in fact, is to keep believers under the influence of religion and the Church. It is seeking efficacious means to halt the progress of religious indifference among large sections of people in all countries. Now the masses are weary of war and the armaments race. And to follow in this wake and compromise itself with capitalism (which, for the Soviets, is uniquely responsible for the armaments race) can only serve to further alienate the masses from religion. This explains the new "policy" of the Vatican.

It may be supposed that this "peace policy" is simply a translation of the Christian ideal of peace and universal love into factual reality. But the author believes that this is entirely false. According to him,

Christian principles have always served and still serve to subject the masses to the arbitrary rule of the governing classes rather than to support the cause of peace. Christians have never prevented any war. One of the fundamental principles of Christianity is non-resistance to evil which means, in fact, the acceptance of all injustices, including war itself. To struggle against war, it is essential to act, and not merely threaten warmongers with the judgment of God (since they are hardly concerned about that, even if they are Christians). Instead, they should be confronted with their responsibilities toward the peoples everywhere.

This diatribe, however, ends with the frank admission that the

declarations of the Council in favor of peace have been like a breath of fresh air. Although they proceed from a love of peace which bears its contradiction within itself, they can play a great role. The question of peace was not included in the Council's agenda, but little by little it imposed itself contrary to the wishes of the organizers and participating members, and it received the response that is now known to us all.

It is not surprising that among the topics discussed at the Council the Soviet journalists all devoted special attention to the liturgy. This subject was given the longest consideration and discussion by the Fathers. It is concrete, and in the eyes of a Marxist it represents the bond which attaches the believers to the Church in a more "existential" way than the dogmas of religion.

In referring to the liturgy, Kolonitski, like his colleague, had recourse to the conference of Fr. Herman Schmidt. It is worthy of notice that he mentioned only the strictly religious aspect, leaving aside the social and communal aspects of the liturgy which might have appealed to him.

To extirpate formalism, red tape and routine from public worship, making the liturgy more interior, more living and more beautiful, is the desire of the bishops. And Kolonitski comments:

The Fathers of the Council want believers to participate more consciously in what is occurring in church during the celebration of the liturgy. They want them to be filled with piety in the presence of the hidden significance of the holy mysteries, and particularly the first among them, the sacrament of the Eucharist, which symbolizes communion with God by means of the manducation of His body and blood.

This could not be said any better, even if we match it with a Marxist explanation: the progress of materialism threatens to extinguish the light of faith. What can be done to maintain it? Establish a closer bond between the Church and the believer by a more active participation of the faithful in public worship. It is consequently important to make the liturgy more comprehensible so that it will revive the fervor of believers with respect to God and the Church. Proposed reforms are then enumerated. The majority of the Fathers are inclined to replace Latin with living languages, if not all at once, at least in successive stages, and if not altogether, then at least in part. Mention is also made of the necessity of adapting the liturgy to the particular traditions of various countries. There is emphasis upon the need for renunciation in order to keep men open to the grace of God.

This last remark is more insidious. The cornerstone of Marxist dialectics against religion is, in fact, the accusation that religion diminishes man by making him look to God for everything he needs rather than depending upon the strength that is found in man himself.

In brief, it is a question of pouring old wine into new wineskins, in an attempt to modernize the teaching of the old dogmas of religion.

This effort seems like a total waste of time to an atheist, and dangerous if it meets with success.

In conclusion, the author inquires into the future. Will the Council and the Church remain faithful to this program? The reactionaries are already beginning to protest. Accustomed to counting on the support of Catholicism, they are astonished by the political "line" the Council has taken. In this they see a rebellion and they accuse the Church of having broken the anti-Communist front. They are trying to revive the flame by speaking about the Church of silence and the persecutions of the Church of Russia. With reference to this reaction, the author mentions the exposition devoted to the martyr Church. He says:

This exposition is only an imposture and falsification, regarding all the actions of Russia against the Nazi armies of occupation during the war of national liberation as being acts of persecution.

Reactionary forces and the rightist press are doing everything possible to lead the Pope and the Council back to the old positions. Those opposed to the "new trend" put all their hope in the Ottaviani group. With external help, and under its instigation, this group will unscrupulously utilize any favorable moment to undertake more decisive action.

What will happen next? It is difficult to say for sure.

But the first session of the Council, contrary to the wishes of the reactionaries, placed itself under the sign of the renewal of the Catholic Church and rejected what was called the position of strength and of international tension and preparation for war. Accordingly, the Catholic Church can count upon the support and understanding of the majority of the faithful, thus preserving its influence over the masses of believers. Catholicism can then seriously examine the problems pertaining to the renewal and strengthening of the Church, and this was the reason for which the Second Vatican Council was originally convoked. It seems apparent that the majority of the Council, and Pope John XXIII at its head, understand this perfectly. The authority and significance of the Council, and of all later activity of the Catholic Church depend upon the steadfastness and fidelity with which the chosen course will be carried out in real life.

This analysis shows us that the Communist world, before the Council, feared that it would produce new divisions among men. However, it now sees that the Council is engaged in a task of peace. The explanation that Communists give for this change is inspired by the Marxist analysis which is unable to take into account the Church's interior life. The Communist authors did not see, or were unwilling to see, that the Council's work for peace derives from faithfulness to the double love of God and of men: *Caritas Christi urget nos:* the love of Christ impels us (II Cor. 5:14). This saying of St. Paul, which inspired the message of the Fathers to the world, also inspired all the Council's activities with regard to the world.

It is certainly true that the Fathers undertook liturgical reform to ensure a more efficacious pastoral ministry among the masses, and to keep them within the Church or bring back those who have drifted away, or who never belonged to it. But it was not a desire to extend the Church's domination and power which inspired the Fathers, but rather a real love for mankind. For Christ loved all men and this love of God, if it is known and experienced, will be for all men a *gift of God,* capable of transfiguring their lives and the life of the world, as the Gospel tells us.

NOTES

[1] We have reference here to Communism and not to the government, and still less to the Soviet people. Although the party constitutes the substance of the government and provides its doctrine and ideology, it is quite obvious that in factual matters and happenings the Soviet government must take into account both internal realities and the world situation. In this respect, there can be no doubt that there is a wedge between the party dogmatists and the empiricists of the government. We need only note the complaints formulated by the dogmatists and the militant atheists against a certain passivity of the administration. The ideological struggle is very intense in Russia at the present time. This results in a repressive climate for believers.

[2] An extreme case is that of Father Lombardi, who became suddenly sympathetic to Communism on the day when his book on the Council (*Le Concile. Pour une réforme dans la charité*) provoked the reprobation of the Curia and reactions of the Holy Father.

[3] This way of speaking shows that the Soviet government attaches great importance to the action of the Churches in favor of world peace (viz., the earlier Peace Conference in Prague).

[4] *Yearbook of the Museum of the History of Religion and Atheism* VI (1962), 28.

[5] *Ibid.,* 29 to 50.

[6] The dispatch added that certain statesmen, known as Catholics, governing countries such as the United States, France and West Germany, are far from following the Pope's counsel in practice. Krassikov doubtless alludes to President Kennedy's letter, addressed to the Pope on the eve of the Council and published in *Osservatore Romano* on October 11th. The letter is very interesting. Mr. Kennedy was inspired by the radio

message of September 11th. He wrote, "We hope that the Council will be able to present in clear and persuasive language the effective solutions of numerous problems confronting all of us, and more especially that these decisions will advance the cause of peace and of international understanding in an appreciable manner." The President was not a bad prophet.

The hopes of Chancellor Adenauer, addressed to *Osservatore Romano,* were even more incisive: "We are convinced that in our era when the ideologies of materialism and militant atheism are becoming increasingly threatening, the Council will give a new and powerful impetus to the unity and strength of Christianity for the well-being of humanity and the cause of world peace."

The Chancellor again spoke of the Council in his message to the German people on Christmas Day, 1962; this address was imbued with a profoundly Christian spirit. He expressed the hope that the Council would produce peace between Christians which, in the past, was so often lacking in Germany, and peace between all men as well. He told of his great confidence in the Council's work, calling it the work of the Holy Spirit. And where the Spirit is, there also is freedom.

appendix III

The Witness of the Russian Orthodox Church

It WAS THE TASK OF THE OBSERVERS TO FOLLOW THE PROCEED-
ings of the Council and inform their own ecclesiastical communities
about them. The delegates of the Russian Orthodox Church had received
a very specific mandate to that effect. In accordance with this requirement, they sent a weekly report to Archbishop Nicodemus and, through
him, to the Holy Synod of the Russian Church.

In the presence of journalists, they would have preferred to remain
silent. However, they could not completely escape them. Earlier we
noted the comments made by the Archpriest Borovoi to the German
journalist, Eva-Maria Jung, concerning contacts between Rome and
Moscow. We also possess a few clippings in which Russian observers
spoke about the Council, or more generally the Russian Orthodox
Church. The Council, in fact, offered the Russian Church an occasion to
bear witness to itself. And we believe that it is useful in these times of
ecumenical *rapprochement* to publish this testimony and to throw light
upon it by certain explanations drawn from history and theology.

The first text is an interview between two Russian observers and Mr.
Brajnik, a special correspondent of the Soviet press agency *Novosti* (The
News), at the beginning of the Council. The second is a very complete
and serious discussion presented in the form of an interview between
the Archpriest Borovoi and the editors of the illustrated Polish review,
Za i Przeciw Pour et Contre (*For and Against*). We are indebted to
the editor-in-chief of that review for the French version of the text.[1]
Finally, we shall present a detailed analysis of the first article which the
Revue du patriarcat de Moscou (Journal of the Moscow Patriarchate)
devoted to the Council.

A Conversation between a Soviet Journalist and the Russian Observers

Almost every morning, and also at noon, the crowd of Catholic dignitaries attending the Council filled the steps of Saint Peter's Cathedral.[2] The black cassocks of the observers sent by other Churches contrasted sharply with the white, scarlet or violet of the Council Fathers. The observers representing the Russian Orthodox Church, Archpriest Vitalyi Borovoi and Archimandrite Vladimir Kotliarov[3] attracted the attention of the conciliar delegates, the journalists and the curious crowds from the very first day. Reporters besieged them.

To understand the reason for this, we must keep in mind the growing authority of the Russian Orthodox Church in international religious contacts, and her fruitful participation in the struggle for peace.[4] The Soviet government recently decorated Patriarch Alexis for his activities in behalf of world peace.[5] Father Borovoi is 46 years old, and Archimandrite Vladimir is 33. Father Borovoi represents the Russian Orthodox Church in the World Council of Churches,[6] and Archimandrite Vladimir is the deputy of the head of the Russian Orthodox mission in Jerusalem. Both men have visited many countries and have met many statesmen as well as religious leaders everywhere.

The flow of delegates to the Council spread over the Square. Bishops got into the special buses that took them to hotels and pensions in the various parts of Rome. Some were hailing taxis, and the Cardinals, of course, had their own limousines. Dignitaries of the Church blessed people as they passed and signed autographs for many. The Russian observers, accompanied by their interpreter, Nikolai Anfinoguenov,[7] secretary of the Moscow representation at the World Council of Churches, went to their hotel on foot, since it was not far away.[8]

It was there that they agreed to answer several questions asked by the correspondent of the *Novosti* press agency concerning the proceedings of the Council.

The Archpriest Borovoi began by making his position clear. He said that because of his status as an official observer rather than member of the Council, and the nature of his functions, together with the rules of the Council in regard to observers, he could not openly take any stand or express any opinions concerning the problems discussed in the Council.

The Second Vatican Council, he went on to say, is an internal activity of the Roman Catholic Church. It was convened to resolve many problems pertaining to theology, the missions, and religious and social questions of concern and importance to the internal life of the Roman Catholic Church. It is natural that observers representing other Churches and denominations take no part in the discussion of these problems, but simply communicate the record of debates to the heads of their Churches. Moreover, Archimandrite Vladimir added,

We voluntarily abstain from making any public comments while awaiting the arrival of observers from other Orthodox Churches. Our interventions in the press might have been considered by certain people who are hostile to our Church, as a desire to speak in the name of all the Orthodox Churches. However, as you can see for yourselves, our hopes and expectations that others would come have not been fulfilled.[9]

Archpriest Borovoi, mentioning the things that would be of greatest interest to readers generally, declined to comment on the purely theological or ecclesiastical aspects of the Council's proceedings.

But I must say, first of all, that from the first moment of our stay in Rome and our attendance at the Council, we have been aware of exceptional cordiality and friendliness towards us both.

Pope John XXIII, the presiding Cardinals, the authorities of the Secretariat for the Promotion of Christian Unity in the person of Cardinal Augustine Bea and Msgr. Jean Willebrands, the heads of many Catholic delegations to the Council, representatives of the clergy and the press at the Council have all welcomed our presence in Rome and our participation in the Council, expressing a sentiment of love towards our Church and her spiritual head, Patriarch Alexis, as also a profound respect and friendship towards our people in their struggle for world peace, and unanimous admiration for the remarkable achievements of our powerful fatherland.[10]

The Archpriest continued, mentioning that, although the Council's agenda did not specifically include as a separate topic the problems pertaining to maintenance of world peace or peaceful co-existence and the strengthening of friendship between nations, this subject is nevertheless touched upon in several conciliar documents, and in the public interventions of Pope John XXIII on the occasion of the inauguration of the Council, as well as in his addresses to the diplomats, journalists and observers, and finally in his radio message at the time of the American threat to Cuba.[11] He also cited the solemn message of the Fathers of the Council to the peoples of the whole world. The condemnation of war, the need to maintain and strengthen world peace, the refusal to use force as a solution for international complications, the necessity of resolving international disputes exclusively by negotiation, and the imperative need to reach early agreement on general and complete disarmament[12]—all are crucial problems of our time which have been reflected, as they deserve to be, in the course of the Council's proceedings.

These positions, taken by the Pope and the whole Council, correspond to the demands of all believers and all nations.

"This encouraging beginning makes us hopeful," the Russian observers said, "that the later proceedings of the Second Vatican Council will make a real contribution to the noble cause of peace and the strengthening of friendship between the nations, and will do nothing that might be detrimental to relations between the Churches or good relations between the peoples of the world."[13]

To be objective, as Archimandrite Vladimir pointed out, it should be remembered that both within and outside the Council there have been certain groups who were not satisfied or pleased with the favorable development of things that we have noted at the Council. Among these objectors, there were a few observers representing the Russian political and clerical emigration and a few Ukrainians also.[14] They are attempting, outside the Council, to darken the atmosphere of our stay in Rome and our attendance at the Council, doing whatever they can to prevent the establishment of good relations. But these efforts have been rare and infrequent, and they have been unanimously condemned by the leaders of the Council and the Secretariat for the Promotion of Christian Unity[15]; moreover, they met with no approval by the press or public opinion, whether religious or social. The plans and hopes of these hostile obstructionists encountered failure. "We hope," said the Archpriest Borovoi in conclusion, "that these regrettable incidents will not be reflected in any way in the results of the Council's activities, and that the

Council will be able to fulfill its mission towards God, the Church and all mankind."

Interview of Archpriest Borovoi for the Polish Review "Za i Przeciw" (For and Against)

Question: The arrival of observers from the Patriarchate of Moscow and all Russia to the Second Vatican Council is an unprecedented event in the history of these two Churches. It has aroused immense world-wide interest in the Russian Orthodox Church. Could we now obtain a little information for our readers, especially with regard to the actual status and organization of the Russian Orthodox Church in the Soviet Union?

Answer: The Russian Orthodox Church lives and works in a complete separation of Church and State.[16] Before the Revolution, the Orthodox Church was a State Church with all the consequences of that situation, affecting both its internal life and its external activity. After the proclamation of freedom of conscience, and the separation of Church and State, millions of people who belonged to our Church only nominally, but who were neither true nor convinced members, left the Church once and for all. Of those who remained with us, there were only the faithful who proved their loyalty to Christ not only in words but also by their deeds and a complete Christian life. At the present time, there are millions of unbelievers as well as millions of sincere and convinced believers.[17] From the State's point of view, the profession or rejection of any religion is a private matter for every citizen.[18] Because of this attitude, we have no statistics that would enumerate Church membership or officially show anyone's affiliation or non-affiliation with the Church. The constitution of our State guarantees freedom of conscience to everyone as well as the exercise of religious practices and the freedom of anti-religious propaganda also.[19]

During the years of the Church's existence under the new social conditions, our Church has faithfully and profoundly maintained her faithfulness to Our Lord Jesus Christ, as also the integrity of the dogmas of the faith and the bases of canonical structure.[20] For all of these years the Church has proclaimed the Word of God to the faithful and preached the Gospel to all who would accept the Good News of Christ and, with regard to people generally, by her whole way of life, the Church has witnessed for Christ.[21] After passing through many deplorable schisms and disruptions, as for instance the schism of the "renewers" or the "Living Church" and others also, our Church emerged from these difficulties strengthened in her faith and in her fidelity to the principles of liturgical life, canonical norms, and Christian piety. Neither in faith nor ecclesiastical organization, nor in our liturgical worship have we departed from anything that formed the very essence of our Church during all the centuries of its existence. We have remained faithful to the faith of our fathers, our forefathers, and our ancestors.[22]

The structure of our Church is in line with what is normal and appropriate for every Orthodox Church according to the sacred canons. His Holiness, the Patriarch of Moscow and of all the Russias, presently the Patriarch Alexis, is first in our Church's hierarchy. He is assisted by the Holy Synod, composed of five permanent members and nine who are changed from time to time.[23]

The permanent members of the Holy Synod are the Metropolitan of Krutytsi and Kolomna; the Metropolitan of Kiev; the Metropolitan of Leningrad; the director of the department of foreign affairs of the Patriarchate of Moscow; and the administrator of the affairs of the Patriarchate of Moscow.

The nine non-permanent members of the Synod are diocesan bishops called by turns—according to a special list—to participate in the proceedings of the Holy Synod. The Synod meets regularly in sessions over which the Patriarch presides.

There are special departments of the patriarchate of Moscow, including, for instance, the department of administration, the scientific committee, the economic section, a department of publishing, and the department of foreign affairs of the Church. Bishops are at the head of these departments, although the scientific committee is under the direction of an archpriest. Employees are either clerics or lay believers.

The whole Church is divided into dioceses. There are more than sixty.[24] At the head of the dioceses there are diocesan bishops who exercise the functions of metropolitans, archbishops or bishops.[25] Certain bishops of large dioceses also have vicars. There are about seventy bishops in our country.

The dioceses are divided into parishes, with a priest at the head of each parish, and an archimandrite for every monastery. The administrative and financial activity of the parish is managed by a parochial council under the direction of a *staroste,* a treasurer and a parish secretary. The parochial council is elected by a general assembly of all the parishioners.[26]

For the preparation of candidates to ecclesiastical life, whether for the monasteries, the episcopate, the organisms for Church government or theological instruction, the Church has ecclesiastical academies. There are two of them at present, in Moscow and Leningrad, and there are now five ecclesiastical seminaries located in Moscow, Leningrad, Odessa, Volhynie, and Minsk.[27]

The patriarchate publishes the *Revue du patriarcat de Moscou* (Journal of the Patriarchate of Moscow)[28] and the ecclesiastical academies put out a theological review called *Les Oeuvres théologiques.*[29] Recently a Bible was published and also the New Testament, a prayer book and many other books considered indispensable for public worship.[30]

Our Church has exarchates, that is to say, dioceses and parishes in foreign lands, among the Russian Orthodox living abroad. One exarchate is in America, with its See in New York: another is in Western Europe, with Paris as the See city; and there is an exarchate in central Europe, where Berlin is the episcopal See.[31] We have an ecclesiastical mission in Jerusalem and representation in Damascus and Beirut. We also have a church in Sofia and another in Belgrade.

The Russian Church maintains many active and friendly relations with all Christian Churches and all faiths the world over. It is a member of the World Council of Churches and has a delegate at the General Secretariat of that organization in Geneva.[32]

[The limited possibilities of this interview would not permit a detailed and complete exposition of the interior life and external activities of our Church. Not long ago, in 1958, the Patriarchate of Moscow published all of this information in a book titled *The Russian Orthodox Church.* It has been translated into English, French, German, Italian, Spanish and Arabic.[33]]

Question: What is the position of the Patriarchate of Moscow in regard to other Eastern Churches, Coptic, Armenian, Maronite, Syrian,

Ethiopian and, especially, the Patriarchate of Constantinople?

Answer: This problem arises under two aspects. The first concerns the attitude of our Church toward the ancient national Churches of the East, separated as a result of the great Christological controversies of the fifth to the seventh centuries, after the condemnation of Nestorianism at the Third Ecumenical Council in Ephesus in 431, and the condemnation of Monophysitism at the Fourth Ecumenical Council of Chalcedon in 451. Other separations occurred following the matter of the "three chapters" at the Fifth Council of Constantinople in 553, and the condemnation of Monothelitism at the Sixth Ecumenical Council of Constantinople in 680–681. Members of these ancient Churches include the remaining Nestorians in Cyprus, Copts in Egypt, Ethiopians in Abyssinia, Malabarese Christians in India, and Maronites in Lebanon. Our Church maintains close, friendly relations with all these national and ecclesiastical groups and with their Churches, but dogmatic and canonical differences have created an obstacle to reunion and the formation of a single Church. Nevertheless, we have ancient traditions of friendship with these various Churches, and together with all our sister Orthodox Churches we hope that sincere, fraternal theological discussions, on a footing of equality, will lead to the overcoming of our heavy burden of old misunderstandings and disagreements.[34]

The second aspect concerns our relations with the Patriarchate of Constantinople with which we are within the communion of one and the same Church. All the venerable autocephalous Orthodox Churches, together with the patriarchates of Constantinople, Alexandria, Antioch, Jerusalem, Moscow, Serbia, Romania and Bulgaria, and the Churches of Greece, Cyprus, Poland, Czechoslovakia, Finland and the archiepiscopal Church of Sinai[35] belong to one and the same universal Church. All together constitute the universal Church, representing the whole of Orthodoxy throughout the world, in its totality and its integrity, from the era of the apostles down to the present day and until the end of time.

We constitute a unity, we are one Church; for this reason we maintain complete dogmatic, canonical and liturgical *liaison*. This is a unity in faith, sacraments, theology, Christian piety, and the Christian life. Each of these sister Churches, however, is entirely autonomous and independent of the other autocephalous Churches insofar as its internal structure is concerned. They are all equal among themselves in matters of internal jurisdiction and authority. However, in matters pertaining to primacy of rank, there is a respect for hierarchy and for the ranking precedence of the patriarchs according to tradition. It is the Patriarch of Constantinople who is first in rank among us. In the ancient, undivided Church of the period of the seven ecumenical Councils, the first place was accorded everywhere to the See of Rome.[37] The second place was granted to Constantinople, the third to Alexandria, the fourth to Antioch and the fifth to Jerusalem. After the division between the East and the West, the first place in the Orthodox East was naturally attributed to Constantinople. Our Church acknowledged this in the past and still does so. In the list of Orthodox Churches, we hold the fifth place. But this primacy of rank has nothing in common with a primacy of authority and jurisdiction. The Patriarch of Constantinople is the first among us everywhere, but *primus inter pares,* the first among equals.

Question: May we ask you, as a theologian, to explain your own conception of the institution of Ecumenical Councils and their role in the history of Christianity?

Answer: Our conception of the institution and importance of Ecumenical Councils for Christendom is wholly in line with the opinion of the early undivided Church of the seven Ecumenical Councils. Nothing, in this respect, separates us from the teaching and practice of those Councils of the undivided Church. According to the will of God, the Church is the "pillar and ground of truth." It is Our Lord Jesus Christ who alone is Head of the Church and is her divine Founder. And in conformity with the unquestionable and unchanging promises of the Lord, the Holy Spirit lives within the Church. For this reason the Church is infallible in the teaching of faith and morals, that is to say, forever faithful to divine truth.

In the Church, there is nothing or no one superior to the Ecumenical Council, that is to say, superior to the universal voice of the whole Church, the voice of the Holy Spirit, but the Ecumenical Council is not superior to the Church herself. The councils are her organ of expression, as the Holy Spirit is given to the Church herself—*as a Church*—and not merely to the established hierarchies or special organs.

Question: Christian public opinion followed with great interest the visit of Patriarch Alexis to the Phanar and the old capital cities of the Eastern Church, Damascus, Beirut and Jerusalem. Did the Patriarch's

,visit and mission have any effect upon the problem of unifying the various national Eastern Churches with the Russian Orthodox Church?

Answer: The pilgrimage of His Holiness the Patriarch Alexis to the holy places of the East, and his visits with the representatives of the venerable, autonomous Orthodox Churches of the East, in Constantinople, Alexandria, Antioch, Damascus and Jerusalem, were in response to the visits made to our Church by the representatives of these patriarchates. Obviously, the cordial and fraternal relations and sincere conversations on problems concerning all of our Churches could not fail to influence to the highest degree the beneficial strengthening and enlarging of reciprocal contacts, and also facilitate the collaboration of all Orthodox Churches when they must make decisions pertaining to the common and contemporary problems of our era. The Pan-Orthodox Conference held on the island of Rhodes in 1961 is the best evidence of this.

Question: The entrance of the Russian Orthodox Church into the World Council of Churches is generally considered as an important success of the ecumenical movement, and this strengthens its authority in the Christian world. What is the opinion of Orthodox theologians regarding the world-wide ecumenical movement and its contribution to the task of the reunion of Christendom?

Answer: The Russian Orthodox Church has always considered the reunion and reconciliation of universal Christendom as highly important. Every day we pray for "the welfare and unification of all the Churches of God." Our Church joyfully welcomes every movement having purposes that are noble and fundamental for the Christian, and we are always ready and willing to collaborate, but there is one essential condition: the movement must be based upon principles that are purely evangelical and Christian. The World Council of Churches has been making great efforts in this movement, and doubtless it has made a very magnificent contribution to the cause of Christian reunion. It labors to become the meeting-place of all Churches, thus enabling them to learn how to live together in community and pursue an ecumenical dialogue sincerely, while also collaborating in the solution of the great problems of the present time, common to all Christians everywhere, upon a basis of fraternity and equality of rights. Approving the purposes and goals of this organization, the Russian Orthodox Church entered the World

Council of Churches to make its own contribution to the task of universal Christian reunion.

Question: Our readers would be very interested in knowing the differences in doctrine which separated the Catholic and Orthodox Churches in the past, and still keep them apart today. Could you point out these differences?

Answer: The differences are generally known; indeed, they are well known. This is neither the place nor the time to indicate or discuss them. Before all else, we must make a serious effort to change the very climate that exists in the relations between the Churches, in order to establish real fraternity, friendship, and good will. In the matter of doctrinal differences—which do exist and they are very important—we must nevertheless lay greater stress upon everything that unites us, and not upon those things which divide us.[40]

Question: The pontificate of John XXIII is known for the human and humanist attitude that prevailed toward all ethnic religious groups, and—what is even more important for the reunion movement—for a critical evaluation of the past.[41] Would you not say that activity of this kind opens up new ways to the Christian world, responsible, like all other world religions, for the future of a humanity that is weary of war and the threat of war?

Answer: Beyond all doubt. The pontificate of Pope John XXIII definitely contributed to the creation of a new climate in our reciprocal relations, and in those of all mankind, including our own Church. He established the hope that new efforts, both positive and constructive—in the task of mitigating our age-old disputes and the present tension—could only exercise a beneficial influence in the strengthening of peace and friendship between the Churches and the nations.[42]

Question: What thoughts come to mind as Orthodox theologians observe the debates of the Second Vatican Council, when references are sometimes made to the time of the first Councils and to the era when, in spite of many disputes, Christendom was still united in doctrine?

Answer: In view of our status here as observers at the Council, we must refuse to evaluate its activity. Consequently, we shall limit ourselves to praise for the atmosphere of full freedom which enables the Fathers of the Council to express different opinions, an atmosphere abounding in good will and fraternal feeling toward other Christians, non-Catholics, and personally we would emphasize the very friendly attitude of the majority of Council members toward ourselves.

Question: Humanity, in a general way, feels the need for unity and for a common solution of the problems of our time. Are the Christian reunion movement, the World Council of Churches at Delhi and the Vatican Council, a kind of manifestation of these efforts? Can they contribute to the creation of an atmosphere of reconciliation among all Christians, and perhaps even among all men of good will, by going beyond territorial frontiers and the negative aspects of the past, so full of exaggerated ambitions and artificial prestige?

Answer: Beyond any doubt, the Third General Assembly of the World Council of Churches, meeting at New Delhi in 1961, brought a positive contribution not only to the task of world-wide Christian re-union, but also to the problem of reducing international tension, the reconciliation of all mankind, the strengthening of peaceful co-existence and of friendship between the Churches and between the nations. We hope that the Second Vatican Council of the Roman Catholic Church will fulfill its task in regard to God, His Church, Christendom and the whole race of men.

The Council has every chance to make a positive contribution to this great and sacred question, but this all depends on the Council itself. We can only express our heartfelt desire and pray.[43]

Question: Is there any possibility that an Ecumenical Council of the Orthodox Churches may be convoked in the near future, as a new and fruitful step leading to the renewal of Christianity?

Answer: At the present time, all the Orthodox Churches are study-ing the problems raised by the Pan-Orthodox Conference held at Rhodes in 1961. In the future, we shall have to do a great deal of preparatory work for the convocation and organization of the gathering which will precede the Council. Only a Council is authorized to legislate in matters that your question includes.[44]

An Article in the Journal of the Patriarchate of Moscow

The *Journal of the Patriarchate of Moscow* in January, 1963, devoted an article on the Council for the first time. It was written by A. Kasem-

251

bek, who ordinarily writes on ecumenical subjects.[45] The Vatican Council, he said, is a most important event in the life of the Catholic Church. (I noted immediately the respectful manner in which this Church was called the *ancient, apostolic Roman Catholic Church*.) The Council is important because the Roman Church covers the whole world and numbers hundreds of millions of Christians. The Councils, according to Catholic doctrine, are the expression of the thought and activity of the Church. The task of the Councils is to give norms to that thought and action in the form of dogmatic definitions and disciplinary canons.

As it was stated on many occasions by Pope John XXIII, whose efforts led to the planning and convening of the Council, the fundamental purpose of Vatican II is to express the authentic and ancient teaching of the Church in new formulations that will correspond to the mentality and the problems of contemporary man, as well as to the objective conditions of his existence today. The author then mentioned the goals assigned to the Council by the Pope in his encyclical *Ad Petri Cathedram*.

Concerning the unity of Christians, the Pope said that it is a difficult task, because it requires overcoming the obstacles accumulated by human deeds, in order that the Church may appear before the world in all its beauty, "without spot or wrinkle or any such thing." Pope John XXIII sees a way to attain this goal in the liberation of the Church from all earthly temptations and temporal interests, in purifying the will to exercise domination over institutions and the wealth of this world, and in being independent of such things. According to the words of John XXIII, the Council must reflect the image of a truly maternal Church, concerned about all who are suffering, a Church that brings peace to all who are overwhelmed by the threat of war and social injustice.

These declarations by the head of the Church have echoed resonantly not only in the world of Christians but also among non-Christians everywhere.

World public opinion is looking to the Council of the Roman Church for a new message that will pacify afflicted mankind, deeply concerned about the division of our contemporary world and the fearful threat of war. . . . Like all Catholics, the Christians of other Churches and denominations hope that the activities of the Second Vatican Council will culminate in concrete action that will heal the painful wounds of our day.

The author then changes perspective and takes up the matter of reunion. The Orthodox Church, he says, always hoped for the manifestation of a desire for unity in Western Christendom. It suffers from the divisions of Christ's flock. Since the time of the ecumenical doctors of the faith, the Orthodox Church repeats the prayer of Saint Basil the Great: "May God put an end to division of the Churches." In all of our liturgies the prayer rises for the peace of the whole world, the well-being of the holy Churches of God and the unity of them all.

Although the autocephalous Orthodox Churches, as branches of the one and only universal Orthodox Church, have not been in canonical communion or liturgical unity with the Roman Church for a thousand years, and do not consider these Councils as ecumenical, but rather as local Councils, expressing the internal life of the Catholic Church, the subjects discussed at these Councils and the decisions taken are of great interest to these Churches.

There follows a short history of the Councils of the Latin Church, occurring after the seven early Ecumenical Councils that were received by both the Catholic and Orthodox Churches. The First Vatican Council, he said,

did nothing to foster the unity of the separated parts of Christ's flock. On the contrary, it merely deepened the chasm between Christian denominations by defining the dogma of papal infallibility. This definition created new difficulties in the relations between Rome and Orthodoxy on the one hand, and with Protestantism on the other. The possibility of fulfilling Christ's prayer that there be only one flock, seemed relegated to some inaccessible region. Although, because of men's deeds, the bond of love was broken between the Russian Orthodox and Roman Catholic Churches, the Orthodox Churches have always acknowledged the mutual likeness and nearness existing between the apostolic Churches as parts of the single Body of Christ.

It is this awareness, the author continued, which explains the seriousness of any step or measure that might tend to increase the distance between us.

In spite of the breach of communion with the Roman Church, the Russian Orthodox Church has always recognized the validity of the sacraments administered in the Roman Church, for this Church has preserved an uninterrupted apostolic succession. In the countless examples of holiness and piety manifested by the faithful of the Roman Church, the Orthodox have

253

always noted the presence of grace and the possibility of reunion in the future.

In the last part of his article, the author examines possible ways for the Council to foster reunion. He points out that the pontificate of Pius XII did little to contribute toward mutual understanding between Christians of different denominations. He emphasizes the difference between the image that generally prevailed when the new Pope was elected—it was said that he would only be a transition Pope and that his election was based on compromise—and the image which the Pope gave of himself by his first decisions and the entire preparation for the Council. And then the author comments about that preparation, briefly mentioning the topics that figured in the agenda of the Council, and commenting upon the opening address which he promised to report more fully in later numbers of the review. He quoted the passage concerning pessimists and reproduced an excerpt taken from the address of John XXIII to the heads of diplomatic missions on the duty of working for peace by negotiation.

He concludes:

The future will show to what extent these ideas of Pope John XXIII will find an echo in the acts of the Council and the life of the Roman Catholic Church. We hope that the Roman Catholic Church will occupy a noble place among the forces working for peace. We also hope that the Fathers of the Council will strengthen the ecumenical atmosphere so that, by the common efforts of the Churches and with the help of the Holy Spirit, the coming of unity will be attained, a unity desired and professed by the faith, uniting all of the faithful of our Lord and Savior Jesus Christ.

We can only be grateful for such a calm and fair dialogue and for such benevolent consideration on the part of the Russian Orthodox Church. We especially like the author's vigorous declaration that the Russian Orthodox Church recognizes the sacraments of the Catholic Church and the examples of holiness to be found in it. In times that are still not very remote, the rebaptizing of Latins occurred in the Orthodox Church from time to time. It should be said, however, that the Church of Russia was always hesitant and reluctant in regard to that practice.

As we formulate the hope, with the author of this article, that the activities of Vatican II will confirm the tendencies manifested during the first session, we also hope that the Russian Orthodox Church will remain steadfast in that ecumenical climate which will foster not only the reunion of Christians, but also encourage greater understanding between the nations and favor the cause of world peace.

We were just bringing this book to completion when, in March, 1963, the *Journal of the Patriachate of Moscow* published an issue in Moscow. It contained an article by A. Vedernikov, author of the famous article titled *Non possumus*. He surveyed the history of relations and contacts between Rome and Moscow, and explains how Moscow changed from a position of reticent reserve to a most benevolent attitude, largely because of the declarations of John XXIII concerning the Council and its task in behalf of all mankind.

John XXIII fulfilled the hope that the Russian Orthodox Church had expressed on the occasion of the death of Pius XII. Paying homage to the activity of the late Pontiff in favor of peace and against atomic armaments, the Russian Orthodox Church then declared its further hope that "the successor of the late Pope would multiply the efforts of Christians of the Roman Catholic Church to establish peace between the nations and the prosperity of all men everywhere."

This association of Pius XII and John XXIII and their efforts in behalf of peace and justice was an act of homage that could not possibly fail to touch the hearts of all sons of the Catholic Church.

NOTES

[1] The magazine *Gente* (Milan) on December 28, 1962, published an interview granted by the Archpriest Borovoi to a Catholic priest of the Byzantine Rite for the review *Oriente Cristiano*. The only interesting part that we found in this interview was Archpriest Borovoi's comments about the situation of the Church in Russia. He said that the Russian Orthodox Church really does encounter difficulties because of atheistic propaganda. But what Church, he asked, does not encounter obstacles today in the fulfillment of its mission? If the problem is atheism in our country, it is immorality, corruption, or religious indifference in other lands. The important thing is for every Church to zealously hold fast to divine truth and defend and preach it. Perhaps the religious situation is better in your country and you ought to thank God for it, but how many of you would remain faithful if you were really put to the test? We have heard criticism regarding the Russian Orthodox Church, as if it had yielded to compromise. But we reject these accusations and we must point out that it is not easy to be Christian and it is not loyal to judge your Christian brothers when they are in a hard situation, especially when you, yourselves, remain in a calm and privileged situation.

What is expected of us? Make your own examination of conscience. When Communists of our countries arrive on visit to your land, they openly profess their atheism. But when Westerners come to visit our country—and there are many of them, including statesmen, artists, tourists and other visitors—why do they never publicly profess their religion? Why do they never say that they are Christians in the midst of a society that is Christian no longer, or one that is still Christian to a diminished degree?

[2] This is a translation of the Russian word *sobor* which, strangely enough, means both a Cathedral and a Council.

[3] Brajnik seems to be little acquainted with ecclesiastical nomenclature. All during the interview he called Borovoi a *vicar* and Kotliarov an *archpriest*.

[4] On October 25th, during the Cuban crisis, the heads of the Christian Churches in the Soviet Union, including Alexis, the Patriarch of Moscow; Ephrem, the Catholicos of Georgia; Vasghen, Supreme Catholicos of the Armenians; Iosif, Archbishop of Moscow (Old Believers); Gustav Turs, Archbishop of the Evangelical Lutheran Church of Estonia; Ian Kiviit, Archbishop of the Evangelical Lutheran Church of Latvia; and Iacob Jidkov, President of the Christian Baptist Council, made a joint appeal to the heads of governments and of Christian Churches. The whole responsibility for the crisis was placed upon the American government. Patriarch Alexis also sent a telegram to U Thant, to Patriarch Athenagoras, and all the heads of the Orthodox Eastern Churches, asking them to lift their voices in protest against the action of the United States.

Archbishop Nicodemus, for his part, wrote to the President of the National Council of Churches of Christ in the U.S.A., Mr. Irwin Miller, and also to the Secretary General of the World Council of Churches, Dr. Visser 't Hooft, expressing the same point of view.

The Journal of the Patriarchate of Moscow (No. 12, 1962) published the reactions to these appeals. Patriarch Athenagoras replied that he also was praying for the peace of the world and the respect of human dignity. Patriarchs Christophoros of Alexandria and Benediktos of Jerusalem replied in a way that was hardly pleasing to Moscow. "The Orthodox Church," they said, "always prays for peace, but we do not think it possible to make protests of a political kind."

[5] On November 8, 1962, on the occasion of his eighty-fifth birthday, and as a reward for his important political activities in the struggle for peace, Patriarch Alexis was decorated by the Soviet government with the Order of the Red Flag. The previous day, November 7th, celebrating the forty-fifth anniversary of the October Revolution, the Patriarch, together with Archbishop Nicodemus, had attended a reception given by the government at the Kremlin.

[6] In this post the Archpriest has recently been replaced by the Archimandrite Kotliarov, raised to the rank of Bishop of Zvenigorod.

[7] It was suggested that the interpreter was in fact the "observer" of the observers! But in the absence of proof, it seems best not to form any opinion.

[8] Like most of the observers, they stayed at the Hotel Astello, 12, Piazza Adriana, behind the Sant'Angelo castle, and therefore less than ten minutes away from St. Peter's. During their entire stay in Rome, they were guests of the Secretariat for the Promotion of Christian Unity.

[9] This statement was made toward the end of October. The arrival of the Russian observers confirmed the Greek Churches in an attitude of refusal. Representatives of these Churches reproached the Russians for trying to monopolize the dialogue with Rome and speak in the name of all Orthodoxy. But the Russian observers denied any such purpose.

[10] This is certainly an overstatement. But the Soviet government obviously expects the Russian observers to produce a good opinion of Russia in the West and throughout the world because of their presence at the Council. It is hoped that Russia will be admired for its "struggle for peace" and its "remarkable achievements."

[11] This way of speaking about the Cuban crisis is obviously very political. Archpriest Borovoi is simply using language that is customary in the Soviet press. What is

more serious is that the reader may believe that the Pope, in referring to the Cuban crisis, was speaking of an American threat.

[12] This enumeration of topics related to world peace appears to be rather simplified. The problem of disarmament, for instance, is not mentioned specifically in any of the documents that he cited.

[13] This is indeed the Pope's wish, and the desire of all the Fathers of the Council who are still seeking the best ways to attain this desirable end.

[14] We do not believe that the term as it is used here should be understood in its technical sense as meaning a conciliar observer, or else it would be quite out of place. No doubt he has in mind certain Russians of the Emigration who arranged for a Mass to be said on October 14th for the suffering Orthodox Church. On October 25th, the Catholic Ukranians distributed a pamphlet concerning Metropolitan Slipyi.

[15] This does not pertain to the press release of the Secretariat for Christian Unity which expressed disagreement or non-concurrence with certain remarks about the Russian observers, for this press release was issued posterior to the date of the interview.

[16] The decree of January 13, 1918, concerning the separation of Church and State, and article 124 of the Soviet Constitution. Commenting upon the significance of this decree, Metropolitan Sergius, head of the Russian Church, in March, 1942, wrote in his book, *The Truth about Religion in Russia,* "The separation of Church and State suppressed the obstacles that were artificially keeping people within the Church, and all the 'faithful' who were so in name only, finally left us."

[17] The number of Orthodox believers is a subject of controversy. Sometimes, in Western almanacks and religious statistics we see the exorbitant figure of one hundred millions. But fifty millions would be a guess that is more likely to be correct. And while there are no statistics of Russian believers, there are none either concerning unbelievers. On this matter, the official documents on atheism simply and invariably remark that the vast majority of the people in the Soviet Union have abandoned all religious faith and practice.

[18] This is not, however, the point of view of the Communist Party. From time to time the Party finds itself obliged to remind certain members that article 13 of the statutes stipulates that for a Communist religion cannot be considered a private matter.

[19] Concerning the separation of Church and State, and freedom of conscience, Kolonitski, editor in chief of the review *Science and Religion,* and special correspondent at the Council, published an interesting article in *Izvestia,* February 7, 1963. We are building, he said, the most just and most reasonable Communist society in which there will no longer be any place for superstitions and prejudices, and where the power of man's enlightened reason will be triumphant for everyone. At present, there are still believers among us, and that is why there are churches and clergy. In its relations with them the Soviet government is guided by Lenin's decree on the separation of Church and State. This decree is the best expression of justice and equity, according to the author. Nevertheless, in the West, there is constant mention of persecution for religious faith in the countries of Socialism. "In Rome, the Jesuits had organized an exposition with the provocative name, *The Martyr Church in the Countries of Socialism.* This was composed of documents that were grossly falsified." In the course of recent years, Kolonitski continued, more than fifty Church delegations have visited Russia. Not one of them discovered evidence of persecution, and the Secretary General of the World Council of Churches himself declared that the Church is free in the Soviet Union.

The basis for these accusations is the knowledge that in the countries of Socialism, scientific atheism is carried on and developed through propaganda. And indeed, we are struggling to eliminate religious prejudices; we make no mystery about this whatever. But this struggle is carried on among us by ideological methods and by means of persuasion or propaganda without diminishing the rights or wounding the feelings of believers.

257

And that, concluded Kolonitski, is the Soviet Constitution on freedom of conscience. If it does not satisfy most Churchmen, that is another matter. Those who desire freedom to propagate obscurantism in order to keep the workers in chains of religious prejudice and spiritual slavery obviously cannot adjust to such a law. But for that kind of freedom there is, of course, no provision in Soviet legislation. Lenin's decree is a law of freedom, not in the *formal* sense, but *authentic* nonetheless. This comment, unfortunately, clearly shows that the Churches are not free to proclaim the Gospel to those who are far off.

[20] This affirmation is essential to understanding and judging the Russian Church. It reminds me of another made by a Russian bishop who complained about the lack of understanding on the part of Western Christians who were accusing the Russian priests of being converts to Communism: "We shall never be Communists," he told me, "and nobody in Russia, neither on the party's side or in the Church, tries to hide the invincible opposition between the two ideologies."

[21] This point was especially stressed at the Third Assembly of the World Council of Churches meeting in New Delhi. The Russian Orthodox Church explained to Christians of the West the particular nature of its witnessing for Christ and more especially its way of proclaiming the Gospel and living it.

[22] The "restored" Church, under the direction of Bishop Alexander Vvedenski and the "living" Church, were first supported by the revolutionary forces against the Church of the Patriarch Tichon (1925). After the war of 1940–45, however, Metropolitan Sergius and Patriarch Alexis liquidated these schisms and they lost all support and official recognition by the Soviet government.

Carried to the extreme, this fidelity to tradition sometimes becomes mere antiquarianism. Archbishop Nicodemus, sharply answering a journalist who asked him whether the Orthodox Church would perhaps adapt its liturgy to the new conditions of life in Soviet Russia, replied, "Never! Never!" Protestant delegations have also been astonished by the peremptory remarks of Orthodox representatives loudly asserting that they have preserved the tradition of the Apostles without any variation.

[23] The Holy Synod of the Russian Church for a long time had only six members: the three metropolitans of Krutytsi (the See of the patriarch's bishop-vicar), Kiev and Leningrad, as permanent members, and three other bishops appointed by turns. This number has just been increased to fourteen, following a recent reform in 1961, in an effort to associate the bishops more effectively with serious matters and decisions taken by the Holy Synod.

[24] The book, *The Organization, Situation and Activity of the Russian Orthodox Church,* published by the press of the Patriarchate of Moscow, in 1958, still mentioned sixty-three Sees.

[25] Certain Sees, like those of Krutytsi, Leningrad and Kiev, possess Metropolitans. The title of Archbishop, in the Russian Church, refers to a person but not to a See.

[26] The organization of the parish was reformed early in 1961 and approved by the Council of the Russian Church in July of that year. This reform tends to liberate the priest from the material administration of the parish, which is entrusted to laymen. In fact, the civil authorities exercise various controls over administration.

[27] Recruiting for seminaries is now the most serious problem and one of greatest concern for the Russian Orthodox Church. Reading the Soviet press and the literature of atheistic propaganda, it becomes quite apparent that the ideological struggle of the atheists seeks above all to obstruct the recruiting for seminaries and monasteries. Candidates are made to appear as mentally weak persons or as parasites or careerists. During the last two years, three seminaries out of eight were closed, including Kiev, Stavropol and Saratov. These facts are sadly eloquent.

[28] This review was published somewhat irregularly before the war. We possess a

complete collection at the *Institut français d'études byzantines,* an impressive witness of the struggle of the Russian Orthodox Church to keep its canonical unity and the integrity of its faith. The review was published again after the war and naturally reflects the political vicissitudes of that troubled period. The review is now making real progress, especially in the field of ecumenism.

[29] Only one issue was published, to our knowledge.

[30] Among others, an edition of the *Typicon* (the calendar with the offices) and the *Trebnik* (ritual) have been published. These books reveal the faithfulness of the Russian Church to tradition and its great love for the liturgy.

[31] Different changes have taken place. Bishop Iohann (Wendland) was transferred from Berlin to New York. Archbishop Sergius was chosen for Berlin. Moreover, a new diocese, comprising Great Britain, was formed in October, 1962, as part of the exarchate of Western Europe. This diocese was entrusted to Bishop Antony Bloom. Until recently, the exarch for Western Europe was Metropolitan Nicolas of Korsoun. We may recall his ecumenical message when he addressed an interdenominational conference in Paris, on August 15, 1962. Referring to the enthusiasm of Christians in their quest for unity, as this was apparent in the three main branches of Christianity, he said, "We are at the threshold of the Second Vatican Council, convoked by His Holiness, Pope John XXIII. We believe that the resolutions of this Council will be directed toward that same unity. The Conference of representatives of all the Orthodox Churches which recently took place in Rhodes, had the same end in view. The World Council of Churches is inspired by the same idea. Consequently, the desire and goal of unity of the whole spiritual flock has become the heritage of all those who call themselves Christians."

On February 14, 1963, we learned in Paris that Metropolitan Nicholas, by decree of the Holy Synod, dated January 14, 1963, was retiring from his post and that Archbishop Antony would replace him. The son of a former Russian Consul General in Teheran, and born in Lausanne in 1914, Archbishop Antony studied medicine in Paris, completing his courses in 1942 as a doctor of medicine. Then he began theological studies and became a monk in 1943. On September 1, 1950, he was appointed to London. In 1957 he was consecrated as a bishop. As a member of the Russian delegation to New Delhi, he showed unusual broad-mindedness on several occasions. He speaks Russian, French and English, and has many friends in ecumenical circles everywhere.

[32] The exarchate of Berlin publishes a monthly review (although irregularly), called *Stimme der Orthodoxie,* which reprints in German a large number of documents published in Russian in the *Journal of the Patriarchate of Moscow.* Sometimes there are articles that have never been published in Russia. The exarchate of Paris publishes a quarterly bilingual review in Russian and French, that is more theological in content: *Messager de l'exarcat du patriarche russe en Europe occidentale,* 26, rue Peclet, Paris, XVe.

[33] *The Organization, Situation, and Activity of the Russian Orthodox Church* (Editions du Patriarcat de Moscou, 1958). This book can be obtained at the offices of the Exarchate, 26, rue Peclet, Paris (XVe), 12 francs. The French title is *L'Eglise orthodoxe russe, organisation, situation, activité.*

[34] The Orthodox Churches, including Moscow as well as Constantinople, are putting forth great efforts at this time to renew fraternal relations with the ancient national Churches of the East. At the first Pan-Orthodox conference of Rhodes, in September, 1961, these Churches were invited to send observers. Regarding these closer relations, we remarked at the time that these same Churches were quite obviously related to Orthodoxy, as could be seen in their rites and traditions. However, the separation originally was not from Orthodoxy, but rather from the early undivided Catholic Church. That is why the Catholic Church is also greatly interested in these Churches. The pres-

ence at the Council of observers representing the Syrian, Coptic, Ethiopian and Armenian Churches was a sign of this interest and a mark of mutual good will.

[35] This list of autocephalous Churches is the one currently accepted by Orthodoxy everywhere. The Churches of Poland and Czechoslovakia are recent creations of Moscow. Albania was not mentioned.

[36] This indicates a conception of the Church that is different from Catholic ecclesiology in which unity of faith and worship finds its expression and basis in union and submission to the same visible authority.

[37] In the event of a restoration of visible unity, Rome, according to the Orthodox, would recover its first place. But this would only be a primacy of honor. There are, however, certain theologians who, by virtue of this primacy, recognize certain functions as belonging to the Pope, as for instance, convoking and presiding over ecumenical Councils, proclaiming infallible definitions and, in a general way, expressing the visible unity of the Church.

[38] The author here is apparently setting forth the theory of *sobernost,* or the conciliarity of the Church, which teaches that a Council is neither universal nor infallible until its decisions have been accepted by the whole Christian people in general. The latter, in their universal, infallible consciousness, somehow come to "feel" the conformity of conciliar decisions with the faith, or their non-conformity, as the case may be. It was for this reason, according to the Orthodox, that the Council of Florence was rejected by the people of Christendom. It is in this conception of ecclesiology that we find the principal divergence between the Catholic Church and Orthodoxy. Reunion cannot occur until there is doctrinal clarification on the infallibility of the Church, as such, and of its various organs of teaching, including the Pope, the Council and the bishops.

[39] This journey was also advantageous to the Russian Orthodox Church. Patriarch Athenagoras pleaded the cause of reunion with the Western Churches, including Rome, in his discussions with Patriarch Alexis. And whereas the spokesman of the Russian delegation had declared in Istambul that he was not interested in what was occurring in Rome, Archbishop Nicodemus, in response to the urgings of Patriarch Athenagoras, made more conciliatory statements in Athens a few days later. The Pan-Orthodox conference at Rhodes (September 24–October 2, 1961) established harmony between the Orthodox Churches. They decided to follow the rule of unanimity in all of their resolutions.

[40] Obviously, the author wanted to avoid polemical argument. He mentioned the problem in the manner of John XXIII. We can measure the progress achieved on the road to fraternal reconciliation if we compare this reply with the complaints formulated in the resolution of the Conference of the heads of Orthodox Churches (Moscow, July 8–18, 1948): "The bishops of Rome have attacked the purity of doctrine of ancient and universal Orthodoxy by the newly introduced dogmas of the *Filioque,* the Immaculate Conception of Mary, and especially by the wholly un-Christian doctrine of papal supremacy in the Church and papal infallibility. As a result of this unchristian innovation, the bishops of Rome did enormous harm to the unity of the universal Church of Christ and, in general, to the task of achieving the salvation of men on earth. We ardently implore the Supreme Pontiff, Our Lord Jesus Christ, to grant the light of His divine teaching to the Catholic hierarchy, helping it to recognize the whole immensity of the gulf of sins into which it has led the Church of the West, by inventing a new doctrine on the supremacy and infallibility of the Pope, as well as utilizing the Church for the sake of a political struggle."

[41] This is perhaps an allusion to the words of John XXIII in his allocution to the pastors of Rome (January 29, 1959). Speaking of the reconciliation of separated brethren, the Pope is said to have commented, "We shall not make any historical survey.

Nor will we try to discover who was right and who was wrong. Responsibilities must be shared between us all. We shall only say, 'Let us reunite. Let us be done with dissensions.' " It should be noted, however, that this statement is not found in the summary of the papal allocution published by *Osservatore Romano* on January 31st.

[42] The question and the answer both tend to emphasize the importance attached by public opinion in Communist countries to the action of the Council in favor of world peace.

[43] These are serious words. We must not forget that, in a cause of such grave importance, it is not men or public opinion that will exercise judgment, but rather the Holy Spirit who decides. Nobody should try to establish conditions for His action or claim that He is absent from the Council if He does not "blow" in some particular respect.

[44] It will be remembered that the Pan-Orthodox Synod of Rhodes had the task of establishing the agenda of the future pre-synod that would then prepare the way for a Council of Orthodox Churches. These are remote possibilities, however, because it takes for granted that a solution would soon be found for the question of relations between the Orthodox Church and other Christian Churches, more especially those which possess a valid apostolic succession and which, furthermore, never have been expelled or excluded from the universal Church by any conciliar decision, (the Seventh Ecumenical Council was held in 787, long before the schism of 1054), should therefore participate in the future Council. This is implied by the very conception of Orthodox theology, of course.

[45] This author is little known. He has published, especially in the *Journal of the Patriarchate of Moscow,* an article in 1961 that was devoted to the ecumenical movement titled *"From Evanston to New Delhi";* in 1962, in the May issue, *"The Russian Orthodox Church and the Ecumenical Movement";* in July, a scholarly essay, *"Oikoumené, Catholicity and Contemporary Ecumenism."* These various articles show that the author has always followed the movement towards unity in the Christian Churches with great interest and understanding.

[46] *Journal of the Patriarchate of Moscow* (May, 1961).

A NOTE ON THE TYPE

IN WHICH THIS BOOK WAS SET

This book is set in Intertype Garamond, a type face considered by many to be one of the most successful ever introduced. Claude Garamond, the designer of these beautiful types, was a pupil of Geoffroy Tory, a leader of the Renaissance in France, a university professor, artist, designer and printer who set out to place French on an equal footing with Latin and Greek as a language of culture. Garamond's evenness of color throughout the font is highly appreciated by book designers. The moderately strong fine lines tend to soften the effect, which is decidedly agreeable to many. One thing is certain, Garamond is unusually pleasing and will distinguish much good printing for many years to come. This book was composed and printed by the York Composition Company, Inc., of York, Pa., and bound by William Marley & Co., Inc., of Philadelphia.

The typography and design of this book are by Howard N. King.